"A wonderful story on life's struggles with grief, sacrifice, and redemption."

—**Fred Burton**, author of *Chasing Shadows*

"Josh's storyline is the great storyline of history: God in pursuit of his beloved. Josh narrates God's grace in the white spaces of his life."

—**Dave Goetz**, author of *Death by Suburb*

"*Heroes and Monsters* is a beautiful book—and an ugly one. Beautiful because it's so honest, and ugly for precisely the same reason. Josh tells his life story with lively prose that explores the paradox of human splendor and wretchedness while dangling hints of redemption. As you read, don't be surprised to find your story in his story, and the divine companion who interrupts his life—the same one who has broken into yours. For Josh, the road traveled with God is twisting, bumpy, potholed . . . and well worth the ride."

—**Drew Dyck**, managing editor of *Leadership Journal*;
author of *Generation Ex-Christian*

Heroes and Monsters

An Honest Look at the Struggle within All of Us

Josh James Riebock

a division of Baker Publishing Group
Grand Rapids, Michigan

Published by Baker Books
a division of Baker Publishing Group
P.O. Box 6287, Grand Rapids, MI 49516-6287
www.bakerbooks.com

Printed in the United States of America

Library of Congress Cataloging-in-Publication Data
Riebock, Josh James, 1979–
Heroes and monsters : an honest look at the struggle within all of us / Josh James Riebock.
p. cm.
ISBN 978-0-8010-1398-0 (pbk.)
1. Riebock, Josh James, 1979– 2. Christian biography. I. Title.
BR1725.R563.A3 2012
277.3′083092—dc23 2011042751
[B]

To protect the privacy of those who have shared their stories with the author, some details and names have been changed.

The internet addresses, email addresses, and phone numbers in this book are accurate at the time of publication. They are provided as a resource. Baker Publishing Group does not endorse them or vouch for their content or permanence.

Illustrations by Derek Geer

12 13 14 15 16 17 18 7 6 5 4 3 2 1

In keeping with biblical principles of creation stewardship, Baker Publishing Group advocates the responsible use of our natural resources. As a member of the Green Press Initiative, our company uses recycled paper when possible. The text paper of this book is composed in part of post-consumer waste.

Veen. This. Is. For you.

Author's Note: Abbreviated

The Thing before the Thing . . .

Most of this happened.
I wish some of it didn't.
I hope the rest does.

Author's Note: Expanded

This is, in its essentials, a true story, except for the parts that clearly aren't feasible, couldn't possibly happen unless one were living in a . . . well, not here. Most of the names have been changed, substituted with the names of artists, musicians, and authors who have inspired me, which I find fun. Also, while this book is written in chronological order, there are a few places where the timeline has been slightly adjusted in order to minimize repetition, confusion, and additional lengthy explanation— Or is it because I'd prefer it if my life had happened this way? Those instances are: (1) Pieces of chapter 3 actually happened following chapter 4. (2) Some of the events of chapter 6, specifically the part about the road trip, occurred later. Though, at this point in life, Gus and I were friends, as stated, and I was facing the included thoughts, issues, and questions, and Gus was playing a significant role in them. (3) Most of the events of chapter 15 actually happened after chapter 16.

Contents

Grateful

Thank you to my family and friends. Thank you to all the writers who are teaching me how to write. Thank you to Baker Publishing Group—Rebecca, Chad, Jessica, Michael, Paula. And to Derek: Thank you so much for everything. Your abilities are, well, just flip through here and see. And thank you to Jack.

I

The Corner of Damned and Divine

I run my fingers over my soft-boiled body, my arms then my face, checking to make sure I'm not broken. I touch my tiny chest and tiny legs, expecting to find a million cracks running everywhere. Then I breathe easy. No cracks. Most of me seems to be in one piece.

Through the windows, the world is dusty, everything tall and rickety, a city of mingling shadows, all of them looking down at me as if to say, *You don't belong here, little boy*. I couldn't agree more.

Shifting in my seat, I unfasten the seat belt, rubbing the imprint out of my waist. It is deep and red, turning pink, turning to skin color. I look out over the dash and see nothing but stalks. They are everywhere, high and dense, like urban skylines and grandma hair, all except for one chunk straight ahead of me. My first growth spurt is still years away, long after most people I know will hit theirs, and from this short man's angle, it looks like— Is that a person? No. Ridiculous. What kind of nut would be out here at this time of night? Grave robbers, escaped convicts, werewolves maybe. I look closer, squinting, squinting, and duh, of course.

Dirty but proud looking, he hangs from his wooden post, sort of floating there above the brown and yellow corn, just beyond the punched-in bumper. Based on appearance, he'd never be my first choice, but then again, we're not supposed to base relationships on that, are we? Besides, this isn't the time to be superficial or choosy. Whether I like it or not, I'm stuck with him. He's all I have now, my only comfort out here. Out here, he's my only friend, my only protection, the only thing separating me from darkness and total oblivion. A lot like God in that way, my mom would probably say if she were here—

What's that noise? Insect? Mutant? I'm being stalked. Oh gosh oh gosh—

Fear rattles through me, so I tuck my feet under my butt, and sure, sure, maybe I'm drawing far-fetched conclusions right now, but they seem realistic and certain. I can see it, all of it . . .

Even if I fend off the lurking nocturnal beasts and survive the night, I'm never getting out of here. So this field will be my new home, which means I'll have to learn how to make fire from rocks and how to find water, and at some point, assuming I grow, I'll have to sew myself new clothing out of beaten stalks. I must be resourceful. A savage. But oh! I will be! Eventually I'll marry a field woman. She'll have pigtails, and I'll call her Dandy, because that will remind me of the way life was before it all went wrong. Together we'll gather food, which will be easy—ideal, even—because corn can be used to make a million meals, so that part will be okay. So maybe it won't be all that bad—

Wait. My family will never see me again. Mom will be so worried. She'll cry at night, I'll cry at night, every night—

Oh, this is grim, so grim, devastating, beyond devastating, and I'm trapped picturing it with no one but him, this man on a post, this field king.

To my left, in the driver's seat, is the only other person here. My dad. The beer version of him anyway. He's just beginning to come to, his face baggy and loose, like falling pizza dough, his inflated, surgical-glove hands puffy and red, his eyes gone deep inside his skull.

I guess, contrary to what anyone says, none of us is immune to becoming ugly.

According to the dashboard clock, we're supposed to be at a party by now, one for my parents and their friends, a catered affair, where everyone will show up just a few minutes late—that way the rest of the guests can yell, "Hey! Look at this guy!" when they walk in—and retell the same stories, talking about their diamond lives and how everything is going just as they planned. My mom is already there with my sisters. Dad and I are supposed to be coming late, just the two of us, theoretically a few minutes behind them, and when the night began, this excited me. It meant that I got to spend more time with my dad, and for me, a little kid, life doesn't get much better than that.

Seaweed Monster, I'm Yours

Every year for my birthday, my dad disappears for hours. And every year, his disappearance coincides with the arrival of some hero of mine, some bigger-than-life figure carrying countless wrapped gifts. One year it was a misshapen Spider-Man, the next year it was a Cookie Monster in gym shoes, and then another year the Toyota Tercel Santa. With that last one, I expected the gift haul to be greater than other years, not only because it was Santa, but also because Santa had apparently abandoned his reindeer and sleigh for a roomier, familiar-looking silver hatchback. So I was disappointed when I received the standard amount of presents, even though it was a great deal of presents, way more than I needed.

We always think we need more than we do, and my dad has always given us more than we need. This could be because he was orphaned as a boy and grew up in a neighborhood that spoke with fists and cigarette burns. Since he didn't have much to call his own, he wants us to have it all. He's convinced we deserve every drop of wonder this world has to offer. Don't we all? For better or worse, he's a gift giver—that's his way. And he, not Spider-Man, not Superman, not anyone else, is my real hero. He even has his own fortress of solitude.

The only way to get there, to our vacation house in Wisconsin, is by dirt road. Dirt roads are the only way in and the only way out, and even better, none of them have a speed limit. But there really is no need for them, because it's in the middle of nowhere. It's like the freaking city of gold, so no one can find it without someone who's already been there. And that's the way my dad likes it. I guess we all kind of like it. In many ways, our family has built our life on privacy and secrets—*behind* them is probably a more accurate way to put it. So we'll happily drive the six hours up to that Wisconsin house and stay for weeks at a time, completely removed from civilization, camouflaged, ghost-town kings, confident that our clandestine lives are safe among the trees. It's not half bad, though. Actually, that's where my dad taught me how to fish.

My first rod was one of those crappy plastic Snoopy rods, the kind that sporting goods stores don't sell, the kind that you can only buy at a toy store, right next to the Silly Putty and Rubik's cubes. It didn't really cast, and the line was always getting tangled up, so fishing with my dad back then was mostly an exercise in holding a piece of string into four feet of water and waiting for just one dumb fish to come and sniff it. Predictably, we never really caught much of anything. But that didn't matter; I didn't go for the fish. To just be within reach of my dad, that's why I went—to watch him, to be surprised by him, to be near him . . .

Oh, he does this thing sometimes, this weird thing, where he'll sneak away from where we're fishing or swimming or whatever, without saying a word. Minutes will pass, and then, out of nowhere, he'll emerge from the water, black seaweed draped over his shoulders and across his face and lips. I think he even puts some of it in his mouth—my dad has always taken pretending very seriously, so he goes all out, that's how he is. Imagination is considered a form of genius in our family. Anyway, he'll growl and throw his arms around like a willow, flex his hands into wide, gnarled tarantulas coming at me. He's supposed to be a seaweed monster, and when he does this, he is. He absolutely is. I can't say that I'm ever actually scared, but I do laugh. I laugh until my face hurts.

My dad rarely knows how to talk about feelings or serious things, and because he works so much and is gone so much, he misses a lot of the everyday parts of my life—the homework, the packing of lunches, the tucking in at night—but he does know how to make me laugh, and sometimes there's no better way to love someone than that.

If you want to know the truth, I love my dad. And I love driving with my dad. For whatever reason, some of our best times happen in a car. It's like a glimpse of him in unfiltered form, the dazzling core of the man. He'll sit there behind the wheel, checking the rearview mirror, adjusting his hair, yelling at cars that aren't really in his blind spot for being in his blind spot, and making up little songs about monkeys, but when he isn't doing all of that, we usually discuss the Cubs.

"Man, are they stinking up the joint or what, Josh?"

"Yeah, it doesn't look good."

And we talk about the Bears too.

"Why can't we get any first downs? It's ten yards. *You* could get ten yards, Josh. Should I call Coach Ditka and tell him about you?"

"Dad, you don't really have his number, do you? Do you?"

"What? Well, I'm shocked you'd think I don't really have his number. Your father? I mean, really—"

"Da-ad."

And we talk about the Bulls.

"Josh, I think you should stick your tongue out like Jordan when you play. It might make you jump higher."

"Yeah, right."

"Hey, I'm being serious here. I know what I'm talking about, son. I used to play a little basketball myself. When I was your age, they used to call me . . ."

And then comes a story that he *insists* is complete fact. But no matter how ridiculous it may sound, he makes it so believable. My dad, a veritable urban legend.

Then after that, he usually transitions into telling a string of bad jokes. I'm not talking about the kind of jokes that make you laugh because they're so bad, and you repeat them to four or five more people because the stupidity of them is funny in their own kitschy way, but jokes that sponge the whole room of energy. Of course, like the fishing, none of that matters either. It doesn't matter that the jokes are bad, it only matters that they're between him and me. It only matters that he's telling me the jokes. Me! *Me!* There's nothing I'd rather be than my dad's audience. I guess everybody wants to be somebody's audience, to be near people who live to make us smile, who rally all parts of their energy and personality for our benefit, their life a tribute to us. Some spend their whole life looking for it. Not me, though. I've got it right here.

Sometimes, when the radio dial lands on a song he likes, he sings the lyrics that he knows and improvises the ones that he doesn't, totally winging it and not even coming close to the real words, all in this tortured clarinet falsetto voice.

Yeah, our car rides are epic. I'd let him drive me all the way to the horizon if he offered. But tonight, being in the car with him wasn't like that.

No, tonight was altogether different.

Old Style

Waiting at home to leave for the party, Dad decided to have an Old Style—the official beer of Chicago—before we took off. He does this often. But tonight, one turned into a few, and a few turned into a few more, and a few more turned into a hollow cardboard box, a table littered with empty cans, and my dad speaking only in a loud, wormy language that I didn't know. By the time we left, he probably didn't even remember my name, but he got behind the wheel and drove anyway.

I always hate when my dad drinks. Or maybe I hate my dad when he drinks. Both are true, I think. Most of the time he isn't an angry guy, but with alcohol, something happens to him. Something terrible is unlocked. And a troll awakens.

I once saw him chase my older sister, Corbett, out the front door. His arm was cocked back, a thick book loaded in his right hand, ready to fly in her direction. His eyes were black.

He was breathing fire. She was just a kid when it happened. A little girl! Oh, she was so afraid. It was written all over her face, the expression of prey—

Some nights, after my dad gets home really late from work or from wherever he was, I'll sit perched at the top of the stairs, listening to him yell at my mom about this and that, about adult stuff mostly, stuff that doesn't make any sense to me. From the sound of things, it doesn't make much sense to my mom either. I can only imagine how she feels afterward when she's left sweeping up the pieces of whatever dishes and mugs he smashed in the process.

After the smashing and shouting stops, I usually go back to my room and lie down on the floor or the bed, and there, surrounded by my posters and stuffed animals, I make up little stories and tell them to myself again and again, weaving words into a rope ladder, into a means of escape— But this is all very normal, super normal! Everyone goes through this! I'm not alone. Surely at some point everyone wants to escape the people they love, right? Sure. Sure— But even as I'm escaping, I'm still never far from wondering what my mom possibly could have done to warrant Dad's behavior. I never do come up with much of an answer.

I don't understand, but understanding something isn't a prerequisite to feeling it. We don't have to understand things in order to be affected by them. I may not understand any of this stuff with my dad, my family. But I feel all of it.

Beyond the walls of our house, no one knows about any of that or talks about any of that—not that I know of anyway. We keep that part of ourselves close to the vest. In fact, recently we were straight-out forbidden to talk about it; again with the secrets, again caring so much about what people think, again gauging our lives by the opinions of total strangers. So from the outside, everything must look so shiny and perfect, a little model life, but inside, something other than perfect, other than shiny, has been growing—something that can't be ignored forever.

The sour storm of Dad's breath rained over me as we drove. I was counting how many cars we'd passed—*seven, no, eight, plus the yellow Beetle makes nine! We've passed nine cars! We're so fast, we're winning*—and listening to a song that my dad thought he knew, when we missed that turn. It was a sharp one, and on that dark country road, I guess he probably didn't even see it. We flew right off the pavement and over a patch of grass, ramming right into that wooden fence, reducing it to kindling and shavings. And we didn't stop there. I wish we had, but no. Our momentum took us clean through it, deeper and deeper into that cornfield, each bump heaving me up, the seat belt unyielding, cutting me in half, my fingers wrapped around it so tight I thought they might explode, legs whipping in the air, noodle-like, my eyes pinched shut, our wagon mowing down stalks and sending others over the hood and roof. When we finally came to a stop at the foot of that field king, everything went black and empty. The engine sort of rumbled for a second and then died, and all I could hear was my heart, beat, beat, beating in my chest, all I could feel was the squeezing of my body, every muscle, all of me clenched up, a possum playing dead—frozen, desperate for protection. Safety. I thought that maybe if I was still enough, the whole moment might pass me by, disappear, that my brain was powerful enough to erase what had just happened. But it couldn't.

I suppose we all hit a point when no one has to describe fear and confusion for us anymore, a point when life carves it into us. This was it for me. This was fear. This was confusion. This was having no idea what to do. This was wishing that I were somewhere else, someone else. This was my entrance into reality, new birth.

A moment later, I pried my eyes open. I looked over at my dad, and he was hunched forward, a toppled tree, of no help to me or to himself. Suddenly the world felt foreign, as if we'd slipped right off the edge of the planet, completely unaware.

Around the Wonderful World

Up until now, though, and aside from the angry part of my dad, my life has been mostly brilliant, a wonder. I have a beautiful, middle-class, suburban life, and it suits me fine. Our yard is big and reaching, and while our neighbors are friendly, they know and respect the fact that we like to be left alone. If only we could leave their property alone.

My sisters, Corbett (older) and Quinn (younger), and I like to sneak into Mrs. Hanson's backyard and eat blueberries. The berries taste fine, but the real taste is the danger. The danger is so sweet! We love the danger! One of these days Mrs. Hanson may catch us, drag us into her dungeon, and stew us in that cauldron we know she has, but at the last minute and in miraculous fashion, we'll break free, live another day, and it'll all be worth it, not only because we'll have lived an adventure, but more importantly because we'll have lived it together.

Yes, we fight, as everyone does, but as much as it's possible for siblings to get along, we do. With all the family secrets and seclusion, we're all we've got, and that sort of imaginative, mischievous, creative stuff is what we do. Every summer, when the Illinois air becomes hot and Saran Wrap clingy, we put on these little productions for our parents and neighborhood—we've done a ballet thing, a Michael Jackson tribute, and something from *Guys and Dolls*, and we've even opened an art and comic gallery that turned a small profit—and when we aren't doing that, we explore the open world together. That's how we interact. That's who we are. We live in fantasy, in fiction. Life is more interesting that way. We get it from my mom, I think.

I've traced Mom's evolution through old photographs. The only child of a steelworker, she eventually became a skunk-haired hippie, a real wild woman. Then sometime in the late '70s she got really conservative and started wearing old-fashioned dresses, like she had to churn butter. Seeing the way people change really is something, isn't it?

Anyway, lately she's been talking about love and God a lot, especially during my piano lessons. Oh, right, that's another thing about my mom: she loves music and art, so it's really important to her that we play an instrument. For reasons that are unclear, I chose piano, and I'm already regretting it. Learning to play has been a grind. My thing is that I don't want to learn to be good at it; I want to *already* be good at it. Tapping away at "Ode to Joy" every afternoon is hideous, and that metronome planted on top of the piano shaking its head at me, back and forth, seems so disapproving. I hate it. Forget that! I want to play big music, stadium music, like Billy Joel and Stevie Wonder! I want to attract the universe with my music, to be the sun, to toast every corner of the world! My mom tells me that if I work hard, one day I could. I believe her.

At night she comes into my room, sits down on the bed, and reads to me from the books she loves, books that she hopes I'll love too, like *The Lion, the Witch and the Wardrobe* and *The Magic Bicycle* and *Love You Forever*. She's a great reader, my mom, using voices, dramatic pauses, and wide, sweeping hand gestures. She's a wizard, the way she can speak the story out of thin air and into my room, conjuring it right in front of me, the characters dancing and swinging from the walls, my bed becoming other towns, lands, and planets. Some of the other kids I know dream about traveling around the world, but I don't need to do that. My mom takes me every day.

Like I said, life has been brilliant. I'm a little boy, and I already have more to smile about than most do in an entire lifetime. Blessings do exist.

Arsonists and Architects

Under the moon, everything is bluish now. Blue stalks. Blue car. Blue fingernails. A Smurf world. As for my dad, he's gone blue too, still dumped over the wheel. My hero cut down—

Rustling and the crunching of hay break the quiet. Wiggling his arms loose of their ties, the field king stretches his neck, tilting it to one side, then to the other, and then upright again. Leaping down off his post, he marches up onto the hood of the car, his rugged boots denting the metal, his frame massive above me. Slowly he crouches down to my level, his coat spread out into a parachute behind him. He raises his hat slightly. Gentleness swirls in his eyes. Through the glass, they hold me tight. He asks if I am okay.

And while I know this whole scene bends life's rules—that this is supernatural—I'm not stunned. My heart is still young, so at this point, life's rules are elastic. It won't be until later that life's boundaries appear to be made of bone and concrete, not until later that I'm resistant to what I don't already know. So for now, this scene makes perfect sense to me, absolutely, and I talk back to him.

I tell him that I'm okay, sort of, I guess. And because I've been taught to be polite, a good boy, no exceptions, I ask him what his name is.

Jack, he says.

I tell him my name is Josh.

He knows that, he says. Then, reading my contorted and obviously confused face, he asks me what's on my mind.

I tell him that it feels like the whole world has gone horribly wrong.

Jack says that in a way, it has. He says something is horribly wrong with the world, with life, and with people too. But then he says that the world and life and people aren't total horror. Jack says there is good in the world and good in people. He reminds me of laughter, of love, and of fishing. He reminds me of the way the sky looks at sunset, sort of watercolored, round scoops of cherry ice cream clouds floating above, the air so sugary you want to roll your tongue over it. He reminds me of the times when everything feels perfect, and then he promises that I'll get more moments like that, moments that he says will feel bigger and higher, moments that will carry me through.

I listen to him, taking it all in, and thinking about it. Then I ask him what it all means. I ask him what the world is, what life is, and about people too.

Jack hesitates, adjusting his position on the hood of the car, arching his back, crunching around and shaking his hands out, flinging bits of hay into the air and sending bugs scattering for cover. He settles again and says that all thieves can be generous, and that even the kindest person hates. Every human, Jack says, is both an arsonist and an architect, marked with the thumbprint of good and the claws of evil, breathing both death and life into this world. Humans, Jack says, are both the stench and the aroma.

I look over at my dad, my disintegrating hero, and ask Jack if that includes him too. Jack nods, says it does, and says that it's also true of me.

A moth flies out of a hole in his shirt, then loops above the wide field toward that party, toward that house of laughing and drinks and glittery happiness where my dad and I are supposed to be, toward the life I'm supposed to have.

Then Jack tells me that this world is actually two worlds combined, one world of everything that I hope for and the other world of nothing that I want. This world, Jack says, is the merging of wonder and horror, of twisted and beautiful, comedy and tragedy, a place where both exist and mingle every day. He says that this world is part heaven and part hell, and that every second, inside of me and out, I'm standing at the convergence of the two, at the corner of damned and divine.

My mom doesn't let me say *damn*. I tell Jack this. He tells me that I have a good mom. Then I ask him if it's like that everywhere, for everyone. He sighs, heavy and full, his chest expanding and sinking, and says yes, for now anyway—

Noises crawl from Dad's mouth. He begins stirring, and with that, Jack leaps from the hood of the car and vanishes into the cornstalk jungle. Slowly, Dad snaps out of it, shaking off the stupor, coming back from wherever he's been. He looks through the windshield, then at me, wiping his eyes, sort of feeling over his body the way I did. Then he breathes easier, because at least for one more night, he dodged oblivion. Slowly, he backs the station wagon out of that field, leaving a pair of deep tire trenches and a splintered fence.

From deep in the passenger seat, I wave to Jack, to my guardian, wherever he is, and strange as it is, while he's somewhere out in that field, I know that he's also coming with me.

Once we're back on the road, I'm clinging to my seat belt again, my fingers crimped and throbbing. There is no music and no laughing. Dad is not performing, and I am not his audience. I am not anything. I'm a ghost. There are things that I want to say. I want to ask my dad why I have to beg to get him to throw the football with me, and why he doesn't like coming home, and what beer gives him that I can't, and if he's ever going to stop drinking, and if he loves me . . . but

I don't. There are certain questions that you don't really want answered— The car cruises along, slow and paranoid, and with each rotation of the tires, I'd almost rather be back in that field, where the quiet wasn't nearly as painful. Dad won't talk to me. He doesn't say anything. He doesn't apologize or console me. Or maybe he does. My mind is too busy running to pay attention, too busy trying to protect itself, so as we ride, maybe he apologizes a thousand times. Or maybe he just bottles the whole thing up and sucks it way down into that part of ourselves where we keep the things we're trying to ignore or forget. I don't know. All I know is that we make it to the party, and all the waxed people are laughing and eating, playing games and smiling, clinking their glasses together, while my sisters and I run around, eating junk food and sliding on the floor in our socks, and everything is back to the way it should be: a little model life.

II

To the Ground, Smoked

This hallway never shuts up. It's been rambling about nothing for years, and now here I am, seventeen years old, and it's still gabbing away as I step across the gummy floor in the northwest corner of the house till I reach the door to the study.

The polished brass color of the knob is gone, but I turn it, giving the door a shove. No luck. It opens only a few inches. I shove again, but still only a few inches. Something on the other side is blocking it, or maybe pushing back against it:

a wild boar, a family of elves, or perhaps a sequestered twin brother of mine, one I've never met, a boy named Egg. Why am I even doing this? I should walk away, forget about this room, but because I have raw teenage determination and am invincible, I can't. I want to see it, so I grab the knob again, lean into the wood of the door, and wedge all of my 150-pound self against it, against it, against it, and ha! It finally slides open, plowing a mountain of boxes and papers and clothes and who knows what else out of the way. Slipping sideways through the opening, I step onto what used to be carpet. Still carpet? There could be anything under here now. The floor is gone forever, buried under years of things that we once thought would save us and make us new, things we thought we wanted. We didn't know what we wanted.

Sometimes I wonder if anyone really does.

This whole mess started innocently enough, years earlier. Mom would come into my room to wake me up. Of course, I fought it, rolling over, cocooning myself in what I believed to be my invisibility blankets, disappearing and pretending not to hear her, pretending to still be sleeping. In retaliation, she'd make all kinds of noises. She'd sing, push me, rip the covers off my body, pull the curtains open, and flash the lights on and off. And when I was especially resistant, she'd . . .

"Come on, Joshy!"

Splash!

"Mom!"

. . . lob cups of cold water on me, which was indefensible.

"Cold, isn't it?"

Splash!

"Stop it!"

"Oh, come on, you big baby. We got a lot of living to do!"

"Nooooo." (I drew out my "no" as long as possible, just to be sure she understood the magnitude of my discomfort and displeasure.)

"Up and at 'em! Let's go! Let's go! If we don't get going, all the good stuff'll be gone!"

"I don't wanna go. Please let me stay in bed. I'm so tired. Sooooo tired."

"I don't think so. I'm going to go get more water."

Splash!

"Fine!"

Our family would stomp out to the van and cruise all over the Midwest. I have to admit, once I was awake and in the van beside my sisters, it was kind of exciting, like blazing the Oregon Trail but with the McDonald's breakfast menu. Hitting every garage sale, antique store, flea market, and auction within driving distance became a noble quest. We were so ambitious! On Saturdays we didn't watch cartoons, we didn't jump in piles of leaves, we didn't sleep in; no, we scavenged through other people's stuff, through boxes and aisles and bins and stacks and crates. And when we found something good—that old-fashioned butcher block, the lobster trap, the sea captain statue that we needed to complete the sea captain statue collection—it wasn't just good, it was like we'd discovered plutonium! We'd struck oil! We were Lewis and Clark finding the Pacific!

By the time evening arrived and we headed for home, our van was usually crammed with lamps, worn books, snowshoes, skis, snowmobile helmets, old toys, bikes, spoons, billiard equipment, records, trinkets, marbles, jars, clutter, blah, clothes that didn't fit any of us, blah, this and that, and other random objects that we were going to forget about twenty minutes after they came into the house. But that's what we did. We were pack mules.

Of course, next came the task of finding a place to stick it all. This was a lot like playing Tetris—the strategic shifting and rotating of objects—and it became a greater and greater challenge as the years rolled by and the closet, shelf, and room space ran out. But we always summoned a special reservoir of creativity and found a way, found a spot, and then continued searching for more bargains. Another rattan chair was added to the living room, where no one sat in the chairs we already had. In the kitchen, where we never cooked, more pots were added. An eighth ceramic windmill, this one coral green, was added to the ledge above the toilet—

I mean, sure, having nothing probably sucks, but I'm beginning to think that having too much is even worse— Why did we do this? And why are we still doing it? Why? Why do we keep filling our house with more stuff? And why can't we ever subtract anything? Just one thing! This isn't normal— For years we've been tirelessly expanding our knickknack empire, convinced that happiness is just an acquisition away, after which we'll never want or need again. But with each thing we add, we seem to become more and more unhappy. I guess happiness is rarely as simple as addition. Is anything significant ever that simple? It doesn't feel that way— But complicated . . . well, these days everything feels complicated, as if every choice and idiosyncrasy and mistake of both my family and my ancestors have been spun—are still being spun?—into an intricate, sticky web in which we've now all been caught—

Look at this place. Gosh, we're freaks.

Slugger

On a table along the wall, the old computer—not our current old one, but our prior old computer—stares at me all blank and pathetic, begging for help. At one time, this was the pinnacle of technology. I sat at it for hours, punching away, sliding and clicking the mouse, those erratic *grrraaaas* and *dadadadas* ringing out from the monitor. I felt so powerful. I ran the entire government from that thing. I was an astronaut. But as I see it now, it's old and terrible. Dust all over its face. A pair of gym shorts flung over the top. A big smear of some black or brown or furry thing on the side. Steak-sized floppy discs and books dumped on top of the keyboard. It's nothing. It's ringing a tin cup against bars, sentenced to forever exist in a world that has forgotten all about it, moved on, become obsessed with the next big thing.

Using my foot as a shovel, I scoop and shift things out of the way, clearing a narrow path for myself. After a few times, it becomes a little game to see how high and far my foot can launch whatever it has picked up, so boxes hit walls, toys smack the ceiling. As I scoop and toss, scoop and toss, I begin wondering if I might find anything interesting, something meaningful that I lost years ago—a great piece of vintage clothing? Maybe even . . . a bowling shirt? Some lost Mayan relic? A genie lamp? But after a few minutes of finding nothing, I stop wondering. There is nothing in here that I want. I hate all of it. It's all junk, and even the stuff that isn't junk is junk to me. Everything has crumbled—this room, the whole house, and our family too.

It happened so fast. It usually does. Blink, and you're a different person, with a different life. On the plus side, this means that every single breath matters. On the negative side, this also means that there's no such thing as downtime. One night/move/conversation/decision really can change everything. Or in my case, maybe one car ride.

Ever since that night in the cornfield, I've been a different person, with a different life. Letting anyone in seems impossible now, and that includes Jack. Weird, isn't it? I figured he and I would be close forever, and for a while we were. But these days I don't think about him much, and I see him even less. Hey, even life's most powerful moments can be forgotten.

And as for my dad, well, in my mind, he died among those stalks. Yes, I gave it a chance. Held out hope. For years I believed that he, my hero, would return, rise from the ashes. I waited for him, but it never happened. And you can only wait so long for someone who isn't coming. Right? Now I've accepted the truth: my hero isn't coming back, and in his place is a monster. Every night, my dad, the monster, walks through our front door. Seeing him, I can't scurry up the stairs fast enough. How do you laugh with a monster? How do you ride in a car with a monster? How do you hold a monster's hand? Won't the monster just devour you? And if I let that happen, how could I live with myself? I couldn't. I won't.

That night in the field was the breaking point. All those years of drinking, being gone, the fire-breathing moments, watching my mom erode—all of it was too much. He's a monster to me now. He's become the seaweed creature that he used to impersonate. He is around more, though, which only makes it more difficult to shove him away.

Going through the twelve steps of Alcoholics Anonymous, a decade of sobriety, and his fading health have all worked to reform him, I guess, enlighten him. So now he tries talking with me. He comes to everything I do—the concerts, the musicals, the soccer games, the basketball games—shouting and booing, so passionate, so supportive, so present. And he tries engaging with me afterward too, starting conversations about my car and my friends and sports, the way we used to, but there's nothing epic or beautiful about it anymore. It's a nuisance to me now. No, he is, like a piece of gum stuck to the bottom of my— Am I being too hard on him? I suppose it's possible that I'm simply casting him as the villain so I have someone to blame for my flaws, for all the ills of my life. After all, blame is how we make sense of our lives. Blame fills in the gaps. In the absence of a true villain in our lives, we're bound to enlist one. Sure, it may not be the best way, or fair, but it does help us explain our stories. Is that what I'm doing with my dad? Maybe.

But whatever the case, I try my best to dodge him, or at the very least to give him as little of me as possible. I'm still locked down. I'm still playing dead. He wasn't there for me when I wanted him. Why should I be there for him now that he wants me? Ugh, it's all so "Cat's in the Cradle" and clichéd and angst-soaked teen that I can't stand it.

All of this absurdity became obvious to me recently during the biggest basketball game in my feeble athletic career. My high school was playing against our rivals, and the whole place was jammed with face-painted people screaming. We started slow and pathetic, and we were down big before we knew it. It didn't look good, but methodically, confidently, we chipped away. As the seconds ticked down, our rally became complete, and we took the lead. The place was in a frenzy, about to pop. The other team had one last chance, a prayer from half court. The ball went up, sailing, sailing, but no! We won! We won!

When the horn sounded, the stands emptied, pouring onto the court, onto us, like ants to sugar. Oh, we were sweet and delicious, the center of the universe. Overwhelmed by it all, I collapsed onto the floor, mobbed by hysterical fans, all of them clutching and shouting and tugging, their mouths echoing our greatness. They wanted us. We wanted them. The hysteria was desperate and enormous, everything. I lost myself, so overcome in what I was sure would be the greatest moment of my life, of all our lives—

Then, from behind, spindly tentacles wrapped around me and squeezed. I couldn't move, but I felt the bristly hairs of a familiar beard poking into my neck, and I smelled the English Leather aftershave.

"I love you, son!"

He shouted it right in my ear, so there would be no missing it.

"I love you, son!"

Each phrase just barely able to wiggle its way through his tears.

"I'm so proud of you!"

If it wouldn't have made a scene, I would have rammed my fist right into his grizzled face, knocked him into the open grave I thought he belonged in. Him there, touching me, felt sick, gross. I was locked in an attic with a million centipedes crawling over me. I had to get away, but I didn't want to panic or draw attention. So instead, I pushed him off discreetly and burrowed my way into the warm center of the crowd, making it seem like I was being gobbled up against my will by the mad celebration. Cold-blooded, I know, but he hadn't been there for me, so he didn't deserve this now. This was the greatest moment of my life, and he hadn't earned his spot at the table. He'd forfeited his share years ago. I'd share it with the entire human race—ex-girlfriends, sisters, friends, teachers, terrorists, convicts, perverts—but not with him. I would not share this moment with a monster.

Vengeance is mine.

But it's not just my relationship with my dad that has crumbled. My sisters and I don't really talk anymore either. Our adventures have stopped, and we live in reality now, a harsh reality where we don't know each other. I suppose that's reality for all of us, including my mom and dad.

There was a night when I couldn't sleep. I came out of my room, looking for a snack—cookies, pudding, anything sweet, whatever—and found my mom sleeping on the couch. No pillow, no blanket, one arm draped off the side, her leg thrown up against the back, like she was sleeping on a park bench, homeless in her own home. I stood there and knew that obviously this had to be accidental. Yes, yes, it had to be—this was just an accident. I knew she'd never choose this. She fell asleep reading or watching a movie that dragged on too long. That's it! I've done that! Everyone has done that! In my mind, that's all this was, and nothing more, nothing more, nothing more. Any minute, my dad, longing for her, would come out and get her, carry her to bed with him, back to where she belonged. Right? Right? But over the next few days, I found out that it wasn't an accident. My mom had moved out of the bedroom. She and Dad were sleeping in separate rooms now, living in different parts of the house: Dad upstairs, Mom downstairs.

Marriage may be how two become one, but this is how one becomes two.

Seeing and living in this tension every day, I've made my oath. Marriage isn't for me. I won't be volunteering for the same war that they've been fighting now for years. Every day it's two sides, two empires, him versus her, endless crossfire. And in this war, there are no winners, just more arguments about where an envelope went and whether or not the phone actually rang.

True, they aren't divorced, not legally anyway—just in the ways of intimacy and tenderness and friendship and partnership and, well, all the ways that matter. Since no else is willing, I've even taken a stab, mentally, at drawing up the divorce papers for them.

The document is long, full of clauses and complicated jargon, complete with an embossed seal in the top center of the page, an owl wearing black shorts and purple suspenders, holding a rolled piece of parchment in one claw and a revolver in the other. Naturally, I'll be the one to deliver the document to my parents, because that way I can make sure they got it and it isn't lost in the metropolis of other paper stacks around the house. Then I'll watch, urging them with my eyes not to think about it, just to sign right there, get it over with, because this is best for everyone, especially the children. And that will be it.

Then Dad will move out, into a crummy one-bedroom apartment with a doorbell that doesn't work and a screen door with a hole in it. The inside will smell like flannel and hairspray and microwave dinners, and we'll eat on paper plates whenever we come to visit, which will be every weekend, then every other weekend, then once a month, until not at all. Mom will stay in our house, and from time to time, a weird man with thinning hair and a turtleneck will show up carrying flowers, give me crappy presents that I have to pretend to like, and refer to me as Slugger while he fiddles with the exposed wires from this dumb old computer that we don't even use, assuring us that he almost has it working again.

Life Sucker

I stand here scanning the heaps. They go on and on. They are a metaphor for us.

Way on top of a bookcase in the corner of the room is a white teddy bear dressed in a white T-shirt. On the shirt, in hurried, hand-drawn marker letters, it says, "Happy Mother's

Day." Even when I gave it to her, I knew it wasn't much of a gift, certainly not one that took any forethought. Mom said she really liked it, but I knew that wasn't true. That's one of those times when lying is a good thing, I guess. Like anyone, she was hoping for something a little more meaningful, hoping for a little effort on my part, hoping for something that she could really be proud of. This room used to be that for her. The whole house was.

There was a time when you could see the floors and the windows were clean, a time when the pantry wasn't filled with trash bags, when the toilets and sinks worked—and didn't resemble Saturn, the rust rings—when the countertops weren't covered in prescription containers, when you didn't have to worry about bug colonies, when patches of green alien-skin mold weren't coming through the ceiling. It was a place with an enviable potpourri smell, a lilac and cinnamon thing, a place where you could invite your friends and girlfriends, a place where you could cook things and celebrate things, a place you could point at and say, "Yes! I live there! Look where I live!" But not anymore. Not even close—

Suddenly I'm punched by an aggressive and all-too-familiar smell wafting from the boxes and floor. The smell is angry and toxic, filling my nose and mouth. I try fashioning my arm into an impromptu gas mask, but it doesn't help. I cup my hands. I hold my breath. It's useless. Nothing helps. The runaway fumes wiggle into my eye sockets and skin, clogging every pore, before chugging down into my throat, scraping my insides raw, the way only airborne cat urine can— Yes, as if all the junk we've collected wasn't enough, we're also the cat family. And we've housed a varying number of the purring rats throughout the years.

Beginning when I was eight or so, we've never had any less than three, and at one point we had as many as thirteen/fifteen, but the exact number always seemed to elude us, which made the feeding process problematic and sloppy. We would dump a guesstimated amount of wet cat food into and near little plastic animal bowls, trusting that the mysterious number of cats were intelligent enough to come and eat. There was always too much there—leaving much of it to harden into thick, brown, fly-attracting floor cakes—partly because the cats began dying off and often we were unaware of it. A striped or all-black one would pass into kitty heaven quietly and with little fanfare, by way of old age, in the basement or garage (two places that no one ever visited), or by way of sneaking out of the house unbeknownst to us and never returning.

Other times, though, we knew. For example, I once walked in the front door of the house to find a big sheet of newspaper thrown over a lump on the floor.

"Dad?"

"Josh? That you?" he shouted back from upstairs.

"Yeah."

"Hey, son!"

"Dad?"

"Yeah?"

"Why is the newspaper spread on the floor?"

. . .

"Dad?"

"Yeah."

"What's underneath it?"

"I think one of the cats is dead."

"You *think* it is?"

"It is."

You know those television shows where people become trapped in their own homes, by their own stuff, by their own lives, and you don't want to watch but you have to watch, because you just can't believe anyone lives that way, and it sort of makes you feel as if your life is in order because their lives are so obviously out of order? Well, that's us. Our disorder is everyone else's assurance. We are comfort for the masses. This is no longer a house. This is no home. This is a landfill, and we did it to ourselves.

I guess it's true what they say: if you don't know what you want to fill your life with, there's a good chance you're going to fill it with everything that you don't—

My chest is burning now, my lungs singed. The urine smell in the room wins, and I can't take another second. Holding my breath, I turn and walk along my path until I'm out of the room, suctioning down the gummy hallway, blowfish-puffed, all the way to the front door of the house, but even here the smell and burning lingers. Everywhere it lingers. Oh, I hate this place. I hate what it's done to us. I hate that leaving home is the best part of my day.

At my feet, my bag is waiting for me. It's time to go. I have a basketball game tonight. And once I'm there, none of this will matter.

For a few hours, I'll be set free by a bouncing ball. Rubber salvation.

The outside of my coat is slick, and water repellent too, I think. I slip it on and step outside into the white and cold. The dang wind cuts through my clothes to my skin. I pull the collar up around my neck, creating a sort of Dracula look for myself. I am a vampire. No, this house is the real vampire, sucking the life out of us. I'd love to drive a stake right through the heart of this place. Someday. I slam the front door behind me, and against the faded, peeling wood, the broken knob rattles loose.

Black-Winged Snake

The wipers aren't working.

I'm blaming them for this, belittling them with breathy words. But they don't change their ways. They don't feel bad. They shouldn't feel bad. It's my fault. I didn't take the proper time to scrape the windshield, so as they click over the thick layer of ice, I'm leaning across the center console, staring out a softball-sized porthole in the middle, like a submarine commander. But because I believe myself to be just a bit extraordinary, I'm not worried. I'm confident in my ability to drive safely while seeing only seven percent of the road. I will sense the activity on the other ninety-three percent!

I am supernatural. I am an idiot.

I'm on my way home from the basketball game—at least I think I am. Every time I'm out, I consider never going back. Someday, I tell myself. Someday. But at least for tonight, I'll return. I didn't play very well. Actually I didn't really play, but we won again. Our basketball team is great this year. The whole high school is behind us, and that feels very good. And now, crawling up Rosewood Drive, I'm bracing myself for the tension of home, the eye rolling, the mess, and the smell, so I'm putting my shields up. By the time I enter, I'll be bulletproof, impenetrable. Nothing will get in.

The neighborhood smells of smoke, and right now fire sounds wonderful. Just to sit by our fireplace—that goodness nearly outweighs the other elements that I want to run away from—

The loud *woo, woo, woo* of sirens explodes around the corner, fast, along with lights flashing red and blue. I pull to the side, still inhaling the fireplace smell, and watch the fire truck, police car, and ambulance go speeding by, off to rescue someone. I wish they'd rescue me. As I pull back out onto the street, the reds and blues continue spinning on the asphalt, bracketed by white snow, and I'm reminded of birthday cake. It's the most beautiful thing I've seen in a long time.

Now thirty seconds from home, I begin forming my entrance strategy. I'll grab my bag, remove the key from the ignition, shut the car door with my foot, run over the snow and ice, shut the front door behind me, and then curl up near the fireplace just long enough to get warm, but not long enough to get stuck engaging anyone, which must be avoided at all costs. And as an added bonus, my proximity to the fireplace will no doubt diffuse some of the vicious cat odor, which also must— Wait. Are the *woo, woo, wooing* vehicles parked in front of our neighbor's house? I hope they're okay! Hopefully they— Oh my gosh, no! They aren't parked in front of our neighbor's house! They're parked in front of our house!

Synced perfectly with this realization, our front door whips open, releasing a winged snake of smoke. Flapping and slithering, it sweeps over the yard and up past the gutters and roof, its tongue flickering, licking everything black and dead all over. From the car, I have an unobstructed view. Drive-in theater. My dad, that monster, comes out the front door, off the porch, and into the snow. Where is his shirt? Where are his pants? He's in his underwear, turquoise, popping his bony knees and arms up and down like a marionette, doing some kind of German techno dance, screaming.

"IT'S OVER HERE!"

He runs toward the uniformed emergency people, pointing back at the house.

"[INDISCERNIBLE YET ELOQUENT JIBBERISH! CURSING?]"

The snow kicks up around his feet. His hands are daggers, jabbing into the air, back to the house, into the air again.

"The fire! It's over here! HURRYYYY!!"

Corbett, Quinn, my mom, and Corbett's boyfriend come running out, coughing, just as the firemen rush past them into the house. Neighbors we don't know are gathering along the sidewalk—nightgowns and robes—whispering among themselves. In slow motion, I step out of the car and walk into the yard. This can't be real. This must be a play. These must be actors, props, costumes, pyrotechnics— The sound of heat on glass bursts in my ears, and my face grows hotter, making me more alert. What should I do? What should I do? I should be saving someone or something I care about: a photo album, a favorite tie, a few cats maybe! Yes! Yes! I should move! Perform an act of bravery! But I don't, so I feel wrong inside. I'm as frozen as my windshield. Staring. Watching our house burn—

My mom sprints toward me with her arms spread wide. "Josh! You're okay! You're okay! You're okay!"

"Mom, I'm fine."

She grabs me, hysterical, eyes clenched tight, sobbing. "You're okay! You're okay! You're okay!"

"Yeah, Mom, I'm okay."

"I thought you were inside, but we couldn't find you. I looked everywhere upstairs and then ran downstairs. I was calling your name, and then I asked Quinn and Corbett if they knew where you were, and your father was shouting like a lunatic, and then he ran outside. I thought—"

She keeps sobbing, squeezing.

"You're okay."

Behind her, the black and yellow rubber-wasp-looking firefighters are yelling to each other, aiming hoses into the flames, the winged snake shrieking and breaking apart in the water.

"You're okay, Josh. You're okay . . ."

A thousand trillion objects we've collected and clutched and counted on for salvation are melting and disintegrating in sweet flames, fluttering up in chunks into the sky, sinking into the ground. I guess everything in life can be reduced to ash.

Mom is still whimpering on and on, so I hold her tight and inhale it all, staring quietly over her shoulder into the orange and black mess of our house. And suddenly I feel only warm inside, lucky inside, the way lottery winners must feel right before they are handed that oversized novelty check.

The back of the ambulance feels the same as a hospital—cold and metal and lonely. They take each of us in, one at a time. I sit with a paramedic.

"You feeling okay, son?"

"I feel fine."

"Are you sure? You light-headed? Any pain in your chest? You don't have like a gravel feeling in there, do you?"

"A gravel feeling?"

"You know, harsh? Kind of choppy?"

He feels my chest a bit and then plays with my head and arm.

"No."

"What about your eyes, any stinging or burning?" He shines a light into my face.

"I said I'm fine."

When I step out of the ambulance, the fire is out. The neighbors are gone. The emergency vehicles are moving on. The snow in the yard is no longer white. Ashy boot prints are everywhere. The front door is still open. The windows are all broken out, and the house is smoldering, caved in, a Halloween pumpkin on November 8. And though it's still freezing out here, I'm impervious to it. I'm bright and weightless, a balloon in the wind, because this event is a gift in disaster's clothing. And I know it.

For years, we've been a white-knuckled bunch, holding on so tight to all our stuff. We couldn't let go of all these things that have been killing us. Somehow we treasured our tormentors. We wouldn't light the match and burn it all down by choice, but now nature has intervened and done it for us. Or maybe Jack did. If I scoured the area, I'd find his footprints, a gas can, an eyewitness, something linking him to this scene, I'm sure— But regardless of who or what deserves the credit, tonight in these flames and screams, we've been given a blank slate. No more mess! No more stuff! No more shame! No more buried alive! Who knows? This fire might even reset our relationships, end my parents' war, get them sharing a bedroom again, talking again, wipe our bitterness and anger away, resuscitate our collective soul, and— Okay, now I'm getting carried away. I mean, sure, our house is a blank slate, but our home isn't, because relationships can't ever *really* start over. Can they? Yes, in song lyrics, in big promises, in a metaphorical sort of way, but not in actuality. Hearts don't work that way, like an Etch A Sketch—

The ambulance pulls away from the curb, and now it's just us, standing on the stained front yard, alone. Shouldn't we hug each other or something? This feels like a hugging moment, yes, a moment when loving families—real families—probably circle up into one of those long-drawn-out group hugs that lasts forever, lasts so long it eventually pivots into everyone standing next to each other, shoulder to shoulder, the way the Rockettes do. That's exactly what we should do! But no. That's not our style. So instead we exchange some shoulder tapping and brief squeezes, making sure that everyone is alright, and then we fan out a few feet away from each other, our breath visible in the air, looking silently together at this open space of a house—this giant canvas that can become whatever we want it to be—wanting so badly for the same to be true of our family.

The Holiday Inn next to the White Castle is the closest hotel, so we drive there. With little to carry in, the unpacking process from the car is quick and simple. We walk into the lobby. At the front desk, we huddle together with our bundles, our tragically smudged faces, and our opportunistic eyes. We are refugees now. The night manager hands us our keys, and without telling him about our misfortune or how much pity he ought to have on us, we shuffle to the two rooms that we'll be living in for the next few months.

Corbett, Quinn, and my mom disappear behind a door. My dad and I do the same. Once we are in our room, I inhale that housekeeping smell, that fresh laundry smell. It's fragrant: the perfume of the gods. Everything should smell like this! Everything should feel like this, look like this! The curtains are thrown open, and there is no dirt on the windows. Whoever took care of the dirt, I want to hug that person. There's an area to walk in, an area to sit in, a mold-free refrigerator, and no excess. I can see the floor. It's green, a bed of clovers against my feet. I think about inviting people over. I can't wait to show off our palace.

I unzip my bag and change into a pair of sweatpants, then I climb into the clean sheets of my new bed. The blankets are soft in a way that I'd forgotten blankets could be. My dad is already in his bed, on his back, with his hands clasped across his stomach, staring up intensely, as if the answer to an important question is painted on the ceiling. I keep watching him as he searches, and for some reason, he looks different than he did just hours ago. For the first time in my life, my dad isn't a hero or a monster to me. He's something in between; he's a man. Just a man trying to find his way, a man just like me, a man who maybe isn't sure how things got to be the way they are, a man who deep down wants them to change, a man who knows we can't start over but hopes that maybe we can move forward, a man who isn't sure where or how to start. Like father, like son, I guess.

And then, right then, instead of just floating distant into tomorrow, I want to talk, I want to connect with my dad, to let him in. Anything would be a step; anything initiated on my end would be something to build on, relationally ground-breaking, positive.

"Dad?"

"Yeah?"

"I just thought of something."

"Yeah? What's that, Josh? And can I get this light?"

"What do you think happened to all the cats?"

"I don't have any idea, son. But between you and me, I know what I'm hoping happened to them."

As he turns out the light, both of us are laughing a bit, his smile shining there in the dark for a moment, like fireflies are glued to his teeth.

Even a sigh reminds us
that we're alive.

EJ

III

A Minnesotan

This is a fourteen- to twenty-hour drive, the majority down one highway, Route 80, all flat, all truck stops, not even a Cracker Barrel or a pass-through Branson to cheer me up. The whole way, rumbling along in my Jeep, I keep repeating the words *transfer senior* over and over in my head. But I have to finish my education somewhere, so I was told, and the first two places didn't work out so well. On top of that, I've backpedaled on all that fresh start and family stuff. I don't know why. I guess going backward is sometimes easier than going forward. I may not like it all that much, but at least it's familiar.

So now I just want to get away, far away, to leave life as I know it in the rearview mirror. I want to find a beautiful place, a place with different people, people who will like me, people I will like, a place where my problems and fears will be different, a place with different restaurants and different smells and a different sky. Everything different, a place where I'll be different, better. So I'm heading west to Colorado, and I'm driving the whole way with the top down, which I'm hoping will accomplish two things.

I'm hoping it will (1) add to my euphoria while placing a symbolic exclamation point on my newfound freedom for all to see, and (2) darken my tan, whereby increasing my chances (hopefully) of attracting potential girlfriends. Oh, I'm excited. I'm ready. I've never lived outside of the Chicago area before, but hey, twenty-one years was a good run.

The house I move into is on the west side of campus. It's a fine house, and clean by my paltry standards, which makes it feel nothing like home. Everything inside is white and fresh, recently wiped. There are no piles. And no endless train of boxes. I don't know how to act in this kind of house, what behavior is considered acceptable. I don't know where I should leave my shoes or how to wipe up spills, so I feel even more insecure around my new roommates. I've never met any of them, but they are already friends with each other. There's Garth from Oregon. There's Nolan, who spent some time in prison, drug related. There's Lewis, an RA. And there's Bon, who may be a Viking. They seem to be normal guys, kind guys, and completely unaware that I am a fugitive running from another life.

They shake my hand, help me carry my stuff into the house, and explain the system by which we'll keep the refrigerator organized. Overall it seems to be a good system, and they are good guys, but I'm not sure if we'll be friends or not, and more than anything else, that's what I want from Colorado.

I don't want the college degree, or the mountains, or the raging, rowdy, college nights. I want friends.

As I left Chicago, people told me that I didn't need friends. They told me that Jack would be with me and that he was all I needed. Because I'm rude sometimes, I laughed at this. Jack and I have sort of fallen out of touch, and that doesn't really bother me right now. To me, he's a fading memory, so I had a hard time taking what people said seriously. And of course, they had the luxury of telling me that and then jumping into a carful of smiling companions, whizzing down the road with the windows open, the warm August air blowing through their hands, their own personal Abercrombie ad. So their advice sounded philosophical and comforting, I guess, but from their position, it was easy to say. And besides, arriving in Colorado, I don't feel that way. It feels like friends are exactly what I need. Right? Yes, I need people to make memories and bad and good decisions with, people to talk to when I'm lonely and vent to when I'm mad, people who know the exact drink I order at Starbucks, people who get my sense of humor and won't require further explanation when I utilize said humor, and people to go out with when I'm bored.

Friends.

Across the courtyard is another house. There is Guy. There is Ewan. There is Vince, who does impersonations. There is Josh (we call him Ralphie since he resembles the kid from that movie *A Christmas Story*). And finally, there is Wallace.

Like me, Wallace has just arrived in Colorado, also as a transfer, coming from Minnesota. We meet and, after hanging out a few times, find that we share a love of football and 1980s movies. We begin hanging out more. During the week, Wallace and I go to the gym together, and at night, at his townhouse, with his roommates and others (including girls I'm trying to impress), we watch all those '80s movies that for whatever reason matter to us. And come Sunday, we watch football, shouting at the television and talking about teams and players and memorable games.

Some might call this a superficial connection, but since I'm alone and in a new place, this superficial connection isn't superficial. These little things we have in common aren't little. They are lifeboats, little rabbit holes of possibility, of potential. They are a sniff of camaraderie and relationship, so they matter. *Fletch* and *Karate Kid* and *The 'Burbs* and *Caddyshack* and *The Great Outdoors*—they aren't just movies. No, no, no! They are so much more than that. Football chatter isn't just football chatter; it's jumping into the seat of a catapult and throwing myself into the chance of a great bond. Yes! It's fishing without a line and hoping, fingers crossed, that someone will bite. It's the possibility of not being alone. And I want that! Everybody wants that! We all want the possibility of not being alone.

The look of grass and streets trapped under frozen glass reminds me of home, the everlasting Midwest cold, but not enough for me to talk to my family. Since I left, we've spoken very little, which means that part of the mission has been accomplished. Corbett has a job doing I'm not sure what, Quinn is in college, studying something or other, and Dad and Mom are still whatever. I'm content with it this way, though, because I have far more important things to think about right now. Winter is here, and since it's been a while since we've escaped campus, my friends and I have grown antsy, and like wedding champagne, we just need to get out! So we're on our way to Kmart.

Rumor has it that they have an arcade that's open all night. That makes it our only option. We can't do anything that will cost much money, since none of us has any. We often use alternative means even to get food. For instance, Wallace and I sometimes go to the local 7-Eleven after midnight because on the night that sandwiches hit their printed expiration date, they are thrown away. Thrown away! Well, ever since Wallace and I discovered this, the trash bins have become our new grocery store. Weekly we gather these throwaway sandwiches, at no cost to us, and we eat. We eat ham and Swiss or turkey and provolone. We eat the way people with money eat! Being poor has made us innovative. And we're going to be poor for the foreseeable future. None of us has a job.

I recently applied for one working the graveyard shift at a nearby gas station. It isn't exactly my dream job, but the white tarp sign with red block letters hanging from the rusted awning said that they'd pay five hundred dollars up front, so it became the dream job for now. I filled out a form, which was followed by a phone interview.

"So," the person on the phone said, "what would you do if someone was robbing the gas station while you were working?"

"What would I do?"

"Yes, as the gas station attendant, what would you do?"

"Well, I guess I'd try to stop them."

"Stop them?"

"Yeah, stop them."

"And how would you stop them?"

"I'd walk over to them, slowly, and tell them that I saw them take the Corn Nuts or the Mounds Bar or the Chapstick, and ask them to put it back."

"And you think that would work?"

"I don't know. I've never worked at a gas station before."

"Is that all you'd do?"

"I'd call the police too."

"Before or after you asked them to put the stuff back?"

"Before. No, I mean after."

"I see."

I didn't get the job.

Anyway, we are crushed when we pull into the Kmart parking lot. As it turns out, it isn't actually open all night, just late.

With nowhere else to go, we sit in my Jeep in the Kmart parking lot, awful and hopeless, our triumphant plans dissolving, a middle-class tragedy. Trying to entertain myself, I begin drumming my fingers on the steering wheel. In the backseat, Guy is biting his nails. He tears off a piece with his teeth, examines the remaining nail, drops the nail chunk onto the floor, and then repeats this sequence. Wallace is sitting quietly in the way Wallace often does, thinking about something profound, probably. I keep drumming, certain that there will be no fun for us— Oh what could we have possibly done to deserve this? To be robbed of such fun? I keep drumming. Guy drops another nail chunk onto his nail pile, which by now is probably visible from space. I swear he'll pay for this! I'm going to make him pick every last one—

It catches all of our attention at the same time. Behind us, one shopping cart is sitting in the cart corral, glistening there, shining like the blood of cherubs, calling to us feral young men, inviting us to improvise. Instantly we all know what must be done. We get out and walk toward the cart. The air is cold and violent. Trying to look tough tonight, to demonstrate that nature has no power over me, I didn't wear a coat, just my grandpa's old vest, but that was stupid of me and now I'm dealing with the consequences. I rub my hands together, then breathe on them. It helps for a few seconds before they hurt again.

At the cart now, we check to make sure that all four wheels still roll, which they do! Obviously this is fate. Such a clear sign that our night can still be salvaged! Guy takes a long bungee chord and attaches one end to the stray shopping cart and the other end to the back of the Jeep. And while Wallace and Guy climb into the cart, I slide over the ice and back to the Jeep. I get in and I roll down the window.

"You guys ready?"

"Yeah! But hey! Just make sure you go straight," Wallace shouts from the cart.

"No problem."

"I'm serious! Don't be stupid! Don't kill us back here or I'll be ticked!"

"How will you be ticked if you're dead?"

The cold is pouring in through the open window.

"I'm serious!"

"I know, I know! You got it. I won't kill you. I'll go straight. Ready?"

"Yeah! Go!"

Then off we go, fast but not too fast, gliding around the icy lot in long, straight lines. From the driver's seat, I'm shouting and watching their faces turn pink in the mirror. The frosty air keeps funneling over me through the open window, and I'm shivering, but I leave it down so I can hear them having fun, so they can hear me, so they know and remember that I'm here too, that I didn't miss out, that this is ours, that I played a part in creating this experience—because if I didn't play a part in creating it, then I wasn't really here—that we shared this experience, all of us!

We keep rolling through the parking lot, and it's bliss, because these guys don't feel like strangers anymore. They aren't. They are my friends, and we are doing what friends do, turning an unfortunate night on its head, making history. And our adventure, our improvisational genius, lasts until I—because I'm fiddling with the radio, trying to find the perfect bungee cart music, which, after much debate, I eventually decide is the Black Crowes—drive the shopping cart right into the median.

Fortunately, my new friends are athletic, and they bail out just before impact.

The Fish Tank and Buddha Man Dimensions

In my hands, the Jeep is a fighter jet, barreling through time, handling the curves of the dark road perfectly. I can forecast every jut and bend and dip. I am Luke Skywalker. I am in a zone. As we ascend the hill, Wallace and Ralphie double-check, triple-check, that we have cheap cigars and a cutter and a lighter. Check. Check. Check. We haven't forgotten anything. I pretend to be happy about this.

Since this is college, I'm acting as if I—like other power-hungry males and those dogs playing poker—enjoy smoking cigars. But I don't enjoy it. What's to enjoy? Every time I try, the smoke gobbles me up and I become helpless, an anxious little flower, worried that my form is bad, that I'm killing myself, that cancer cells are migrating, that I'm gulping mounds of ash down into my stomach, which now resents me for putting it through this pointlessness, this utter— I'm just not a cigar guy. But my favorite place to pose as one is this spot high above Denver.

We arrive, park, and roll down the top of the Jeep. Wallace passes out cigars. We try to blow smoke rings. None of us can. But still, we are mile-high titans.

From here, the city is a fish tank. The streetlights, headlights, and windowpanes are scattered little pebbles, and each person, each life, is a fish, swimming around without any distinguishable rhyme or reason, doing things that we can't understand. Beneath the endless sky, we sit and stare at life in this fish tank, smoke our cigars, and talk till our clothes, hair, and skin all stink of cigar, till the city lights begin to die out one by one.

And like always, our conversation on this hill tonight is different from the bulk of our conversation off it. We are different people up here. Truer. Simpler. Up here, football isn't the focus very often, and neither is pop culture or our history survey class. Up here, we talk about family—yes, I make sure that they are aware of how imperfect my family is and how good they have it, how thankful they ought to be—and we talk about whether or not we will all get married, about the people we are becoming and the things we might want to try someday, like being a dad and building something out of wood and writing music. Up here, no topic is off limits. We even talk about Jack.

Since he and I are still drifting apart, I don't really bring it up, but Wallace and Ralphie do. They visit with him frequently. Initially, this surprised me. They don't seem like the friends-with-Jack type to me, but they are, and have been for a long time. They love talking about how they first met him, which of course is very different from how I met him. Apparently no two people meet Jack the same way.

A deeper layer of life happens on top of this hill, a layer that I've rarely reached or experienced before.

Once we are yawning and thirsty, we head back down the hill and into the fishbowl, driving with the top of the Jeep still down, the air rinsing us of the cigar stink, until we hit the stop sign at the bottom. It's quiet. No one is around. I roll through the intersection. And rolling through it, I figure this is why Jack created friendship. I imagine him looking on from wherever he is, peeking out, observing, enjoying people, watching us go places together as friends, visiting dimensions of life that we wouldn't ever find on our own. I imagine him taking it all in, so happy when someone realizes that much of life happens in places that can only be found with friends, so happy when someone realizes that once you have friends, the world becomes a much bigger, much more profound place, a place where you almost want to live.

Thursday in Colorado is unusually peppy.

I'm walking home from class, carefree, in perfect orbit, when I pass Wallace's house. The windows are tossed open, and I can hear the music from the courtyard. An early jump on the weekend is the way I figure it. Woo-hoo! The guys are already blowing off the steam built up from another week of classes that we mostly skipped! The wildness has begun! Gorgeous people dancing atop tables, a pig roasting, the wallpaper peeling off the walls in long curls, the scent of the last night on earth hanging in the air, our living room resembling legendary old West saloons—speakeasies! This is a wonderful idea! I decide to join in, so I hop up the stairs, practically flying, and open the front door, ready to make my entrance, to deliver a clever line or dance move, to steal the show, ready to—

But once I am inside, there are no guys. There is no party, no yelling, no carrying on or video games, no ruckus, no girls who brought a friend, only Wallace.

Picture Buddha. That's how he looks.

Sitting on the couch, he's leaning forward on his knees, and his eyes are closed, total calm. He is somewhere else. I look at him, perplexed. What in the world is he doing? Wallace, what are you doing? I want to crash this serene moment and ask Wallace to explain himself, to tell me what's going on. I want to cough, maybe clap, anything to break this silence, but this dingy college living room now feels like some kind of hallowed ground, so I keep my mouth shut— What is this music? It's unfamiliar, a departure from our usual playlist—our Kid Rock, our Jay-Z, our Guns N' Roses. I lean toward the speakers. The lyrics say something about Jack, and while most Jack music I've heard triggers an immediate eye roll, for some reason this music doesn't. This music is oddly reverent. Believable. It isn't bad, or fluffed, or regurgitated. It isn't trying to medicate the world's problems away through happy rhymes or sound spiritual. It just . . . is. These lyrics, they sing of a desire to know that love exists in the world, a desire to engage people more deeply, a desperate cry from someone struggling to become who they know they are meant to be.

I lean away from the speakers, and Wallace keeps still as the words wash over him and soak deep beneath his skin. Behind his eyelids, a tear crawls out, meanders down the front of his face, and disappears into the jagged five o'clock shadow around his jaw— Hold everything! Is he? No. Yes! Wallace isn't just listening or observing. Wallace is singing. Quietly, he is singing in a monastic, focused kind of way. Aware of this, I now know what Wallace is doing. This peculiar scene has become clear. Wallace is worshiping. He is gone in meditation, and I get uncomfortable—

I should tiptoe out, yes, slink away, and never speak of this again, think of this again. I will. But just as I'm about to, I catch my smudged reflection in the window. Then right here, in front of Wallace and the speakers, the room alive with the breeze . . .

"Everybody worships something, Josh."

"Yeah, I know."

The reflected me and I have a conversation. We've been doing this for years.

"Well, what about us? What do we worship?"

"Ha, you name it, we worship it. Fame, the right amount of money, the right amount of power—"

"That's a real buffet."

"Yeah, but that doesn't even count the people, the celebrities, the authors, our friends! Look at this." I point at Wallace. "We worship him, and we worship ourself too. We worship so many things that it's hard to keep track."

"So then what are we?"

"What do we believe? I mean, our head tells us we're one thing, and that's what I tell people, but our actions say we're a little bit of everything."

"We are, and that's the beauty of it! Josh, don't grieve that. See, you're missing the bigger picture! Our poor friend Wallace there is pinned in. But our way of worshiping everything makes us the cup of unlimited options. I'll tell you what we are: we are the true everyman. The last of the open-minded. And that's what we want, isn't it? I say he who worships everything is ruled by nothing. Worship everything and you rule the world."

"But what if the point isn't to rule the world? What if there is something, one thing, that deserves to be worshiped?"

"Oh, Josh."

"What?"

"Don't tell me you believe that fairy tale. You're better than that. You're better than him."

The reflected me points at Wallace. I look. He is singing still, crying still, calm and content still. He is sitting in the presence of something that he knows, something that I used to know but has now become invisible to me, and he is responding to it, not to put on a show—he still doesn't even know I'm here—or to gain someone's approval. This is who Wallace is. This is his heart, and something about it is extraordinary to me.

I never knew that a friend could make me so uncomfortable, but I guess a really good friend is willing to do that.

"No," I say to the reflected me, "I'm not better than him. But he seems to know the one who is."

Without saying another word, I creep out of the house, down the stairs, and back to my place, feeling a bit disturbed, a bit thankful, a bit something that I'm not totally familiar with, wondering why, on a Thursday afternoon, love and Jack are on Wallace's mind and so wildly far from mine.

When I get to my bedroom, that soulful, worshiping picture of Wallace is still printed on my bones. And it isn't going away. For the first time since I've been here, I sit at the college-provided desk, and as expected, the chair is crap. Hard. Unexciting. But this neglected chair has a purpose now. It's going to help me.

I fold my hands and close my eyes, and as the outside world vanishes, a swarm of squirrels begins leaping around my insides from organ to organ, shaking free all sorts of questions and desires and realizations. As each of them tumbles down into the dark, I'm completely aware that my friend, this Minnesotan, is changing my life.

And through the open windows, I can hear the Jack music still playing.

IV

A (My) Hand Was in My (His) Chest, So I (He) Swam

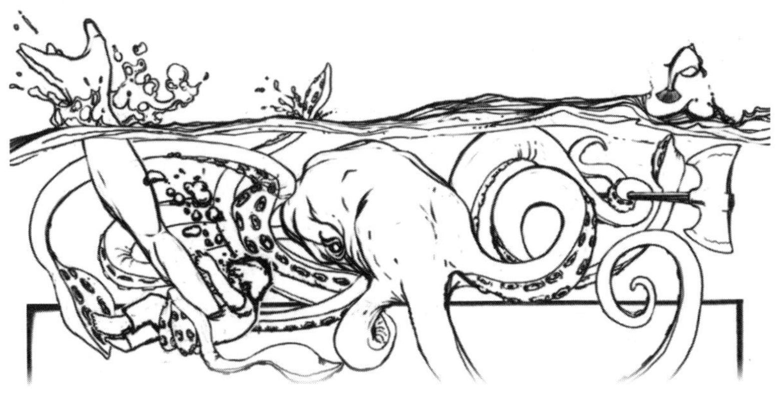

You may not like me, but you know me. Even those who don't know me, know me. In the chaos of the wind and in the perfect cadence of the tide, you know me. In a bride's happy giggle and in the stampeding rhino, you know me. And you feel me. And something deep inside you wants to return to me. I know this. So when you cry for help, for hope, for some kind of relief, for your insides to be warmed, for destiny, for something, you are crying for me. When you're not even sure who or what it is that you're crying out for, you're crying for me. Whether you know it or not, I am, I am, I am . . . all that you are crying for. Call me the boundless one, the braiding of thunder and elegance. I've been around since forever, and I'll be here long after all the trees are replaced by holographic projections and your country is absorbed by a smaller one across the way. I go by a lot of names, some more appropriate than others, but mostly I am, I am . . . Jack.

Wait. Look at this. Come look.

Blank heads attached to bodies are nodding in rhythm, as if conducting orchestras with their chins. In the back, the one being annoyed, that's Josh. Because he's a bit of a follower, he's nodding too. That man in front receiving the nods—with the white hair and wrinkle-free skin—is talking about baptism. Behind him is a swimming pool, and behind the pool are the mountains.

Gorgeous, right?

Wallace and Josh are on a weekend retreat with a bunch of people from their college, a getaway and get-to-know-other-people kind of thing. Each night, gathered in a small auditorium, the whole lot of them have listened to Mr. Wrinkle-Free speak, but tonight, since it's the final night, they've gathered outside by the pool.

Josh's face tells the whole story, doesn't it? For him, this entire thing is a rerun. He's sat through plenty of these.

Josh got his first Bible when he was ten years old. It was signed by both of his parents. Opening it, he nodded to his mom, silently thanking her for it, and also for adding his dad's signature, whereby letting Josh believe that his dad was the man he wanted him to be. When it wasn't summer, and when they weren't too tired, and when they were certain that they wouldn't see anyone they were working so hard to avoid, and when a worthwhile guest host on Saturday Night Live didn't keep them up too late, they went to church.

Josh hated church. Other than that, Josh went to soup kitchens, attended private schools, and was convinced that anyone who didn't was a terrible person, a devil in disguise. This was his life. And now, after two decades of submersion, he has this life down.

He could tell you when to smile and how to squeeze your eyes shut, what to do and what not to do, what to say and leave unsaid—everything the exact way. The routine has been mastered—

Okay, so right now Mr. Wrinkle-Free is saying that in baptism, a person is claiming, "I really believe in Jack, and I'm going to do my best to follow him." Yeah, Josh knew this part was coming. In his mind, he could get up there and do this, say this, be strategic with his pauses and inflections—he can be so smug—but one thing he can't do is claim this for himself.

Just because he's grown up in all of this doesn't mean that he believes it. Knowledge and belief are sometimes worlds apart.

But every day, he keeps on with the routine anyway, acting the part. It's mostly a charade, but even I have to admit that it's a well-intentioned charade. Josh does all of this publicly not because of a belief in me, but because he doesn't want to be abandoned. Josh thinks everyone has abandoned him, and that those who haven't already, will. Josh sees himself as an old, embarrassing sofa, ready to be tossed out and replaced. He thinks that if he doesn't put on the religious face that other people expect, they'll abandon him too.

Sadly, they might. Believe, affirm, act, conform in order to belong. That's how it's often done. In that way, I hurt for Josh.

He doesn't believe in this. He's just dying to belong—

Oh, watch this! See Mr. Wrinkle-Free bursting with enthusiasm? He's the yin in this picture. And then there's his yang, Josh, drowning in boredom. He hates the predictability of all this, so now he's leaning back on his elbows, puckered up toward the sky. Up there, he can see every single constellation that he's never learned. Up there, he can see the magic of life, the infinite energy and dimensions. Up there, he sees the faith he's read about, heard about. Up there, he's reminded of the faith he once had.

Let me tell you about it.

Years ago, in a field where a rumbling car didn't belong, Josh and I met. It was pretty simple, really: he needed me, so I showed myself to him, in a form that would speak loudest to him in that moment in time. Call it personal attention. And afterward he believed. That's the wonder of the young heart; it's big enough, tender enough, to house a belief in the impossible. But now, older, that wonder is nowhere to be found. Josh's heart has been downsized, remodeled, demodeled. And I exist to him in only one place: his imagination. He's chalked up our encounter to his fear running wild and bringing out his creative best. I am just another fairy tale to him now, a story he told himself in order to survive. To Josh, I don't think or feel or talk. I am a statue, a commemorative figurine that would sit politely on his mantel or coffee table if he had either.

People really can convince themselves of anything.

Okay, see the way Josh is holding his arms over his knees? And the way his caterpillar eyebrows are crawling down into the center of his head? Subtle, but let me translate that body language for you. He's saying, Get baptized? Follow Jack? Please. He's convinced that the people surrounding him know this same truth. He's convinced that like him, they're just pretending I am real for reasons they don't fully understand.

Immovable Object

Yes, he's an exaggerator. Unbelievable. Like right now, trying to stay warm against the wind, Josh is bent in all sorts of positions—the mantis, the swan, the lotus—and all of this is taking a toll on his body, but not nearly as much of a toll as he thinks. Look at him, rolling his eyes, big dramatic breaths. Classic. He's going to write about this one day, guaranteed. He'll say things like, "My spine is steel cable, my butt like frozen veal. I guess everything comes at a price." Catchy. But a bit over the top.

Okay, so now Mr. Wrinkle-Free points to the pool and kindly asks if anyone wants to be baptized. No one moves. Josh is convinced no one will. He's about to be proved wrong. There, that boy isn't stretching; he's responding, standing. Watching him move toward the water, Josh recalls meeting him at a party, recalls him being a witty guy, and now Josh is wondering whom he's trying to impress.

The answer: just one.

Mr. Wrinkle-Free takes the witty guy into the water. Here it comes. Mr. Wrinkle-Free puts his arms around him, and—

Smack the surface. Disappear. Gone forever. Smack the surface. Reappear.

I came up with this a long time ago. I wanted something visual, and the water was perfect. But did you know that in some places I've inspired people to do it other ways? For example, in some jungles, they swing from one tree to another on a rope or vine. In the mountains, in the east, they throw a rock off a cliff, watch it grow smaller, smaller, smaller, till it's gone. It's all the same picture. Newness.

Now, see that girl weaving her way toward the pool? Yes, the one Josh is shamelessly drooling over. I know, I know, he won't stop staring, and it's kind of gross that he's checking out a girl who is about to be baptized. But Josh can't believe that she isn't interested in him. Now that he's lifting weights, he considers himself to be way better-looking than her boyfriend. Vanity isn't pretty—

Smack the surface. Disappear. Gone forever. Smack the surface. Reappear.

If you knew this girl's whole story, this would be even more moving. So many details led to this moment. Belief is the culmination of a million seemingly innocuous breaths. Absent one day. Present the next. A traveling circus. Belief catches everyone off guard. Well, everyone but me.

Okay, see how it's becoming contagious? See the others standing? Here they come, all of them, making their way toward the pool, to me–five, no, six. No, more than that are heading to the water now, to me.

Smack the surface. Disappear. Gone forever. Smack the surface. Reappear.

As for Josh, no, he hasn't moved. But he is confused. He won't admit this to anyone, but he wants more out of life. Something is missing. He knows. And now, trying to clear his head, he's looking up into the sky again–

It's time.

I whisper.

Josh isn't sure where I am, where I am coming from. Through the trees, over the mountains, from beneath the water? Inside of him? Outside of him? Am I passing through him? He can't tell. No one can. But my voice does sound familiar to him, as if I am a part of him, which I am. My voice is triggering a memory now. He may not know where I am coming from, but he knows that it's me. And he knows that I am telling him to get in the water. Now.

Oh, right, Josh has never been baptized.

Pride keeps people from doing all sorts of things, drives sane people to the asylum. Like right now, Josh is too proud to even talk back to me, so I am being ignored. That's okay. I am not stopping. I never do.

I whisper again.

Again, Josh won't budge. Yes, I saw this coming. Like most, he wants to be in charge, which means I have to . . . no, I am not giving him a heart attack, but Josh probably can't tell the difference. The thing is, I am not just a voice. I have hands too. And now I have one of my hands in his chest, and I am squeezing him, squeezing his heart, his ego, his future, his past, all of him, and it hurts.

Look, I never said I always play gentle. Brawling is one of my love languages—

There's Mr. Wrinkle-Free, and he's shaking his hands dry and asking once more if anyone else wants to be baptized. This is the last opportunity, he says. Josh can't wait to be dismissed, because after this he's sure I'll leave him alone. He's sure that the squeezing in his chest will stop, that my whisper will vanish in the wind.

Sigh. People always underestimate my persistence.

The thing with Josh is not that he doesn't believe in me. Not completely. He believes that I have good ideas. He believes that I even have some decent plans for his life. But he, like a lot of people, just happens to believe in his ideas, his plans, and himself much more.

When pressed, most people think they are more real than I am.

Amen.

Now, with the prayer done, everyone is standing—Wallace too—heading back to their cabins. Not Josh. Josh is staying behind because he wants to be alone, and with the last person now gone, he thinks he is. On stiff, wooden legs, Josh clunks to the edge of the pool and looks down into the water. He sees straight to the empty bottom, and being so introspective, he relates to the water. In ignoring me this time, Josh expected to feel proud, more complete, a conqueror of worlds, but instead, he feels empty, haunted. He thinks he's now gone to a place from which there is no coming back.

But I am about to show him that such a place doesn't exist.

The Shattering Million

This camp has what I guess could be called staircases running between the different buildings and locations—thick, rough logs half-wedged into the dirt. Walking these trails, these staircases, I think about Paul Bunyan chopping down trees, yelling "Timber!" and Babe the blue ox dragging them into place, hoofs pounding them three feet into the ground, then Paul winking back at Babe, the two of them sharing a drink from the river, laughing, sharing so—

Wait, here he comes, see—Josh is lunging from log to log. I whisper again, but he keeps walking.

Now I squeeze. His heart is a tennis ball in my hand, and I ask him why he's afraid to believe that I am real. Still walking, lunging, he wants to blow me off again, but he can't. Not anymore. He knows I'm going to follow him, that I'm already wherever he might go, that I'll outlast him. So he concedes to a conversation.

Josh tells me that there is a tremendous appeal to his life as it is. Life is more convenient this way. Contained. Explainable. This way, Josh tells me, he doesn't have to rearrange his life. Things stay just as they are.

I hear this often. Sure, sure, people claim that change is good. But most will do whatever they can to avoid it. Tin men. Josh doesn't want change. And now he tells me that he doesn't have to worry about where dead religion will take him.

I can't argue with that.

Squeezing again, my fingers drawing closer together around his heart—the teeth of a bear trap—I ask him if his life is any better because of his castrated beliefs, his stifling religion.

Down another log, he clutches below his neck, shaking his head. No, life isn't any better.

I ask him if he's any different because of this faith he has, and immediately he's tempted to go into charade mode, to give the answer that he's supposed to have. I'm different! Life is fuller! Look at me NOW! But that's not his answer. He knows it. I know it.

Because the logs are closer together now, Josh is walking as if his ankles are tied together. He says that he has questions for me. I tell him to go ahead and ask me. I've never run from a question. Fine, he says, and then he asks me why things are so much different from the way they used to be, why I used to seem so real, and why I now seem so imaginary.

That's my cue.

When he hears the snapping of branches, Josh assumes it's someone on the retreat, strolling through the woods. Wrong. The light hits my face, and immediately Josh's head shrinks around his eyes. Stumbling back over a log, his legs sail toward the sky. He smacks the ground in a cloud of dirt and goes into crab mode, scrambling in reverse.

Behind me the moon is blushing. I step forward. Standing over him, I ask if I still seem imaginary.

Josh shakes his head.

Crouching down next to him now, I tell Josh that I haven't changed at all. I tell him that he's been waiting for me to show up in order to engage me, so here I am. I showed up. The thing is, from now on, I want him to engage me even when I feel imaginary and invisible, and if he does, he'll see me more and more clearly. I tell Josh that if he comes with me, he'll see how close I am all the time.

You know, most people will live their entire lives unaware that I am only inches away.

With Josh still in the dirt and me still crouching, there's something else I have to show him. I take his hand and spit on it, and just as Josh is preparing to be grossed out and offended, yes, he feels it. The cold. He feels the cold on his skin and in his veins, the heaviness, as if his bones are made of lead. Rolling over into the light, Josh sees the color bleeding out of him, his hand turning gray, skin and knuckles and elbow turning gray, and he shouts, What have I done to him? What's happening to him? I take no pleasure in this– Struggling to his feet, Josh is still shouting, his breaths halting and quick, the cold spreading over his body. Help! Help! Josh lunges at me and grabs the meat of my neck, bending my throat between his hands, screaming now. So I take two fistfuls of his T-shirt and slam him to the ground. On impact, pain shoots through his back and into his skull–there will be lasting bruises–and I pin him in the dirt, tell him that I haven't done anything. But oh my, he's an electrocuted worm now, flailing and twitching, and in his panic he can't hear me, can't take it–reality is often a detestable thing–so I hold his cold, gray, writhing body and tell him to listen to me.

But he's still fighting me, clawing at my eyes–

Don't move, I tell him–

Slipping an arm free of my grip, Josh throws his fist, and since I don't try to duck, his knuckles plow deep into my chest, popping the wind right out of me. Regaining my breath, I wedge the weight of my body against him, lean close, and tell him to listen to me; I am trying to help him. Just listen—

But he's still shouting, What have you done to me?

JOSH! LISTEN! TO! ME!

And now he goes still. I have his attention.

I tell Josh that I am trying to undo what's already been done. Josh, I tell him, I've always been real. I was never an inanimate object.

And as the last of his skin vanishes in stone, I tell Josh that the inanimate object has always been him. He's the statue; he just didn't realize it.

Then, reading his mind, I tell Josh that without me, he always will be a statue.

And as much as something this implausible can make sense to someone, Josh gets it. Decades of realities are finally felt.

He starts nodding, and with each nod, tears come loose, his lips repeating, How could I not know? What have I become? How could I—

For a human, discovering that their perceived reality is inaccurate sends a tremor through their soul. And the most jarring truths are the ones that were right in front of someone, yet they missed them. That realization demonstrates just how limited a human is and leaves them wondering what else they're missing. As far as that goes, all I can tell you right now is that it's way more than most people think—

Josh taps out limp in the dirt, his tears making his shirt a wet mess.

I let go. I sit beside him.

Except for his crying, there's no noise for one, two, three minutes.

I am gentle when I take his wrist. As I slide my hand up his arm, warmth begins to pour through him, peach swallowing the gray. The heaviness lifting. Slowly Josh sits up. He turns his hands over, moves his fingers, and breaks into that kind of weeping-laughing-smiling-ugly-beautiful face implosion that happens only a few times in our lives, if we're lucky. That moment that is too big for one emotion, for one expression, for one heart.

Josh lunges for me again, but this time he's not trying to choke me. He hangs on to me. He won't let go.

Josh, I tell him, I want you to come with me. I tell him that he's more alive now than he's ever been, but coming fully alive is going to take a while.

Come with me, I say.

I already know his answer.

Josh may have declined a million times, but not this time. He understands now: stifling religion leads only to stifling places. And humans weren't made for captivity. Life is more than that. Josh wants more than that. He wants what he senses deep in his spirit, what he sees in the sky, so through his tears and sore body, he says yes, yes, yes, he's coming with me, and from ear to ear, I smile and tell him what to do first . . .

When he swings the cabin door open, he sees his friends. They are scattered, dotting the floor and camp beds, playing cards, that musty-boy wilderness smell. He's as real as anyone in this room, Josh says to himself.

In the corner, he sees Ewan and heads straight for him, talking fast, Josh telling Ewan that Ewan has to baptize Josh, which, duh, freaks Ewan out. He looks at Josh as if he's down on one knee proposing, but then Ewan gathers himself and says that he will. The two of them invite the rest of the cabin to come along, and seconds later, everyone is throwing on jackets.

They hike up Paul and Babe's staircase.

Log, log, log.

Ewan mentions that he's never baptized anyone. He says he doesn't really know how. Josh tells him that he doesn't know how either, but that he kind of likes it that way.

I do too.

The water is colder than Josh anticipated and hurts the skin, but I find it kind of refreshing. Up to our waists we go– Uh-oh, now Josh is distracted, nervous about getting water up his nose, dwelling on what breathing technique to use. Does he use the one-handed nose plug? The two-handed? He doesn't want to look foolish and regrets not paying attention in swim class–

Ewan's voice comes shaking out of his mouth.

"Well, Josh," Ewan says, shifting his weight, "we're here to baptize you. I mean, I–I'm here to baptize you. I'm not sure why I get to do it, but this is awesome, and I'm pretty sure I'll remember this for a long time."

Ewan exchanges a look with all the guys lining the pool deck.

"So, Josh, because you believe that Jack is real, and because you want to go with him, I baptize you."

Ewan's left hand cradles Josh's back, his right hand presses down onto his chest. As he shoves,

Josh goes weightless and falls back, and along the side of the pool, a row of smiles glows down, and somewhere, both far away and inside of himself, Josh can hear it—that sound of wonderful smashing, the smashing of a million statues, a million gods being thrown to the ground, a million of his plans shattering, his stone skin cracking a bit more—and then Ewan plunges him down in the water.

Smack the surface. Disappear. Gone forever . . .

To the Bottom of the Sea

Once, twice, Josh blinks his eyes open to a herd of seahorses fanning their way through reefs, blowing coral trumpets, the notes appearing and floating up to the surface. Submarine commanders, starfish, powder monkeys, killer sharks, hermit crabs, and squids surround him, cheering. Pirates and mercenaries and priests fire pistols and cannons. Creatures of all varieties and backgrounds are celebrating, holding signs saying, "Jack is real" and "The stone Josh is gone" and "The new Josh is here." With everyone so excited for him, Josh feels cozy, like he's in the womb again, awakened to a world that just a few hours earlier didn't even exist, to a world that—

Cannonballs in the Night

. . . Smack the surface. Reappear.

In a shower of chlorine diamonds, Ewan rips Josh out of the water. He's soaked, Ewan is hugging him, and they're laughing. The pool deck has been transformed into a grandstand, his friends clapping, whistling, arms pumping, perfect soccer hooligans, rioting, tearing down the sky. It's such a stunning sight that for a moment, Josh thinks they could be angels. He's almost right. Sometimes humans can get sort of close.

The chlorine is stinging Josh's eyes, and he's got water up his nose, so he's blowing air and liquid out of his nostrils, wiping his face. Because he's blind and deaf, he'll never know who went first, but one of the poolside hooligans lifts himself into the air in a tight ball, soaring, and plunges down into the water. By the time Josh's eyes stop stinging, a chain reaction has been triggered, launching cannonball after cannonball, turning the surface of the pool into a thundering explosion of noise and wet spray.

We splash on and on, all of us, still shouting, loud, laughing, dunking one another, flapping our arms in an aqua rave, and Josh feels alive. My breath has given him life. True CPR.

Eventually we stop, and soaked and shivering, still in the pool, they all begin talking to me. They thank me for being real, not a statue, and they thank me for bringing them to life. Then Josh's friends ask on his behalf for my help, because they know that engaging me can be tough, and they want Josh to engage me even in those tough moments—especially then, especially when I seem far away. They want Josh to go where I want, when I want, and they know he'll need my help.

And yeah, you may not see me here in the water, but I am here, soaked right here, the visible invisible, and right now, all I want from Josh is one thing. Just one. I just want him to wake up in the morning and remember that I am real.

Vomit

Vomiting is inevitable. It's all coming up now, in chunks, the Pop-Tart I ate for lunch slogging in reverse through my digestive pipes. I only hope I don't choke on it. In my hands, the phone is a missile, heavier than normal and dangerous. I reach to hang it up. I hesitate. I reconsider. The phone comes back to my ear. I'm praying he won't be there to answer, but who am I kidding? I'm praying for the impossible. Of course he'll be there. The phone is right next to his bedroom chair, and with his Parkinson's and his heart transplant, standing up is exhausting for him. He's attached to that chair now. He rarely leaves the bedroom. Sporting those jean shorts and that oversized, unwashed polo shirt, with his beard unkempt, he'll be sorting through junk mail and watching *Jerry Springer*, or the History Channel maybe. After the phone rings, he'll see my name on the caller ID, which will surprise him. He'll think that it can't possibly be me, that his eyes are worse than he thought, but then, motivated by wishful thinking, he'll answer.

Holding the phone, I'm lopsided, and I feel like only half my body is working, so I sit down on the couch. Jack's hand is in my chest again, and it's been pushing me toward this for a while. Days? Weeks? Longer? I knew this would happen! This is exactly what I was afraid of! This is part of why I resisted believing in Jack. I knew that he'd bring me here, to this moment, this place. I knew Jack would want me to deal with this. And this is only the beginning. What other black holes will he lead me into? What other haunted houses?

I want to vacate the premises.

Standing up, I move into the center of the room and tell Jack I don't want to do this. This hurts, I say. I'm scared. I'd rather not.

Jack tells me that he knows how I feel.

Don't make me, I say.

We begin arguing.

And because I often think I'm smarter than Jack, I tell him that this is a bad idea. I tell him that this sick old man isn't going to listen to me, that it's too soon. I tell Jack that this should be his responsibility—he should know better. He's an adult, for crying out loud! He doesn't deserve it, I say. He doesn't deserve me, I say. And besides, isn't all of this his fault? Yes! He chose alcohol! He chose to never be around! It's his fault! Not mine— No, I don't need time to think it over! I've already made my ruling! Yes, I am the Supreme Court, actually, and I want justice! Reparations! I deserve that. He deserves nothi— I can't do this, revisit this. The pain is too much, my anger is too hot, and my anger is the only thing I've got! It's the only thing protecting me, my suit of armor— Wait, I've got it! Maybe this will all go away. Yes! Ta-dah! If I leave it alone, I'm sure it will go away! Our father-son issues will wane! This too shall pass! Just like—

Oh, I'm a Rolodex of excuses, but Jack's hand squeezes me delicately, wisely, and tells me that I'm great at answering all the questions he *isn't* asking. He isn't asking me if it's a good idea or how it'll work out.

There is only one question: will I do it? This is his only question right now. Will I do it? Am I in?

I'd rather dive into a volcano, sip lemonade from a diaper, poke out my eyes than press these buttons, but reluctantly, slowly, I do it, all ten of them. Once I hear ringing, I start walking in circles around the living room, rapidly, formulating what to say, how to say it. Where the heck do I start? On the third ring, I'm still circling, a blur now, as if I'm flowing down a drain, and I'm really thankful that none of my roommates are home—

"Blast! Well, how are you?"

My dad calls me that sometimes. He gave me the nickname as a kid.

"Hey, Dad. What's going on?"

"Not too much. How are you?"

"Dad, I need to tell you something."

Jack cares about me. He brought me here, and I'm reminding myself of this, and though I don't know how, he's helping, interacting, guiding, loving, real. And though I don't want to do this . . . I do. No I don't. Yes I do. Badly.

"What's going on, son?"

I drop the phone away from my ear and hold it at my side. I want to bury it in the couch cushions, bury myself there too, and tunnel my way to China. Since I'm no longer made of stone, I'm more vulnerable now. Yes, even healing has a downside. I'm afraid. Weak. Forming words has never been this hard. I can speak only in fragments.

"Dad . . . you've screwed up my entire life. Your drinking. You not being there. Everything. And I've hated you for it. Haven't been able to get past it . . . haven't really wanted to. But for years now, I've been doing the same thing to you. I haven't been there. Pushed you away . . . I don't want it to stay this way. So . . . I want to ask for your forgiveness. And I want you to know . . . that I forgive you . . . all of it. Dad, I forgive you."

"Oh my God . . . Oh my God . . ."

A thousand miles away, a withered face is whimpering, unable to speak. I imagine his upturned head, his veiny hands wiping at wet cheeks and wide eyes.

"Son, son," my dad says, also speaking in fragments, "I love. You. So much."

He's imagining my face too, I'm sure.

"I love you too, Dad. I want to be your son, and I want you to be my dad."

"That's what I want."

A few minutes later, the phone is cradled on the receiver, my face is slick, and I'm on the couch, watching two decades' worth of scenes and emotions as they flash in my head, until I'm brought back to the present. No, Dad and I aren't fixed. Our crap still smells, and it will for a long time because, among us humans, some wrongs can't instantly be made right. It's only on television where resolution happens in twenty-two minutes or less. Microwavable forgiveness. This isn't television. But it is a start. The next step. It's getting better, newer, and that's what this is about. Yes, yes, yes, epiphany! I'm now certain that this moment wasn't intended only for my dad and me. No, of course not! This moment was also for Jack and me! Sure, I'm choosing to interpret life's events a certain way, as we all do, but I'll bet that's it! I'll bet Jack brought me here to reassure me that he knows better than I do, that he's in my life, making me new—all of me, even the places that seem so destined to rot—taking this existing space and opening it up, a complete overhaul, and laying down something better, making me and my dad into intersecting streets of gold! I'll bet he brought me here to reassure me that, sure, he may at times be invisible, but that doesn't make him any less involved! And if that's the case, well, it worked, because I am reassured.

On the mountain, on my back in the dirt, he told me: as I go with him, I'll realize again and again that he's close and very, very real, the most real thing this bizarre world has to offer—

Flinging open the door, my roommates walk in. They are loud, discussing rap music and Tom Green's most recent shenanigans, ha-ha-ha. They ask me what I've been doing. Keeping it all to myself, I say that I've been doing nothing.

Jack and I, we've been doing nothing.

V

Starry-Eyed Art

My television is worth two hundred dollars. I know this because I recently sold it in order to acquire the gas money that would get me from Denver to Chicago.

Thus far, post-college life is horribly anticlimactic. Where is the fanfare I was promised, the high-powered employers vying for my services, the chandelier that I should be swinging from, the car chases? I may have a framed piece of paper saying that I accomplished something, but I feel like I'm wandering aimlessly, and if I don't have any direction, does that mean I've done something wrong? Everyone tells me that wandering is bad. But is there ever a time when I'm supposed to wander? I'm hoping there is.

I'm hoping that sometimes it's only through wandering that we can find our way. Right now, that's the best I can do.

Back in Chicago, I'm living at home with my parents—who still aren't talking and have returned to their hoarding ways—and it's weird. Everything is weird. I have no money. I don't know how to pay my bills, make a doctor's appointment, or cook nonmicrowavable food. And I recently found out that I have bad credit. A threatening yellow envelope came to the house, letting me know. I glanced at it and then tossed it on the floor with the rest of the things that overwhelm me, and I haven't seen it since. I'm not worried. If it's that important, I'm sure I'll receive another.

I do have a job, though.

For a while now, I've been working at a church as a youth pastor. I'm not entirely sure how this happened, or what my job description actually entails. Going to work, for me, amounts to eating meals and drinking coffee with people who aren't much younger than I am, and then, when I run out of people to spend time with, I sit in my office, not answering emails and unsure why people do this for a living. Because I know that my co-workers are nobler than me, I can only assume that they do this out of some sense of calling. Not me. I'm doing this because it's a job that doesn't require me to wear an apron.

It isn't bad, though. The hours are flexible, the conversations are always unpredictable, and if nothing else, working for a church is teaching me that every pastor, every holy man and holy woman, is no different from anyone else, no matter how hard they try to be.

No matter how hard I try to be.

Right now, my church job means that I'm preparing to leave for England, a two-week trip with thirty teenagers. We leave in three days and I've never been to England, so logic says that I should be excited, but I'm not. Actually, I don't even want to go. I want to stay here because, well, as schoolboy as it sounds . . . I've met someone.

Yeah, in *that* way. Like, I've *met* someone.

Kristen and I grew up in the same neighborhood, but we hardly know each other. I'm five years older than she is, so you know how that goes. Anyway, I recently asked her out on a date. We're going to a movie tonight. Of course, I'm thrilled and have that giddy kind of nauseous feeling inside. Though I deny it and hide behind bawdy talk about autonomy and being a "lone wolf," something in me wants to fall in love. I feel this. Something in me wants to be chosen by another person. I want to be somebody's somebody.

But along with that, I'm also freaking out. The thought of being in a relationship still frightens me. Along with my parents' marriage and some disastrous relationships of my own, I attribute this feeling to a traumatic childhood experience.

I was at the mall with my mom. While she was trying on clothes in JCPenney, taking forever, I grew restless and snuck into the women's dressing room. I'd heard rumors, interesting things. I had to find out. Thick, serious curtains fronted every stall, deep, apple-colored ones that left a two-foot gap between their end and the floor, just enough space to . . . I couldn't help myself! Not knowing what wonders I would find, I naively peeked under, and when I did, and I saw what I saw—the woman parts, the woman objects, what I saw!—I was sure that I was going straight to hell, would be leading the demonic parade, acting as grand marshal, and that upon my arrival I'd receive a standing ovation and a medal, be promoted to a ruler of some sort, mayor maybe, or deputy.

After that, I stayed away from the idea of sex and girls for years.

The closest I came was listening to a set of educational books on tape about sexuality with my mom. Talk about horrific. She sat there on the floor with me, making sure that I was paying attention, studying my face for signs of confusion and not taking the material seriously enough, and then asking if I had any questions. Yeah, right.

I heard all about puberty and hormones. Side one of the tape ended. She flipped it over.

I heard all about the canyon of inferiority. Side two ended. She inserted the next tape, and so it went.

The whole experience left me believing that sex happened in a musty room with no lights in order to minimize the odds of anyone seeing something that they liked and therefore wanting to touch it.

But then I turned thirteen. Things started to change at thirteen.

The flimsy, glasses-wearing, fluffy-haired me was on a school bus, wearing a red choir sweater, sitting, of course, in the backseat next to her. Maybe it was the way our knees were touching, I don't know, but somehow I knew it was coming— Wow, the nerves were unbearable. I felt like I was about to disarm a bomb. My hands trembled, and the clock in my brain ticked down so loudly that I half expected someone to ask me to turn it down. I didn't know how to do it, how long to hold my face against hers, how tight to keep my mouth. Will it feel good? Will I break a tooth? Can that happen? What if I do it wrong? I'll be made fun of. I'll be called names. Terrible names— My lips were steel wool covered in wood chips, so I kept licking them, prepping them, but they only became more and more dry, desiccated. I considered fashioning my red sweater into some kind of parachute and jumping out the window. I wanted to play in a sandbox, play video games, anything less adult, but then, with the sudden boldness of an eclipse, I closed my eyes, tipped in her direction, aiming blindly, and EUREKA! Our lips met! We were kissing! Kissing? Kiss— Afraid I might overplay my hand or be reprimanded by a bus chaperone, I pulled away. The whole thing happened so fast I hardly even felt it, but still it happened, oh yes, and up to that point it was the crowning achievement of my life. Instantly I felt stubble poke through my chin. I was ready to shave, to drive fast cars, to smoke my first pack of cigarettes. I was all that is man. I think I may have actually stood up on the bus and thrust my hands into the air, shouting. Pearl was her name, and she was my first love.

Since I wasn't allowed to date until I was sixteen—Mom's rule—our relationship was based mostly on phone calls and mixed tapes and note passing. Limited, I suppose, but it worked for us. She taught me how to say "I love you" in French. After that, I closed every note with "*Je t'aime*, Josh." Through her, the world became an enchanted place, very Disney, but still, even at thirteen, romance wasn't easy, simple, or painless.

Every time I saw Pearl I wondered if she was mad at me, if she was still interested, if I was still interested, if we were going to last, how the physical element would progress, if at all, and how I was supposed to discern any of that. And of course, I wondered how to deal with the hurt once things ended.

From the beginning, romance has been more of a gamble than a science, a high-stakes version of Pin the Tail on the Donkey. It's been awkward and complicated, and it's rarely gone the way I've wanted it to go. Chances are, it probably never will. I want love without drama, romance without pain. I want intimacy without vulnerability. I want a guarantee. I want something that doesn't exist. Maybe we all do.

Maybe we're all chasing unicorns.

Running Red Lights

I pull into the theater for my date with Kristen wearing a wrinkled plaid shirt that just earlier today was balled up on the floor in my room. I've ironed it down with my hands, and I look good. I check the dashboard clock. I'm early, way early, way eager, desperate? Kristen pulls in, and suddenly I'm sweating everywhere, from unnatural places. She'll think I've gone swimming. Crap. She gets out of the car, her face turns yellow under the parking lot lights, and I try to be psychic. Is she happy to be here? As happy as I am? Tired? I can't tell. But I can see that she looks better than I do. That part is obvious.

Her sweatshirt is gray. Her jeans are sky blue. Half of her blonde hair is pulled back behind one ear, accentuating her narrow blue eyes, her summer skin, and gosh, look at those cute freckles across her nose. She is the effortlessly gorgeous girl. She is *that* girl. Hands stuffed into her sweatshirt pocket, she comes bouncing toward me kangaroo-like. I wave to her and forget my name, along with what town I live in. I can't feel my legs.

Beauty can be paralyzing.

I want to skip the movie just so I can keep looking at her, count her nose freckles, so we can elope—

"Hey, Kristen."

"Hey."

We sit in the last row of the theater, way up, and a few minutes in, the dialogue fades and it becomes a silent movie to me. The characters' lips are moving, but there is no sound. The only sound I hear is Kristen's laugh. I can't get enough of it. As the movie continues, I want to be closer to her, to devour the air between us, split the atoms. I must, so I lean across the armrest at random times and whisper pointless things, and each time I feel free inside. Before I know it, the credits are rolling, and by the time we walk out of the theater, I'm convinced that *Dodgeball* is the greatest film in the history of American cinema.

Love makes even the dullest things sparkle.

The rest of our night is spent at Dunkin' Donuts. We sit in plastic chairs, talking. Our conversation is natural and limitless, as if we've been doing it for years. Midway through my second donut, Kristen mentions that she wants to go to Italy. I note this. I tell her that I've never been either, but in my head, I know we'll experience it together. We talk about music and philosophical things and soccer and our mutual friends, exchanging funny stories about them.

Employees clock out. New ones clock in.

Time gets muddled. Hours and seconds have no place, and gravity may have ceased to exist. This table between us should not be here; it's only getting in the way, so again I lean toward her. She reciprocates the lean. Yes, we are seamless, enjoying the gift of a lull-free connection.

Obviously these are all signs.

When we get back to the theater parking lot, I turn off the engine and we walk toward her car, slowly. Then, just to prove how chivalrous I can be, that I'm not all clever banter and forced insights, I open the door for her. But she doesn't get in. Sweet! She doesn't want to leave. Neither do I— If ever I needed life's pause button, it's now! Surely this is what all of those awesome '80s ballads have been saying to us! Poison and Firehouse, melodic prophets— Again the space between us is shrinking, and we're talking about casual things. On the surface I'm so casual, so cool, but inside, weighty and eternal things that I've been resisting for years are stirring. Inside I'm wondering if I might be falling in love with Kristen, if she might be someone I could spend my life with. And I'm wondering why, with her, that doesn't scare me. I'm wondering how it's possible that in just a few hours, she's made me into a braver man. I'm wondering how I became so fortunate, because as far as I can tell, the brightest star I know has slipped from the sky and fallen right into my arms. And yeah, yeah, I'm probably getting ahead of myself, being lofty and bohemian, a tad ridiculous, viewing all life as poetry, but love will do that to a person.

Kristen is tilted back against her car, and I think I'm about to disarm another bomb. The clock is ticking. We both hear it, and the wheels of the bus are going round and round, because here I am, feeling like a kid again, with Pearl again. Should I kiss her? Does she want me to kiss her? Yes. Of course. Yes! Kissing is good! That will cap this night perfectly! Seal this night in the annals of romantic hist— But wait, Kristen is beautiful, and I'm only me, embarrassing me, ugly me, looking

the way I do, smelling and sweating the way I am, betrayed by my deodorant. She won't want me, I'll disappoint her—

Kristen steps toward me. I read her body language. She wants to be kissed. Right? Shoot, what does this mean? Who cares! Now is the time, now! Go! The window of opportunity is closing, the way all windows do. In life, in love, there is a time to act, a time when urgency and speed are necessary. This is one of those times!

I reach out. *Go, you animal Tarzan man, and be primal or whatever! GO!!*

But instead of a kiss, I shake her hand.

Chicken.

But oh, even this is heavenly. Her skin is soft and warm, like a towel spread over a tropical beach. Our fingers linger together for longer than necessary, intertwining, delaying goodbye for as long as possible.

I say something about something and she laughs, and then we decide that date number two must happen tomorrow night.

It does.

We decide that date number three must happen the next morning.

It does.

Date number four, that night.

It does.

Date number four ends, and I'm left sitting in my Jeep. I feel different, as if my head has been replaced with someone else's head, my heart with someone else's heart. I feel as if I'm someone who isn't afraid of a relationship anymore, as if I'm someone who now believes that romance is possible for me. How could I not? Our whole lives we lived so near each other, but it's only now that she and I have merged.

This must be how love stories happen, just like this—out of nowhere, while we're just sort of living our lives. Why does it happen this way? Maybe because we can't manufacture love on our own. Maybe this kind of love is imported, doesn't originate here but in another realm, and maybe only a resident of that realm can bring this love to us. Maybe we can hunt for love all we want, but it only shows up when the heavens decide. Or maybe those are things we just tell ourselves in order to justify our feelings and strange behavior. I don't know, maybe I've seen *Jerry Maguire* too many times.

Fastening my seat belt, I remember—dang it—that I still have to pack for England. I'm leaving tomorrow morning, but only physically. My mind isn't going anywhere. I know this. While my body is moving around England, my mind will remain here, focused on Kristen, on what she's doing, on what color toothbrush she has, on if she sprinkles sugar on grapefruit, on whether she's talking to someone about me, on if she's falling in love too, on the nature of her penmanship, on—

I drive home thinking only of Kristen, unaware if I'm stopping at all the red lights or running them completely.

An Unending, Jumbled, Blurred, Hard-to-Read Season

Somewhere over the Atlantic Ocean, while I'm crammed into a plane with a group of teenagers, most of them trying their hand at British accents and impersonating Austin Powers, the early stages of romance take over completely, making life a transitionless scene where everything happens in run-on sentences and questionable punctuation, in a jumbled flurry of difficult-to-discern events and emotions, beginning with landing in England, seeing Parliament and Big Ben, and thinking about whether or not Kristen and I are compatible, because she's an ESTJ and I'm an INFP; is that okay? And what will she look like when she's old? And does she get along with Jack? How do I know for sure? Oh gosh, how do I know that our relationship won't end up like my parents'? So icy and parallel and— I'd die, just die, but then again, it may not ever come to that, because am I absolutely sure I'm straight? I'm nearly positive, 99 percent, I'd say, but hey, I've wondered— Three days later and I'm still in England, out in the foggy countryside, talking with Jack about Kristen. He tells me that he likes her and the idea of us very much, and seeing how beautiful the landscape is, I'm wishing that she was here with us, with me, not just because, you know, we could talk about it while holding hands, but because I don't want to experience this without her. No, it's more than that! I don't want any more of life without her, I want to share life with Kristen, and now, AHA! I figure this is what love is, when you're ready for your life to belong to someone else, yes! That's it! Love is a blissful hijacking, and standing here in England, I tell myself, *I'm going to marry her*—

Back in the US, love makes Kristen and me stupid, and we stop referring to each other as "Kristen" and "Josh" and instead use substitute names such as "sweetie" and "kiddo" and "babe," which obviously means that everything is going so well and that we are so Moulin Rouge, which is only further proven when Kristen and I start discussing the future, our future, and then even further proven when Kristen introduces me to sushi and I not only eat it but like it, and I can only assume this not because of the mushy/fishy/perhaps E. coli–inducing food itself, but because Kristen introduced it to me, because our love is great enough to create jealousy within a city of cupids, because we are daydream believers, because we are the relational equivalent of the Sistine Chapel— Hold everything, because in a shocker, a lightning bolt strikes out of a sunny sky, and WAIT, we hit a snag that threatens to derail our fairy tale, the snag being that I'm terrified Kristen is going to leave me, and obviously I should've seen this coming, but I didn't! My love for her has only heightened my fear of losing her, which means, simply put, that I can't trust her, and naturally—because blaming others is always the right thing to do—this is her fault, and I'm keen to let her know this by saying things like, "You don't love me well enough," "You don't make time for me," "If only you were more [fill in the blank]." But none of this is accurate because Kristen hasn't done anything wrong, no, no, my lack of trust is a piece of my baggage that comes from my parents' marriage, my ex-girlfriends, and being made fun of as a kid, and my baggage has instilled me with what a psychiatrist might call a fear of abandonment, and the thing is, I was hoping that our love would act as an elixir and make all of this baggage go away, but it hasn't. Love hasn't fixed my issues, it's exposed them, exposed me to the reality that I don't trust anyone—and with good reason, right? Right! No one can be trusted! Everyone is a turncoat! Indubitably! But still, all of this catches me off guard, because I thought trusting her would come as easily as falling in love with her did, but wow, I was way off, and then I figure out why: because love is confidence in my feelings for someone else, but trust is confidence in someone else's feelings for me, which, in my case, makes trust harder than love, because I have been set free from the Matrix and know the truth that everyone is out to get me, that everyone will eventually leave me if given the chance, everyone—

Yes, I'm paranoid! I'm aware! But paranoia fuels the world! We operate primarily in the hypothetical, in contingencies. I'm doing that now! I know! But I can't stop because trust feels impossible, trust is the beast, a beast I can't overcome, so now, out of mistrust, my inner arsonist is torching our relationship. I'm smothering Kristen, at first with phone calls—two a day, then four a day, then ten a day—and then following the calls with pop-ins, you know, swinging by her house unannounced because I was "in the neighborhood," and sitting in my car down the street, just beyond the glow of the streetlamps, hidden in shadows, snacking on jerky, like I'm on a stakeout, waiting for her to come home. And when I'm not stalking her, I'm waiting for my phone to ring, and since I don't want to miss a chance to be with her, I don't go out with my friends or go to work at the church or do anything but wait for her, and through my actions I'm putting massive pressure on her—save me, save me, save me—and then, of course, when she doesn't meet my needs, I give her guilt trips, which I'm good at because I have years of experience from the inner workings of my family, and though I swore I'd never do that, I'm now copycatting the things I despise. I'm finding that destruction runs in my blood, that fear can be hereditary, that monsters breed monsters, and while at times it seems that my smothering Kristen is working to hold her close, it's a mirage. The truth is I'm pushing her away, and since Kristen is a strong woman who will become who she is destined to be with or without me, she backpedals out of a hug while we're standing in a parking lot and tells me that I'm smothering her, and then out of her mouth march the words that I've been afraid of my whole life: "I need some space"—

BOOOOOM! Grenade to the heart! Oh, these words are my nightmare because, well, my parents needed "space" from each other, and "space" was code for "get out of my life," so when Kristen says this, I'm thrown into a panic, I go into crash position, and I antagonize her and try to get her to dump me on the spot, in the parking lot, practically daring her to do it. Why? Because I'd prefer this ruse of a romance, this hexed love, to end sooner rather than later—better to be decapitated than drawn and quartered or boiled in oil or disemboweled or flayed— But since Kristen is less impulsive and less spastic than I am, she says that she isn't breaking up with me—reassuring me that she loves me—and then tells me that this pattern has to change, because if I can't trust her, we won't make it, so I'm instructed by Kristen not to initiate any conversation with her.

"For how long?" I ask.

"Until I say so," she says.

And beginning that day, we see each other only when she initiates it, which lobs me out of an invisible plane and sends me plummeting toward earth, the wind as hard as copper, hoping that my chute—which I have not been trained to operate—will open before I face-plant onto the heartbreak cactus growing larger by the second, the second, the— Wait! Because as I'm falling, nearing impact, something strange happens. A phenomenon? Maybe. The descent stops, and instead I hover in midair, flanked by clouds and pigeons, because while I'm afraid—and about to experience everything I've worked so hard to avoid—I realize that I don't want to smother Kristen, no! Unlike so many of the other girls I've been with—girls I lied to, girls I told that I was an assistant coach for the Indiana Pacers, girls I told that I was a goalkeeper for UCLA, girls I told that I was from Ireland and therefore spoke to in a fake Irish accent—I genuinely do want to love her, and I don't want her to drink my homemade poison, so for three months, I don't call her or stake out her house or guilt-trip her, and at first, as expected, I struggle, slip into a moribund state, my own fermenting, whereby I'm eyeballing the unmoving hands of the clock, waiting for her call, sure that she won't call, sure that she's moved on to someone better, to a cop probably, Officer Something-or-Other, or maybe a taller guy with a nice car who doesn't wear clothes off the floor and who can afford to go skiing because he actually knows how to balance a checkbook. Yes, that's probably it. These are certainties, and I also know that I'm not laughing anymore, that humor has become extinct, and my church office is empty for days on end, and I know that I'm wasting away in this lover's rehab, in romantic withdrawal, and I know that my hair will probably turn gray soon, not to mention the oceans that are drying up—

But then, lo and behold! I wake up one morning and I'm not dead, and things are becoming easier, better, little by little. After a few months, when snow begins falling in Chicago, I go play in it, I go out with my friends again, and I hang out with Jack again, just us being us, and I'm also engaged at my church job again, and Kristen is pursuing me like she said she would! She's not saving me, but she's initiating time with me, loving me, and now I really know and believe that she loves me, that I love her! And could it be? Drumroll . . . yes! Finally! I trust her. I have no reason not to, and so another piece of baggage that I've been carrying around has been thrown off a bridge, down into a quarry—one of those places Fred Flintstone works—and buried under an avalanche of redemptive rock. Yes, the trust beast has been tamed! And it needed to be tamed, because love is a force furious enough to require a conscience, and trust is that conscience—the only thing that keeps love from killing, because without trust, love murders.

So now, on a midweek day just before Christmas, my mom and I go to a store with a jingling bell over the door, and we stare down through a glass case, saying no, no, no, no to the recommendations of a heavyset guy with the uneven mustache, until here it is. *That's it*, the right one! We all agree, so I empty my bank account—the check bounces twice before clearing—and it's mine, mine, mine, and then I put it on her finger and it's hers, hers, hers, and when I ask her to marry me, she says yes, yes, yes!

Broken Vow

Life returns to normal speed. And in easier-to-read scenes now, a string quartet is playing popular radio music, men dressed like lawyers have their legs crossed, and I'm wearing an orange tie and black tuxedo, standing in a row of other tuxedos worn by Jack, Wallace, and my bald high school friend, Norton. We could be a boy band. Next to Norton, Corbett and Quinn are holding tiny bouquets. I feel handsome. I feel as if I belong. Just a few feet away, in the front row, my parents, acting civil. Mom is blazing in an orange and brown wrap, an African queen sort of thing, her style and flair in full bloom. Dad's wadded-up skin is sagging over the collar of his overpriced suit. It's Frank Sinatra meets "Thriller": hard to stomach, but this is the best he can do now.

Every inch of him reminds me of his health battles. The Parkinson's, the arthritis, the brain surgery, the heart transplant. String and pills are holding him together now. He doesn't do much walking anymore, but tonight he wanted to take his legs out for a spin, so he's using a cane. Being so Dad, he doesn't want anyone to help him. No, he wants to do it alone, to stride to his seat and to the reception by himself, unencumbered by assistance, to hug Kristen on his own two feet. I don't understand what he's going through. But I do. This fragile man, he wants to be strong, to show the whole world that we can still lean on him. He is an eggshell masquerading as a tank. In my own way, so am I.

But what if he falls? Can you imagine? Him crumbling in front of everyone, his combed head coming apart into antlers of hair, his hip and dignity shattered, his head split open, the perfect irony of blood spots in the wedding aisle. People we hardly know knocking over chairs and crowding over him, covering their mouths and commenting on how this was inevitable, how they would've handled it differently, thought ahead, then judging us for our lack of foresight, pitying Dad like an invalid. Us left wondering if we should go on with the wedding or delay it so we can be with him at the hospital.

No, he doesn't want that attention. I don't want that attention. So a plan has been put in place. Norton—who lost his dad in middle school and sees my dad as his own—is Dad's personal usher for the evening, his human handrail. The whole thing is painful to watch, but at the same time, I wasn't even sure Dad would live to see the wedding. Just the fact that he's here is a miracle. Shouldn't I just be thankful for that? Probably. But still, it sucks.

I've come to enjoy this man, to understand him, to love him, and now that I don't want to lose him, I'm going to, soon. Time doesn't negotiate. What a harsh lord time is—

The string quartet starts playing U2 now, and flash bulbs go crazy in a red carpet kind of way. Guests stand, stretching their necks sideways, arching onto their toes. I guess everyone wants a glimpse of true love. To keep from fainting—and as instructed—I'm bending my knees, reminding myself to breathe. Dad makes a hand gesture that I don't understand. I nod as if I do, but then it doesn't matter, because Kristen, in white, comes around the corner, smiling as big as forever, and one piece at a time, the room collapses until it's just the two of us staring down the aisle, riding swan-shaped boats toward each other—our tunnel of love.

Out of the wedding party line, Jack lunges forward, whispering how amazing it must be to know that she is giving that smile to no one but me.

Yes, I have the power to make someone smile, to physically alter someone. Amazing.

Keeping my eyes on Kristen, I thank Jack out of the side of my mouth for being here, for making this day happen. He's happy to do it. And because Jack can be sappy and is a sucker for love, he tells me to accept her smile and cherish it always.

Kristen is next to me now. We are being stared at, cried over, photographed. I reach for her hand, and just like the first time, she feels like a warm towel spread over the beach.

"Hey, babe."

"Hey."

Over the week of late nights and out-of-town friends, she's lost her voice, so she sounds like a chain-smoking Muppet. Perfect. I glance back at Jack. He winks. Our inside joke. Earlier at the hotel, he asked me if I wanted anything from him today. Yes, one thing. In our tuxes, in the hotel, I asked Jack to make today memorable. Jack squeezed my shoulder, real father-like, and said he would. Already he has. But now, hearing Kristen's unforgettable Muppet voice, he's going above and beyond. It's almost as if he's taking more pleasure in this day than I am.

"Kristen, you look . . ."

Words are lost. Sometimes they just aren't big enough.

"You're amazing, Kristen."

"Thanks. You too."

"I love you."

"I love you too."

We exchange vows, and in doing so, I break an old one. Sure, I swore I'd never get married. But I guess life is a matter of knowing which vows matter most and which ones you're better off without. Sometimes it's the broken vows that let us know how far we've come.

Why walk down the stairs when you can slide down the banister?

EJ

VI

Dog

Are we human? Or are we bear dogs?

It is our duty, our responsibility, to raise and foster something beautiful. As human beings, this is our grand privilege, our opportunity. Responsibility? So Kristen and I, young married lovers, young humans now living in Texas, embrace it. Because the idea of having children is currently unappealing and terrifying, we adopt a dog and name him Ditka. Since he is ours, he is, of course—to us and probably everyone—brilliant, impeccable, never late, the pinnacle of cuteness, more advanced than other dogs his age, and more liked by all of creation. He has an inner ferocity, a bigness, a bearness, but he's physically small enough to thrive and romp in our one-bedroom condo.

We've fallen into our unique roles as parents like second nature. Kristen is a loving disciplinarian, offering affirmation and structure, and I'm more of an adoring pirate, encouraging a bit of anarchy, enforcing fewer rules, and lavishing excessive treats and affection upon Ditka. One of the things I've started doing with him is singing. Fully aware that this is a bit quirky, I've mostly kept this behind closed doors. I don't really talk about it.

Like most people, I'm afraid to be weird, so I'm always concealing my quirks, which is a shame. Our quirks are the very things that draw people to us. Our quirks make us who we are. Our quirks are all we have. Without them, we're boring. Hide your quirks and you're a Volvo.

One day I'll stop hiding this quirk of mine. One day I'll stand in the shadow of all things and be able to say, in my most revolutionary voice, "Give me weird over boring any day!" And on that day, I'll mean it. Oh, that will be such a great day.

Anyway, for now, and mostly in private, what I do is this: I take my favorite songs—in this case, something by the Killers—and change a few of the words, personalizing it for Ditka. So instead of, "Are we human, or are we dancer?" it's "Are we humans, or are we bear dogs?" Entertaining him is my gift. The gift is letting him be my audience. Wow, I never meant to be, but I really am my dad's apprentice. I suppose each one of us is an accidental apprentice, unknowingly studying under someone, learning the craft of being them. So I guess that makes this my attempt at a seaweed monster. That's fine. It's worth it. Every now and again as I'm singing to Ditka, he'll cock his head to one side, which as far as I can tell is dog for "thank you." Most of my songs end with giving him a rub, which could be why he likes the song so much to begin with. The song is the promise of what's to come. The appetizer. Ditka would do anything for a rub. My dog, the rub slut.

It's late. I feel it. My posture tells me. I'm drooped down, my chest slumped into my stomach, the rest of me spilled across the couch next to Ditka, finishing a song while working on his shoulders. He rolls over onto his back, shutting his milk-dud eyes, those little paws reaching for the ceiling, his mouth creasing in the corners. I sit up. I give his puffed belly a scratch, then his neck and his boxy chest. He guides me, telling me where he needs it. I find this satisfying. Just knowing that he's enjoying my gift fills me. I'm not sure who's enjoying the rub and song more. Is this how my dad felt when he dressed up as Spider-Man and Cookie Monster? Is this how Jack feels when I smile?

"Ready for sleepy, tiny man?"

I already know the answer to my question.

Barely peeking up, Ditka lets me know that he's ready. I scoop him into my arms, his head nuzzled in my neck, and kiss his fuzzy snout, whispering, "You're so sleepy," and set him on the bed, down near Kristen's feet. Two seconds and he dozes off into dreams about chew toys and bacon and riding in the car with his head out the window. Bending to my knees at the foot of the bed, I run my hand over his ears and quietly—so quiet only a dog can hear—I tell him, "You're my best friend, Ditka, and I love you, buddy. I love you so much." In the bathroom, I brush my teeth and wash my face, and then I crawl under the sheet next to Kristen.

She's asleep before me. This is unusual. I'm always out first. But tonight I enjoy being second. I put my hand on her back, and the heat of her body grows. I blink hard just to make sure I'm not hallucinating, that she's real, that this is real. I still can't believe I'm married. I'm not old enough to be a husband. I don't know enough about mortgages or auto repair to be a husband. I don't own enough collared shirts to be a husband. No, I won't share any of this with Kristen. No need to ignite a family panic. No need to appear unprepared, in over my— Ditka shifts to get comfortable. I pull the sheet toward me, and as I do, I can't help but wonder if this little animal understands anything that I communicate.

Does he have any idea what I mean when I say "I love you"? Does he have any idea *why* I pet him, carry him, squeeze him, give him water, throw the ball to him, wrestle with him, take him for walks, and feed him those chicken and liver treats that make my hands reek like a dead hamster? Ditka exhales big, and I'm wondering if he knows how much I love him, how badly I want him to know, and if I'll be able to rest until I'm certain. Yes! It's that essential! He needs to know that I love him, because obviously that moment will prove mystical to him! That moment will ease his heart and light his way and rescue him from self-doubt and so many misguided quests! Or maybe it will do that for me. Maybe I believe that the moment this creature knows beyond question that I love him, then my heart will be eased, my future illuminated, that I'll be rescued from so many misguided quests. Maybe I believe that once I truly love something well, I'll have fully existed, emerged from a vaporous state, become present, served my purpose—

Gosh, I want Ditka to know how deeply I care, and how hard I'm trying to tell him. But does he?

Jack must wonder the same things.

Even in the dark here, I feel Jack with me. Weird, but I do. And I know—I'm not sure how, but I do—that even through this darkness, Jack is telling me that he loves me.

Somewhere deep inside, I know this to be true, and I know that darkness is only one of his ways of saying that. Jack does so much to tell me that he loves me: sunny March days, zebra stripes, wasabi sauce—the way it explodes in my nose and mouth—great paintings and books, bold coffee, and naps on the couch. He says it a million ways, speaking it in a thousand languages, but in every language, it's always the same message. All of these things, these gifts, these moments, are his way of shooting up flares, signaling me and everybody about his love. Of course, like Ditka, most of the time I have no idea what Jack's trying to say.

Knowing that Jack is real is one thing. Knowing that his love is real is quite another—

Ditka, as he does every night, stands up on his paws, turns in a circle, and drops back down into a ball, letting out a big bear dog sigh, and just as he flops onto the mattress, I'm reminded how often the greatest challenge of love, any love—man to dog, parent to child, friend to friend, husband to wife, stranger to stranger—is to communicate that love. Communicating that bonfire within us, and communicating it in a way that someone can feel, in a way that someone can understand—that's the challenge—

Ditka's eyes close again, and now I'm feeling a philosophical wave rolling toward me, so I paddle out and surf it, understanding mysteries for the first time.

Love without communication is guessing.

To love is to be intentional. To love is to innovate.

Inventive love is divine.

Without creativity, love doesn't exist.

Every true lover is a creator. If I'm not creating, I'm not loving—

The cold of the room gets me—why do we turn the thermostat down so low?—so I turn, mummifying my body in the sheet. I look past Kristen, out the window. Our room is calm, but out there, it's an all-out frenzy. Out there, Jack and his intentionality are evident, everywhere. His new and specific ways of letting me know that he loves me are all around. Lightning bugs doodle on the air, passing secrets among themselves in their disappearing ink, stars puncturing the sky, the faint whistle of the wind.

I love you. I love you.

Oh, Jack is being obvious with me—not only obvious but new. Yes, new! Even now, in this moment, he's trying other things, different things, maybe in case the other attempts don't get through to me. I smell Thai food wafting from the restaurant across the street, and I feel the joy of a resting body. I hear Kristen breathing next to me, and our first date comes to mind— That's another one! I have the ability to remember! In that too, in giving me a memory, Jack must be saying, *I love you, Josh. I love you. I. Love. You.*

He's always trying something new. Jack: history's most innovative lover—

I yawn and roll over. My eyes start fading, but I understand now. I understand. This bittersweet world muddles the message of love, so like Jack, and in an effort to be as good a man as he is, I must innovate in order to communicate it. The call to love is the call to create ways of loving, and I will do just that. Like an unmanned bobsled, here I come! I'll be one of those buoyant rebels who are crazy enough to believe that they can get through to people! With Kristen, with my friends, with this world, I'll conceive new ways to love! Ha-ha! Life is my lab, and invention will happen! With this little furry guy, I'll continue singing and rubbing and holding him and whatever else I haven't thought of yet—maybe a new park? Longer walks? New tricks? Wait, how about more spontaneous wrestling matches? Rearranging the blankets in his crate? Dropping to all fours and acting like I'm a dog, his kin? Absolutely! I'm going to explore ways to tell Ditka that I love him, and tomorrow will be another attempt—

My face is elastic as I yawn again. The day is finished.

Tomorrow is another empty lot where I can build a love tower for him. Tomorrow I'll love him in fresh ways, in ways he'll understand, ways that fit him just right.

Another yawn, and now the edges of the world go fuzzy. Tomorrow will be . . . tomorrow will be . . .

A bus just ran into me, but it's more like I ran into it. I must be dreaming because it doesn't hurt at all. In fact, the bus got the worst of the collision. The whole front end is crunched, dented, and the entire casts of both *Saved By the Bell* and *Dawson's Creek* are staring out the windows, applauding and wearing terrible '90s clothing. Something nudges my ankle. I spin, and behind me, pressed against my shoes, Ditka is panting, his pink tongue strung out like taffy in a big dog grin. I just saved his life by jumping in front of that bus. On cue, and befitting the moment, the chorus of that song "Hero" by Enrique Iglesias begins playing on a crackly hi-fi, the needle skipping periodically. Now I sweep Ditka up in my arms that are more muscular than normal, and wings unfold from my back, giving him all the shade that his furry body needs, and together we stride down the middle of the street.

"Thanks, Dad," he says.

"You're welcome, son. I love you so much."

"I know you do, Dad. I know you do. Hey, Dad?"

"Yeah, pal?"

"You want to sing a song together?"

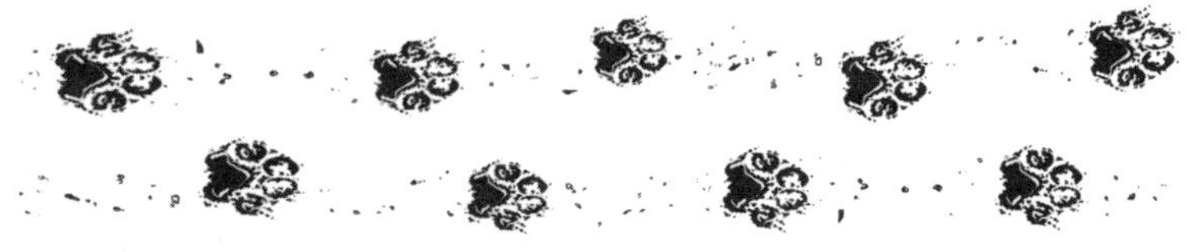

VII

A Minnesotan and a Southerner

Gus is teaching me about country music.

This is Randy Travis.

This is George Strait.

I don't understand it, so I'm having a hard time keeping up, but there's nothing between Austin and Lubbock. It's like driving on the moon, so this passes the time. And besides, he's being so patient with me.

This is Jerry Jeff Walker.

It goes on like this for hours.

Kristen and I have been living in Austin, Texas, since we got married. Some people move because they have to. We moved because we chose to, because we craved a fresh playground, the chance to yet again reinvent ourselves, and because we wanted to prove to the world that we could survive outside our Chicago cradle, that we are not in over our heads, brittle, made of leaves— Obviously it was time for something new, something opposite of where we were, and Austin was about as opposite as we could find, what with the glut of hippies and organic foods. Almost immediately after we arrived, I met Gus.

Within the first hour, I was sure that we were horribly mismatched. After all, he's from the south, Texas, and I'm from the north. Also, he wears shorts, which is troublesome to me since I don't wear shorts anymore, can't possibly, on account of my bony thighs and Slim Jim calves. Sure, sure, these tiny differences seem petty, but often it's the small things that separate people, isn't it? Most wars are fought over slivers.

But since we've gotten on with it, neither difference has been much of an issue. Actually, it's been quite the learning experience. I'm teaching him about hot dogs, cold weather, and the saying "thanks a ton." He's teaching me about boots and that a ten-gallon hat isn't actually a specific hat size—versus, say, an eight-gallon hat or twenty-gallon hat—but rather a general statement emphasizing that a hat is large, and, of course, he's giving me a country music education.

This is more Jerry Jeff Walker.

And then Gus is also teaching me about an unexpected subject, a subject that I find very unfamiliar . . . me. It's true, at this point in life, the real stranger is the person sleeping inside of me.

I'm on the backside of my twenties—practically forty!—and I know so little of what I'm like, of what I like, which probably explains why the last decade has been a blind shotgun spray of different ideas and fashion statements and catchphrases and elaborate handshakes and hairstyles and tattoos and girls and college majors, most of which seem to swing from one extreme to the other, each personal fad lasting only until it has taken me as far as it possibly can, until it becomes painfully evident that my most recent self-personification no longer represents who I am, nor does it appeal to the public at large, and has, in fact, become so contrived and shamefully unphotogenic that I'm left with no other option but to don an alternate image and continue searching for myself in other places. And so here I am, still searching. How is it possible to spend all these years with myself and yet understand so little of who I am? This is just another answer that I don't have. But I do know this: through Gus—whether he knows it or not—I'm slowly getting better acquainted with me. He's helping. Friends do that, I suppose. More than anything else, they show us who we are. Without friends, we'd never know ourselves. Show me someone who knows himself, and I guarantee he has great friends.

This is Merle Haggard.

This is Merle Haggard again.

And in all of this, as I'm learning more and more about me, and as Gus is too, I'm confident that he enjoys being my friend, that he likes me, and not the refined pretend version of me that I trot out for job interviews and church and virtually all pressurized social interactions, not the version of me that doesn't really exist, but the actual me—as well as I know the actual me anyway—the me I'm still getting to know. I never feel as if he wants me to be anything else, and while that feels quite good, freeing even, it also freaks me out and leaves me suspicious, turns me into a fountain of questions: Is it safe to be myself? Do I even want to be myself? Aren't I better off being someone else? What the heck is wrong with Gus that he wants me to be myself? Psychosis? What's his angle here? But at this point, my desire to find answers to these questions is greater than my fear of them, so a road trip across a third of Texas through barren terrain is a welcome opportunity.

This is more Randy Travis.

We're picking up the little animal that will be his new dog—that's why we're on this road trip—and Gus already has a name picked out: Landry (as in Tom, the former coach of the Dallas Cowboys). It's a perfect name, considering that she happens to be Ditka's sister from another litter. Naturally, Gus and I find that special, and we've already spent significant time trying to figure out what that makes us. It has to make us something more! If our dogs are siblings, then we must now be connected in a new way through them, perhaps as third cousins, or step-something-or-other—

Out the window, the world is flat and brown, miles and miles of paper sack. I think we're still moving, but since everything looks the same, it's difficult to tell. Country music continues filling the car, and suddenly I feel something in my lower half. I glance down. Is my foot doing what I think it's doing? Yes! It's tapping, and now I'm humming along to all the words that I don't know, bobbing my head, gripped with an instinctive urge to strum the air banjo. Oh, this is precarious. If I'm not careful, I'm going to get hooked on this country music that I've been mocking all these years.

I turn to Gus. He's swaying just a bit, into it. We keep talking about Ditka and Landry but are unable to make a final decision on our new relationship label. So for now, Gus and I just know that we are friends, friends who are becoming less afraid of being ourselves, and that makes us closer than blood.

Twist Project

The oil derricks and family restaurants stare at us with a *duh* look on their faces as we drive by. Here in Texas, Dairy Queen is the only public meeting place outside of the large cities, so the breeder chooses to make the dog-for-cash exchange there, which makes it feel like a drugs-for-cash exchange, which makes me feel more like an outlaw than I have in my entire life.

This is Waylon Jennings.

We arrive right on time—because Gus is always on time—just as the breeder does, and we hop out of the car. Whoa, it's cold! And again I haven't dressed for the weather, but neither has Landry, poor thing. Her hair is still thin, and carried by the breeder, she is lumped into a tight fist, a little monkey fist, shaking and trying in vain to keep warm against the gray wind. I hug myself. I'm turning blue. Gus hands the breeder the money, takes Landry in his hand, and after a second to collectively *awwwww* the puppy, we are off again, back the way we came.

This is Willie Nelson.

This is earlier Willie Nelson.

This is later Willie Nelson.

This is Clint Black.

Within hours, the sun is setting and we are the last people on earth, driving across Texas, listening to more and more of the country music that I'm now growing tired of. The novelty has worn off. Apparently my fondness of it (immunity to it?) works only in small doses, and now I'm officially overdosing, so I'm noticing every nuance and nook and cranny that I don't like: the warbling vocal inflections, the hick lyrics, the jerky rhythms. And since I'm noticing them, and since they're making my skin crawl, I feel compelled to voice these complaints, make them known. Obviously that's the right thing to do. I want Gus and Landry to be aware of how flawed this music is. I want to criticize it. I need to criticize it. Deep in his subconscious, Gus is silently counting on me. He needs me to tell him all the reasons why country music isn't good, why it are-you-kidding-me sucks, why he shouldn't enjoy it, and why he should feel terrible about himself if he does.

One chorus later I've reached my breaking point. I have to tell—no, not just tell, but educate, liberate, enlighten!—Gus about what good music is and what he should like, and awaken him to the staggering error of his melodic preferences! He needs to branch away from this whiskey-drinking, pickup-truck playlist! He needs other things, fuller things, better things, my things! Right? Right!

I mean, come on, where is his '80s pop? Where is his Andrew Lloyd Webber? And his off-the-beaten-path singer/songwriter music? Huh? Where is it? It's nowhere. He's nowhere. I need to help him. Yes! That's why we've been brought together! This is my spiritual voyage! Like a Sherpa, I'm meant to guide him. I'm obligated to guide him. I need to twist him in a different direction, into different interests, different preferences, the *right* preferences, into something else, someone else, someone more like me. Oh, he is in such luck because this is my specialty! I've got years of experience with this!

Rich. He was my first twist project.

As middle school friends, we were fans of video games, Michael Jordan, and Weird Al, but this wasn't friendship as in *I like you.* This was friendship as in *I'll like you once I get done changing you.* This wasn't a person-to-person relationship. This was a sculptor-to-marble relationship. I, sculptor. He, marble. So I analyzed him. I studied him, watched him. I climbed around him at lunch, at parties, and in the school hallways, scrutinizing the angles, holding my chisel and hammer, chipping away at him—his music, his style, his opinions, his personality, his fashion statements—smoothing him, shaving away the imperfections, the things I didn't like, adding the things I did like, crafting him to be better, so very supreme. More like me.

An Adonis.

Yes, he was the first, but I've had plenty of twist projects since then, even Kristen. Clearly this project is still ongoing, but it's taking much more time and effort than I was anticipating. She can be so stubborn—

Seriously though, why does she have to be a high heels girl? I don't like high heels. I don't care if they make her calves look toned and deer-like, or however that works. I want her to be a flats girl.

"Why don't you wear your Pumas, Kristen?"

"Because I like wearing my heels."

"That doesn't make a lot of sense, not with the walking we're going to be doing."

She's a going-out person. I want her to be a staying-in person.

"Let's go out, Josh."

"Nah. Don't you want to stay in?"

"Not really."

"Come on. We could watch a movie? Order food in?"

"We did that last night."

"And we had such a good time!"

She's a physically affectionate person. I feel she'd be better off as a verbal communicator.

"Kristen, you need to tell me this stuff."

"I do. Why do you think I take your hand? I want you to know that I want to be close. I just say it differently from the way you do."

"Well, you should say it too, though, right?"

Just like me.

It wasn't always like this, though. No, no, no. During the genesis of our love, she could do no wrong. Every inch and detail of Kristen, every peccadillo, only added to the masterpiece. She was incapable of improvement—to even consider alteration was blasphemous—but then, somewhere in our relationship and marriage, maybe in that U-Haul between Chicago and Austin, things shifted, and I began trying to make her into someone else. I'm still trying. I want her to talk differently, to think differently, to throw in the "right" jokes and refrain from low-hanging, obvious ones—the "wrong" jokes. I want her to agree with me, to have the same opinions about Jack and people and art and finances and politics—even though our political engagement is mostly limited to comedians impersonating real politicians—the same opinions about cars and ideal vacation destinations and home décor— Yes, my style is better than hers! And not only better, but more economical! Less materialistic! Nearer to ideal! In all ways, I want Kristen to conform to the image of me. And yes, I think I'll be happier this way, that she'll have a better life this way, my way! Yes, through her conformity she'll be rescued! And of course, by seizing control I too will be rescued! But it won't stop there, no! I'll then, in turn, be able to rescue us all. Once I am manning earth's switchboard, pushing all the buttons, the human race will finally enter the utopian potential that has been eluding us, the perfect harmony of all species, cats and mice sharing plates of cheese, weather systems and traffic lights never acting out of turn, permanent smiles tacked onto faces worldwide—

This is George Jones.

Landry is sprawled across my lap and has been sleeping constantly, the way all infant fuzzy things do. At just the perfect pressure, I'm stroking her back and ears, adding to her sense of peace and comfort. She feels safe with me. I can tell. Every few ranch properties that we pass, Gus stretches his arm over to check on her. He smiles at his new canine daughter and brushes his fingers over her, which is sweet, but something about the way he does it—I'm not a fan. First the country music and now this? He's doing it wrong. Pressing too hard. Not pressing hard enough. And his voice, it's too loud, too low, too Darth Vader. That's not how it's done, and I know it, so I feel compelled to bestow this knowledge on him, tell him how to pet his own dog. After all, I have a dog. I've had multiple dogs. I've watched television programs about dogs. I have a book about dogs at home. I am an expert! I know how to do it. He doesn't. I can show him how he should do it, how it's supposed to be done, how I do it, the way to do it. I will. Yes, I'm going to. Right now.

This is Robert Earl Keen.

This is Garth Brooks.

But then my heart is shot full of toothpicks, and I stop. I don't say a word, because I hate what I'm doing. I'm so controlling, with Gus, with Kristen, with everyone. And what I hate even more—even more—is that being in control feels so good. These days, I only feel good when I'm in control. My parents' house is out of control. My parents' marriage is out of control. I'm out of control. I have no control!

So now, driving along, I want what I don't have. Control feels safe. Control feels stable. Control is a drug, and I'm constantly getting high and then hating myself for it. Oh, I despise this slimy puppeteer version of me, and the thought of living this way forever is depressing. I can't bear it! I wish I could just stop, but my mind is disobeying me, doing everything that I don't want it to do, whetting my appetite for further manipulation, reeling off a list of ways that Gus is an idiot, unlike the way he should be. I feel sick to my stomach. If only I could roll down the window and spit these tainted thoughts and coercive ways into the chilly Texas wind, then I might experience relief, the control tumor removed, a fleeting moment of personal symmetry.

Gus has never asked me to be anything other than myself, but so often, that's exactly what I'm silently asking him to be: anything but himself. And I hate it. Why is it that I struggle so much to enjoy people for who they are? Why, if I'm so passionate about not conforming, do I press others to conform to me? Am I that convinced that the world would be better off with more of me in it? And why am I so sure I'd enjoy people more if they were like me, when I don't even like myself?

What Happened at the People-in-the-Basement Motel

Suspended high above, the moon rules the sky, the monarch of the night. I don't know how late it is, but Gus and I are so freaking tired, and in Texas, when you're driving and tired, you take whatever hotel or motel you can get. Get too choosy, drive too far, wait for the next stop one too many times, and you'll be trapped for who knows how long with no options. Aware of this, we take the next place we see, which is a rundown, B-list-horror-film-cliché of a building, complete with a flickering red neon vacancy sign. Perfect.

We park the car and walk into the lobby.

"How many dead bodies do you think are stacked in the basement of this place, Gus?"

"Ha, yeah."

"I'll bet it's more than five."

We check in, the two of us plus Landry, who is still balled into a monkey fist. Having seen many television crime dramas, I strategically take the bed by the far wall, leaving Gus the bed nearer to the door—the one the serial killer will approach first, leaving me time to scream and escape. Both of us are worn out, dragging, and ready for sleep, so we brush our teeth and change, check beneath the beds for specters and syringes and severed limbs and rusty medical equipment, close the curtains, examine the durability of the door, apply the bolt and latch, and then hit the lights, but keep talking.

"Gus?"

"Yeah, man?"

"So I'm pretty sure I'm an introvert."

"Is that right?"

"I think so. It's a new revelation. I'm sort of just figuring it out."

"That's good."

"Yeah. Actually, I'm not sure how I feel about it."

"How's that?"

"Well, it's just that, sometimes I feel like that's not okay or something, like I should be different."

"Like more social?"

"Yeah. I guess—"

The sound of Landry making a high-pitched, squeaky noise interrupts us. We turn the lights on to make sure she's okay and that Gus hasn't accidentally rolled on top of her. She's fine.

The lights go off again, which I prefer, because here in the dark, without Gus's body and face, I can have this long-overdue conversation with anyone—everyone I've ever wanted to have this conversation with. So suddenly I'm not just talking with Gus. Suddenly I'm calling an impromptu summit, a mass gathering.

Clipboard in hand, I stand at the door, checking people in. The guest line extends into the parking lot, snaking around the block, but no one will be turned away. We will accommodate all. And then one by one, I cross each name off the list, and soon the motel room is near capacity. All invitees have arrived.

I see my third-grade teacher, who was a beast of a woman, and I see Wallace. I see my dad, of course, and my mom, who uses guilt to control and manipulate me, to shape me. And there's Corbett, and my current boss, who terrifies me, who I'm confident considers me a terrible excuse for an employee, who I'm still trying so hard to impress. And in the corner, huddled together, are all the kids who used to make fun of me for being scrawny, for crapping my pants that day we jumped hurdles in gym class, and for not knowing anything about sex, the slang terms. Leaning against the dresser are the people from my dad's AA meetings, and they're flanked by former United States presidents, by guys who've appeared on the cover of *Rolling Stone* magazine, and by each of my ex-girlfriends, and oh, Kristen made it too, and my father-in-law, along with Quinn and my middle school friend Rich, and the bank employee on the other end of the phone telling me my account is overdrawn. Even my 1.6 GPA from my first semester of college showed up. And there, sitting below the window is my fifteen-year-old self. He's holding hands with my not-so-slowly-approaching-middle-age self, and my barnacle-skinned old man self. And by the front door, alone, I see Jack.

Everyone is here. So I call the room to order.

In the dark of this motel room, where so many have gathered, I'm asking each of them, all of them, if it's okay to be me. That's why they've been summoned. I make this clear to them. I have to know if they think I'm a mistake. Am I? Well? Is all that you see in me wrong? Would you prefer me if I were someone else? If I were you? Is what I see in you the way I'm supposed to be? How long must I dance? I have to know! Please! Tell me! I have to know if it's okay to be me, or if I need to be someone else, someone better, someone who isn't such a—

"Why do you feel like you need to be more social, Josh?"

The way Gus asks this question makes me feel safe, as if I can speak freely. I temporarily adjourn the summit to answer.

"I'm not sure. I worry that it's a bad thing to enjoy the world of ideas and imagination so much. And I do enjoy it. Really. You know that. I love writing stories and making things up. But sometimes I feel bad about that, like I should be different, like it's not good."

"And what would be good?"

"What do you mean?"

"Well, if being introverted and creative isn't good, then what is?"

"I don't know. Kristen's really social, and so are you. I feel like everyone I know loves being around people. Sometimes I feel like I'm a bad person because I like spending so much time alone, because I like daydreaming and reading, because I like artsy things, like musicals—I love musicals! I love things that stir up my imagination, but sometimes it just feels as if all of that's a waste of time. And so many of my friends have corporate minds. They can organize things and break it all down. They can read graphs and spreadsheets. They're good in meetings, but when I'm in a meeting, I want to put a bullet in my head. They talk really official and keep calendars. I keep everything on random sticky notes and scribble reminders on my hands! And I love pop culture, knowing it, memorizing television theme music and throwing movie quotes into real-life conversations, and learning obscure sports facts—I don't know why, but I do. And I couldn't tell you a thing about cars and I'm fine with that, and I'm such a skeptic, and I like to stick it to the man—whoever 'the man' is. I don't take things at face value. Some people do, and that's fine, but I don't. That's not me, you know? But I feel like I'm trying to be all that, all that everyone else seems to want me to be. Even when someone tells me they like something—*The Fresh Prince of Bel-Air*, cantaloupe, steamed carrots, whatever—I'll usually say that I like it too, regardless of how I actually feel! Gus, I hate cantaloupe! And I think *The Fresh Prince of Bel-Air* is so annoying! But I say I'm into it. And why? Because I'm convinced that being like someone else, thinking like someone else, is better. Right. So I keep trying to do just that."

"Sounds like you're wearing yourself out, man."

"I am. There's nothing more exhausting than pretending to be someone else."

"So then why do it?"

"I don't know. At this point, I'd rather be accepted for what I'm not than rejected for who I am."

"You seem really confident that the only way people will accept you is if you hide who you are, confident that *good* is everything but you."

"I guess. Sometimes it feels like that, yeah. You know, in my head, I have this recurring picture of Jack sitting me down on the couch and telling me how much I embarrass him, telling me how much of a disappointment I am. And while I sit there, I feel terrible, and he tells me that he wishes that I were more like his other sons. His athletic son. His business-minded son. His great-in-a-crowd son."

"Josh—"

"His less skeptical son."

"Josh—"

"His less-messed-up son. His whatever son."

"Hey, Josh." I hear Gus sit up in his bed. "That's a lie."

"It doesn't feel like a lie."

"But it is. You're you, and that's good. You thinking about ideas and getting alone and being creative is good. You asking questions and challenging things is good. You reading the books you enjoy and expressing yourself is good. And yeah, sure, any of those things can become unhealthy, and you have to be aware of all that, but the only thing that isn't good is you being someone else. So you're not the most social person. Fine. So you aren't Mr. Corporate. Fine."

I'm already preparing my apology. I feel bad for strapping this burden on him. I feel bad that he has to coddle me, tell me that it's okay to be me, but I need him to. My heart needs him to. I need Gus to wear multiple hats. I need him to be Jack's voice, because I can't hear it on my own. And I need him to be my dad, my mom. Yes, I need my friend to be my parents. I'm sorry, but I do. I do, I do. I'm so sorry, so sorry, forgive me, please— This whole thing has to be the greatest proof that life can make people crazy, that it's made me crazy. I'm a married man, making a decent salary; I can buy a gun and fight in a war and vote and have children (medical evidence has yet to prove otherwise), but I still need someone else to tell me that it's okay to be myself. Children don't even need that! Children don't even think about that, because in some backward way, children are more grown up than I am! Children may need permission to cross the street, but I still need permission to be me. In that way, maybe children have more license than adults.

"Thanks, man."

I say this, but I'm not thankful, far from it. I want my mattress to grow steel teeth, to transform into a blender, to suck me in and chop me to bits, because I should be above this whole squishy thing and I know it. I'm not a woman, for crying out loud! I'm an alpha! I shouldn't struggle with this—whatever "this" is. I shouldn't need identity augmentation and cosmetic esteem surgery, shouldn't talk about it, should tell Gus to forget the whole thing. Yes, just forget it, it's nothing, ha-ha, kidding, kidding. I'll belch or fart or tell a dirty joke, and we'll both forget this whole conversation—

"No, I'm serious, Josh. Really serious."

"Okay."

The lights come on, and Gus, with Landry tucked gently under his arm, is leaning toward me now, his face serious, all business.

"Josh, I'm serious. You *have* to be you. Don't not be you. Jack didn't put you here to be anyone other than you. If he needed another me or another Kristen or another someone else, he would have made one. But he didn't. The only reason you're here is to be *you*. That's why Jack has *you* here, and all of us."

With my head against the pillow, I smile. Oh, I want badly for everything Gus is saying to be true. Gus sees me smile. He knows that I heard him. He turns out the light. And in the dark of the room once more, I reconvene the summit.

The gallery reappears before me, their arms folded, lips pursed, impatiently checking their watches, wondering how much longer we're going to be. Not long now. But before they vanish, I want all of these people to know that Gus is right.

They are not leaving until I see their heads nodding, smiling in agreement with Gus. I tell them this. I want all of them to learn from him, and I want to learn from him too. I guess I already am. I'm learning that Gus is a much better friend to me than I am to him. I've been trying so hard to change him, and he's been trying so hard to make sure that I don't change.

The summit concludes, and each attendee files out. Gus and I are done talking.

It's quiet now, and a sweaty serial killer may be outside, ear pressed to the door, petting the handle, grinning all crooked, but I'm too tired to care. My eyes are garage doors, coming down, closing, but my concept of friendship is expanding. I know now that a friend isn't someone who lets us be ourselves. No! A friend is someone who will die to keep us from becoming anyone else, someone who fights for us against a world that is constantly trying to shrink us into shelved canisters labeled "how you're supposed to be." A friend does everything possible to make sure we become who we are made to be—nothing less, nothing more.

Gus is doing that with me—he has from the beginning—and I suppose it's time for me to start doing the same. For too long, my curse has been believing that I need to be someone else, and in response I've been cursing others, trying to control them, trying to convince them that they need to be me, convincing them that they are wrong, that I'm right, and then I feel good. But no more. This curse dies here, in this seedy motel. Tonight I will be the serial killer, the Butcher of Nowhere, Texas, slashing curses, slashing all my twisting tendencies. And tomorrow—assuming we survive the night—instead of cursing Gus, I'm going to fight for him. And I'll have the whole forty-thousand-mile ride home across the moon to start.

THIS. IS. HANK. WILLIAMS.

THIS. IS . . . zzzz.

VIII

The Difference between Humans and Cows

The green and black IKEA chairs were all wrong, spoiling the image I'm trying so very hard to create, the precise blend of everyman and artistry. So I replaced them with two of the original seats from Soldier Field, home of the Chicago Bears, and now here they are, violent orange, loud, smelling of fifty years' worth of spilled beers and blue collars, perfect, enhancing everything.

Like most days, I'm here in my non–corner office, '80s music playing, door shut, blinds closed. Natural light is banished.

The to-do list is eternal—sermon to write, leadership structures to build, marketing plans, accounting, meetings, fires to put out, phone calls to return—never to be completed, the equivalent of a thirty-mile dog paddle—

Unannounced, a hairless head pokes into my office, shining under the fluorescent light. I've never seen this man. His clothes don't quite fit. Does he know they don't fit? He sits, I sit, the desk between us, and I ask him what I can do.

His wife is probably leaving him. Money is short. Can I help?

For him and others who have to talk to someone, I play the part of someone. So I listen, stroking my chin, Freud-like, while they talktalktalk about how their sky is falling, and inevitably, in the midst of the tears and sighs comes a pause, and they comment on the Bears seats, how interesting they are, how they like to rock back and forth in them. And here I am, trying to engage, be in the moment, respond with some nugget of Aristotelian wisdom, repair a derailed life, only beginning to understand that I'm way too young to grasp anything of weight but unable to confess that, and still genuinely wanting to help, give hope, let them know they aren't alone, that they are loved, that there are groups they can join, groups with accepting people who have been there, can relate.

An hour passes. The bald man walks out, likely regretting that he came, and as the door shuts behind him, the noise of the gray cubicle shantytown spills in.

Just beyond my office is a chaotic hive of ringing phones, muted whispers and giggles, slamming drawers, keyboards smacking, stapler clicks, purring fans, bundled computer wires, unwashed coffee mugs, and framed family photos, all way too much hyperactivity for my taste. The staff is an entertaining bunch, with experimental facial hair, big hearts, and big ideas. One of the pastors is a drummer and soccer player, usually tanned; another is a brilliant businessman, has this Jedi quality about him; the guy in the office next to me is always on some kind of lemonade cleanse, swears by it, thinks I should try it—yeah, right; one of the administrators has a life-sized cardboard Johnny Depp in her area, and I tell her how much I like his movies; and T.J., the watchdog of the church grounds, is always emailing me funny videos and doing spot-on impersonations of Arnold Schwarzenegger.

In many ways, this place doesn't feel like a church, and not just on the inside but on the outside too. The buildings are carnival colored, warmly screaming to anyone driving by, *Hey! We don't suck! We are living in the present and understand what you want! See! See!*

And of course, Sundays happen, and this place becomes a wide-spanning menu of people, each wanting something different, some unsure of what that is, some unsure why they're even here. If forced to label myself, I fall into that last group.

Yes, I enjoy working here. This is a fine job, sure, attractive to many, I keep telling myself, and I'm probably stupid for not loving it, for not cherishing the paycheck and health insurance. It's probably because I'm spoiled that I'm not on my knees thanking someone for giving me a chance, for placing even the slightest shred of responsibility into these hands. I'm probably just whining, but . . . I just don't want to be here.

I find myself daydreaming about other jobs a lot, fantasizing, sort of mentally cheating on this job with others. And while the dreams are scattered, the mistress I frequent most often is writing. Sweet writing. I dream about writing.

Since I can remember, I've always had a bit of a crush on words, admired them, envied them, the way they can come together as the ultimate team, the ultimate organization, elastic in every way, capable of so much, capable of anything. Words can walk through walls. They can make things disappear. They can raise the dead. Words are giants, able to lift people up, carry them to the stars, and tear planets apart, grinding even the strongest person into dust. These are things I've known for a long time. I come from a family of storytellers, so it's a part of me, my bones made of paper, ink rushing through my veins. Words, stories, imagination—they've sustained me. They sustain all of us—

The murmur of the cubicle shantytown enters my office again as another head pokes in.

Yes, I tell her, I saw your email. Yes, I'll get back to you ASAP.

She leaves.

My red office phone light is blinking, burning. I have a message. Since I haven't checked it in days, I'm sure it's multiple messages, all sorts, follow-up messages even, the old "Hey, I just thought I'd try you again . . ." I should listen to these. But I really don't want to. How important can they be? I turn on my computer and begin playing Solitaire.

I feel no grand sense of purpose here, no mystical bond between my heart and the work, no inspiration. Of course, maybe I'm not supposed to have a sense of purpose in my job. It is called *work*. All this stuff about passion and soul is probably an idealistic invention of egomaniacs or postmodern young people who subscribe to the philosophy of movies and therefore fail to grasp reality, who live forever-convinced that we are getting less than all that we deserve, unfairly thrown onto the cosmic back burner. Or it could be the misconceived notion of wealthy, privileged Americans who have no idea what it's like to really work in order to survive, to sweat and toil in a factory or on a farm in order to feed the mouths that are banking not on our unbridled passions but on our discipline, our work ethic, our unwavering commitment to providing. Surely that's it. My perspective is mangled. Absolutely. It's supposed to be this way, supposed to— But I do want a mission, an expedition, a quest, something that I *must* do. I do want a fiery ring that I must take to Mordor, an opera that I have to get out of me! Because if I don't have that, what am I here for? Without that I'm just ordinary! And I'd rather be dead than ordinary! Oh, sure, for some, church work is their thing, whether that's because of passion or paycheck, and that's wonderful, great, go for it, I say, but this isn't me, and I don't know why. Maybe it's Gus's influence, or something else, Jack maybe, but I want to find what my thing is. I want to be inspired. I want my quest, my purpose.

Every time I'm in my office now, these thoughts hitchhike across my mind, and no matter how many times I tell them to get out—that this is as far as I can take them—they impose, insist. They keep riding along in my brain.

Curiosity Doesn't Kill Everybody

When I wake up the next morning, the sun is coming through the blinds in horizontal lines. I'm stretched across the bed, lips sagging apart, arms limp. Stick a hook through my cheek and I'd be a dead fish. Sweeping my hand over the sheets for Kristen, I find nothing. She's gone, already at work.

My eyes move up toward the overhead ceiling fan. It's silver and sleek, as if installed by a handyman from the future. I look at it, consider my future, look at it, consider what I'm doing now, and look at it again, considering the picture of me turning fifty without having ever pursued a dream, having left my dreams behind and the long list of excuses that I used to justify it. This is a future I don't want. This isn't how it's supposed to be. I'm supposed to be different, to rage against the machine, to overthrow the pattern of Xeroxed living, to run in a herd of elephants, stomping mundane things into pancakes beneath us! This isn't right! This future must be altered! So I make an abrupt and impulsive decision: I'm playing hooky today. I'm not going to work. And if I find the answers that I'm searching for, then bam! I may never go to work again! Today I'm going to drill down into myself, into the way-down places where my passions and dreams live, to see what I find, and whatever I find, if that is writing or something else, I will make it my quest.

Suddenly I feel carbonated. I burst out of bed, and without brushing my teeth—because there is no time for such trivial things—I begin wandering around the condo, thinking and wondering, ready to bask in the glory of my rising future.

Three hours later, my dream is still evading me, and my stomach is a pack of growling dogs. Lunchtime already. I order Greek food, tipping handsomely just to prove that I am not only generous but also doing quite well financially. On the couch, I eat my gyro sandwich without chewing, hoping rapid food consumption will stimulate my heart and mind.

The phone rings. It's Garth. Obviously this is a sign.

With his bright eyes and scruffiness and backward hats, Garth is my most handsome friend. People often comment on how handsome he is. A face jockey, Gus calls him. Garth is a painter, and he acts like one would expect a painter to act: forsaking shoes, smoking cheap cigarettes, telling it like it is, asking unconventional questions, wondering how things work, all that. His heart is as gracious a host as a dream could ask for. No wonder so many dreams chose to live inside him. For a dream, Garth is the Ritz.

I wipe cucumber sauce from my chin with my sleeve. Garth's name keeps blinking on my phone.

Garth is one of the most fascinating people I've ever met, and I know why. He's fascinating because he's fascinated. This has been true since forever. The most fascinating people in the world are the people who are most fascinated by the world, and those same people are the ones who change the world. No one who's ever influenced this planet has ever done so without being remarkably curious. Oh, if only someone were here to listen to these things that I know—

I ignore his call. There is no time. I set the phone aside, and I keep drilling, down deeper into myself, into my passions. What do I want to do? I keep asking myself the question, but only because I'm hoping that if I ask myself enough times, my answer will eventually change. I keep asking only because I want to walk away from what I already know to be true. No. I don't like my current answer. My dream is obvious. So obvious! I want to be a writer, and that's beautiful in a thousand ways, but not realistic. It's on par with wanting to be a ninja, a ventriloquist, a Ghostbuster. Clearly I need to scale back, find something else, something more grown-up, more attainable.

From a cluttered drawer, I grab a pen and begin scribbling alternative ideas:

Work at a different church. (Bigger church?)

Different position in a church, possibly my current church.

Starbucks—PT? Construction—PT?

Garbage man?

Start a cover band? Must find people to play instrum—

I throw the pen, stupid pen. Everything about this list is depressing. This is the most unimaginative list ever written. It is pathetic and wrong, worse than the IKEA chairs, worse than— Maybe this whole dreaming thing just isn't for me. Maybe I should go back to my church job, which is a good job, by the way. Really! I should be so lucky! Yes, I should forget about all this. I will. I'll get dressed, brush my teeth, and go to work. I'll sneak up the back staircase and play it cool as if I've been working hard, squeezing from my brain's udders every last drop of creative milk, preparing something massive, all for the sake of our cause. No one in the office will have to know what I've been doing, all will be forgiven—

Someone is knocking at the front door. I open it.

"Hey there."

I don't say anything back.

"Hello?"

Again I say nothing, but I smell everything. He's pungent and smacking his lips over and over and over. And his body, well, his body occupies half the hallway with his massive head, and his nose is wet, flaring. I'm staring. I'm conscious that I'm staring. I can't help it. I've never seen a talking one before, and sure, you'd think that by now no amount of absurdity could surprise me. But that's one of the greatest marvels of this world. Life has a limitless supply of rabbits in her hat. In this world, the things that can't possibly happen always happen. I'm still staring.

"Everythin' alright?"

"Oh, uh, I'm sorry. Can I help you?"

"Can I come in?"

"You want to come into my house?"

"Well, yeah, if that's alright."

"Um . . . it's just that, you're a . . . a . . ."

"Yeah. I am. Got somethin' against that? Would this be easier or more plausible if I was an invisible spirit? Or maybe if I wore a monocle? Arrived in a DeLorean?"

"What? No. Come on, of course not. Why would I care if you're . . . hey, it doesn't bother me. It's not like that."

"Good. Then it shouldn't be a problem if I come in."

"But, it's just that . . . you're talking to me."

"Wow, nothing gets past you."

"Well, what do you want?"

"Jack told me I should swing by."

"Jack said that?"

"Yeah."

"What for? What are you doing here?"

"What are *you* doin' here, Josh?"

"I—"

"Josh, ya know what the strangest part of bein' alive is?"

"Uh, I'd have to think about it. I'm sure it's a matter of opin—"

"None of us chose to be. Strange, ain't it?"

"I suppose."

"Shame, but some can't accept that, they can't accept that this was somebody else's choice, somebody else's idea. Got news for you, Josh, you didn't choose to be here, in this world. Neither did I. I had about as much to do with bein' born as I did with the construction of the Egyptian pyr'mids. And for you—let me guess: yer parents met, some date to a park maybe, necked and snuggled and then some, settin' science and a string of miracles into motion, endin' with you. You entered this world, not against yer will, but certainly not because of it."

"Okay. So what are you saying?"

"Yer here, and that's that. That part wasn't yer choice, but the rest is. Yer here, and you get to decide what yer gonna do now that you are. Out of the million different lives you could live, which one you wanna try? I want to talk to you 'bout yer passions, yer dreams."

Of course he does.

"Well, Josh?"

Racing through my mind is that old adage about curiosity and cats. Surely that applies here. A kindergarten teacher would point that out. Yes, there are a million reasons I shouldn't let him into the house. I get it. Curiosity kills. But can't the lack of curiosity also kill? This, after all, could be the missing piece, the missing element, like oxygen for a fire. Aha! Curiosity is oxygen for the dream!

And with that, I forget all about going back to work and my terrible alternative list. A breakthrough is beginning now; I know it, because every dream begins with a simple act of curiosity. Every scientific advancement, romance, new taste, and burning bush starts here, with a simple act. This will be my simple act!

I move aside, and he clomps in, chewing and chewing, his hooves tracking mud all over the floor, and he sits down on the couch. Oh gosh, it's leather. I'm hoping that won't offend him.

Hoof to the Chest

The leather couch sinks to the floor under his body, and I know that I'm a horrible, horrible person, making him sit on the remains of his own friend or sister, a tactic almost certainly condemned by the Geneva Convention. To distract

us both from the couch situation, I offer him something to drink, but he politely declines, saying he isn't thirsty. I'm thirsty. My throat is like sand. I pour myself a glass of water and take an Advil.

"So," I say, swallowing the pill, "what do we do now?"

"What's the difference between you and me, Josh?"

"Are you serious?"

"Yeah."

"You've got to be kidding me."

"I ain't."

"Well, let's see." This is ridiculous. I play along anyway. "You're, well, you're what you are, and I'm not."

"Yes, u' course. What else?"

"Hooves." I point at him. "Hands." I point at me.

"Sure, sure. What else?"

"You have a tail. I don't. I can talk, you—"

"I can talk too."

He shoots me a coy smirk between chews.

"Just because we don't all speak yer language don't mean we don't talk. Anything else?"

"I have a family—"

"So do I."

I'm oddly comfortable around him, so even though he's taking up most of the couch, I wedge in next to him.

"Ah, got it. You're—and don't take this the wrong way—you're a . . . commodity. To us, you're a form of goods."

"Ha."

He laughs and his whole body rolls, as if he's filled with water.

"What's so funny?"

"We are commodities . . . and that ain't true of people? Stop trying to sound so noble, as if everyone is a unique and precious snowflake to you. What can he do? What does she look like? Is he hot? What you done for me lately? You ain't foolin' anyone. I see it play out. Keep someone till you find somethin' better, and then you trade. You do it all the time:

girlfriends, teams, employees, friendships, spouses . . . This obsession with movin' up in the world reduces other people to a box of goods."

"Okay, okay."

"What else?"

"Just hold on. Give me a sec."

He crosses one meaty leg over another and rests his front hooves across his midsection.

"What about this? You're—and I feel awful saying this, but you're food. My gosh, I've probably got your cousin in my freezer right now. Just the other day, with relish and ketchup, the bun all toasted, I ate—"

"Josh, yer kind eats a lot of things, but seems to me that yer preferred taste is each other. The most cannibalistic species on the planet is the human race. You bulk people up, process 'em, make 'em fat and happy and famous and powerful, give 'em everythin' they want, tell everybody 'bout 'em, how and why they the best. And then soon as they reach the top, you devour 'em, tear 'em down, and then move on, all in order to satisfy some cravin' inside yerself. We're food? Josh, you feast on people every day. No different."

"Well . . ." And now my mind has gone blank. He sees things I don't, understands things I don't.

"Look, Josh, I guess some of the things you mentioned is differences. That's fair. But hooves and hands—that ain't much. A tail? Whatever. You want to know the biggest difference between us?"

He's got me captured. I'd lean toward him if I could, but we're already close enough. Each time he exhales, I'm sprayed by the wet off his nose.

"Josh, the biggest difference between us is that yer given the power to dream."

He scoots to the edge of the couch, his tail snaking up behind him.

"That power to dream, to pursue a passion, is within you. 'S part of what makes you human." He aims his hoof at my chest and begins poking me again and again. "Sadly, most of you never use that power."

With one final hoof poke, he collapses back into the couch. I start rubbing my chest. It hurts. From the poking or the statement, I'm not sure which.

"The way yer livin', yer no more human than I am. Yer eatin' grass, grazin', just bidin' time till yer slaughtered, and all the while somethin' within you is waitin' to get out."

"You say that, but what if there isn't anything inside me? What if I dig down into these places within me, roll away the rock, and find only a hole? What then?"

"Keep drillin'. You keep diggin'."

I swig the last of my water. "Couldn't you just tell me what I should do?"

"No."

"Why not?"

"Because I ain't in the thievery business. Tellin' you would rob you. And yet most folk want to be told what to do. Most want someone to sit behind a big desk, the way a principal or banker does, and tell 'em what to do. Most don't want the responsibility of livin' they own lives, makin' they own choices. Most'd rather have someone else do it on they behalf because they too afraid to do it themselves. 'Tell me what to do. Tell me who to be.' Sad, though. There ain't much joy to be found in livin' someone else's dreams. Josh, if I told you what you should do, you'd hate me for it in the end. Besides, don't need me to tell you. You already know."

"Writing."

The leather of the couch farts as he slides off the cushions, coming to his hooves. In no rush whatsoever, he heads for the door.

"You've always known, Josh. If only we acted on the things we know, our lives would be so different. For you, now it's time to act."

"You know, I never imagined that someone like you would help me with this."

"Yeah, reckon you didn't. U' course, sometimes dreams is ignited by the most unlikely voices."

He wedges himself back through the door frame, his hide rubbing against the wood on either side. I step into the hallway, watch as all of him trudges away till he turns the corner, and his clomping becomes so soft that it might not be him anymore but rather someone tapping coconut shells together in order to pass the time, or maybe because, like me, they're desperately wanting a more interesting life.

While She Washes Her Hands

The sky is split, light and dark, and Kristen comes in from work. Ditka runs to the door, excited that she's home. Kristen kneels down and rubs him. His ears go back, disappearing into his head in pure joy. I feel a bit jealous over how excited they are to see each other. I'm a third wheel. Kristen drops her keys on the counter, kicks off her shoes, and takes a cluster of grapes out of the refrigerator. Popping them into her mouth, she asks me about my day.

"Oh, fine, babe, it was fine."

Resisting eye contact, I don't mention that I didn't go to work, that I need to quit my job, that I want to be a writer, or anything about the one-ton houseguest that I spent the afternoon with. Please. Where would I start? Besides, I've mopped the floor, aired the place out, lit candles—vanilla candles—and fluffed the couch cushions, so she'll have no reason to be suspicious. I have been smart and strategic, thoroughly covert, so James Bond.

Kristen whisks into the bathroom to wash her hands, trailed by Ditka. I follow them. I want to tell Kristen about the earthquakes happening in me, but I can't. How can I? She'll think I've lost my mind, she'll regret marrying me, she'll tell her mom that she was afraid of this, my impulsive lean, then they'll reminisce about the levelheaded guys Kristen could've ended up with, followed by a comment about "the pants," and questions regarding who is wearing them. She'll probably say I'm irresponsible, that I'm impractical, that I'm—and this would be worst of all—lazy. Yeah, I've heard that before.

I have that speech my dad gave me about needing to do *something* with my life running on a constant loop in my head, his disgusted expression framed and hanging in the den of my heart. Naturally, he did it in front of my mom and my friend. It was as if he wanted to hurt not just me but all of us. Three birds with one stone. A bargain killing. Am I about to relive that moment with Kristen? What if she crushes my dream? Oh, that would be so predictable! That would be just like this world. Too many dreams die young, and right now my dream is so young, so helpless, delicate, a wrinkly newborn. Right now it's crying for protection, for guidance. Right now it must be nursed. Right now my dream can be destroyed so easily, and by sharing it, I'm only inviting it to be destroyed.

Maybe I won't tell her. Maybe I shouldn't tell her. Yes, it's probably better not to, better for all.

"Kristen."

She pumps the soap into her palms.

"Kristen."

"Yeah, babe, what's up?"

Slicking the soap into foam, Kristen looks at me, gives me her full attention. Yes, sharing my dream with her risks destroying it. But on the other hand—

"Um, Kristen, I think I'm supposed to quit my job. I . . . I want to be a writer."

My dream can't live without her. Dreams can't live alone. Sharing our dreams with others may risk destroying them, but without sharing them, we destroy them ourselves. Most dreams aren't murdered. Most dreams commit suicide.

Kristen turns the faucet off. She dries her hands, hangs the towel on the rack. Smiling, with a waterfall of blonde hair splashing down her cheekbones, she places her arms around my waist. Her touch has a sudden jumper-cable effect on me, sending a confident jolt through my body. And as I surge, surge, Ditka stares on with a twinkle in his eyes, perhaps admiring me for my willingness to set out on this heroic quest, for setting such a good example.

"Yeah," Kristen says, "I think you're right."

Shortly after, I meet with my boss at the church, and I quit.

IX

Good Night, Dad; Good Night, Mom

My laptop screen is blank—has been since early this morning, has been since I quit my job. I'm trying to write, to live the dream, but I can't right now. Across the room, Kristen is in sweatpants, comfortable, huddled with Corbett and Quinn and Corbett's husband—the other Josh—watching episodes of *The Office*. For hours they've been watching.

I walk over to the vending machine. My feet squeak on the buffed, sterilized tile floor. Two people in blue scrubs approach, smiling, upbeat, hoping their expressions can wipe away my circumstances, make me forget where I am, turn anxiety into joy, turn water into wine. They go by. Farther down the hallway, the faint sound of their whispers rumbles against the walls, slow and ominous and amplified, a coming storm.

Crap. Of course the vending machine is mostly bare, raided. I'm too late.

Defeated, hungry, I sit in the closest chair. It's blue. I take off my hat, my oily hair plastered against my forehead, and I hold my head in my hands. Kristen sits down next to me, puts her arm around me. Everyone else is taking a break from *The Office*, going up a floor to get coffee, the better coffee. She asks if I want to come along. I tell her that I'll wait here. She leans in, squeezes me, which feels good, kisses my unshaven face, which feels good, tells me she loves me, which also feels good, then leaves with everyone else, toward the oversized elevator. The doors beep open, then close them out of sight.

I'm so sick of hospitals. The last two months have been nothing but hospitals. First it was my dad.

This wasn't his usual hospital thing, the normal thing that we've come to take in stride and not get too worked up about. This was hospice: the final frontier. Immediately after we found out, Kristen and I drove to Chicago, twenty-some hours, crying, all gas pedal—Ditka sitting unaware in the backseat, giddy in his ignorance, the Jeep weaving through traffic—drunk on Red Bull, not talking much, the night eventually giving way to morning as we barreled into Chicago and headed straight to the hospital on no sleep. We spent every day with him for a week, waiting, fetching him cups of ice chips, Coke, Jell-O.

For the first couple of days, he seemed completely unfazed by the approaching end and put on a real show, an encore, taking one final bow. He asked questions, about me, writing,

Kristen, the Bears. He shared stories. And of course he told jokes too, but I wasn't sure whether or not I was allowed to laugh. If the nurses saw me laugh, they'd think I didn't love him, wasn't struggling, that I was calloused—

A young, blonde, ponytailed hospital worker comes around the corner, removing a pencil from her hair. Through red lipstick, she tells me that I have a phone call from our doctor. Relief! This is a good sign, because before this day started, he said it would be an eight-hour surgery and that no complications were expected. Smooth, he said. She's in great shape, he said. And here we are, eight hours later. Right on schedule. So this is good, obviously, very good—evidence that things have gone according to plan, evidence that the breaks have fallen our way. And they had to fall our way, because we deserve it. Absolutely we do. After everything with dad, we've done our time.

I am handed an old yellow phone with a corkscrew tail. I bring it to my ear.

"Is this Josh?"

"Yes."

"Is your whole family there?"

"Uh, no, they went upstairs to get some coffee."

"Well, I really need to see your whole family."

While he gives me further instructions on where to go, I feel the blood run out of me. My face turns white. This doesn't feel right. All wrong. We're so eager to give good news. We're made to blow surprises. But bad news, oh, we drag our feet, we stall. Why do I get the feeling that the doctor is stalling? Because he is, that's why. He doesn't want to say . . . can't bring himself to do it. It can't be, though, because Mom is healthy, strong. The doctor told us! We were assured! Oh, please, Jack, please. Really? Dad first, now her?

Minutes later, we are in the consultation room, fingers crossed, rocking anxiously, exchanging looks of dread. The door swings open—

Oh, please, Jack, please, help, help, don't let this be what I think—

The doctor steps in, but he doesn't say anything. He doesn't have to. We read his face. Without telling us, he's telling us—

My head falls back into my hands. I shake it slowly, back and forth. Oh no, Jack, no, please please please, this can't be happening, this can't be happening—

"I'm so sorry, but we lost her." The doctor drops his eyes, running a trembling hand through his graying hair, and as he explains what happened, chaos blooms.

Complications, he says. Quinn curls up on a chair, fetal. Undetected cancer, the doctor says. What? She doesn't have canc— Corbett crumbles to the floor, mouth pressed into the carpet, shouting. She fought, the doctor says. There was nothing they could do. I'm so sorry, so sorry, he says, but she's gone. Screams fill the room, more sobbing. We can go in and see her if we like, the doctor says, but she looks different, not herself. The cancer was everywhere—stomach, liver, lungs—it took over, her body stolen by malignant bandits. The doctor can't coax himself into looking at us. Kristen reaches for me, but all touch is pain, a reminder that I'll never feel my mom's touch again—Dad's either—so I run, thrashing, for the door. Someone calls my name, maybe Kristen, but I don't stop. I sprint across the hallway, eyed by bewildered spectators, and into the bathroom, locking the door. This isn't fair! Who's writing this twisted story? Jack! Jack! Not her! Not her! This can't be— The toilet catches my fall, my head down into the bowl, my breath rippling the surface of the water. The muscles in my abdomen brace themselves. Am I going to vomit? Yes, I am. Please, let me! Let me vomit this moment out of me! Let me flush it! Forget it! Escape! My body wretches, violent, one massive spasm, but no, it's just dry heaving. And again heaving, heaving. I fall back, crying. The tile floor is cold. Wet? I begin screaming at the walls, at the sky, at the sink, at the doctor, at my parents, at Jack, at life, at this horrible life where it takes decades to build something and only seconds to lose it. People in the nearby waiting room must be alarmed by the commotion, the shrieking madman, clutching their loved ones, feeling fortunate to have avoided our roll of the dice, our lot, because our lives have fallen apart.

In just seventy days I've lost my dad and my mom.

Yes, I knew that life could be cruel to people, but I never knew it could be this cruel to me. To me! To people around the world, sure, people living under barbaric regimes, people who inspire telethons, people down the street, bad people, other people, faceless people, but not to me, not to me. I expected preferential treatment. I thought I was special. But I'm not. And now, on the bathroom floor of this hospital, wet and cold and alone, I've fallen apart. And I know that putting it all back together will take much longer.

Putting back together always takes longer than falling apart—

The door shakes. The hospital chaplain is pounding on it, frantic, begging me to open up, to not harm myself, and for someone to find a key, to hurry, please.

These Talking Walls

For the next few days, we are zombies.

Corbett, Quinn, Kristen, Corbett's husband—the other Josh—and I are staying at Corbett and the other Josh's house in Chicago. It's a bit awkward, since my sisters and I haven't done much talking over the last ten years, not about anything substantive. Of course, we aren't doing much talking now anyway. Just crying mostly. Interacting is, on the whole, more than I can do, and the same is true with eating. When did I eat last? I don't remember. I'm wandering around the house a lot, never really asleep but never really awake either, mostly just staring off into nowhere, the way people in nursing homes sometimes do.

A few times a day, thoughtful and compassionate people come by the house to drop off meals and Kleenex and toilet paper, all the things we've forgotten about. It's as if they're hoping that by giving us these simple objects, they can give us even the tiniest piece of my parents back, heal us, give us life, fill the void. Now that I think about it, it's actually quite insulting, disrespectful! They think this stuff can help? I wish they'd go away, stop meddling in— No. They are good people, doing a good thing. But no matter how approachable they appear to be, we don't answer the door or speak to them or move. We nod to them through the window and they understand. I can tell that they understand. We exist in alternate universes now. They can't cross into our world. We can't cross into their world. Once the car pulls out of the driveway, we drag ourselves onto the porch and bring in the grocery bags, and even that is exhausting. Every drop of energy has been taken from us, stolen by grief.

Grief is such a kleptomaniac. It'll steal anything it can get its hands on—fun, faith, hope, relationships, sanity, serenity, rest, careers, passions, normalcy, identity. Grief will take it all and not think twice about it, unremorseful. One thing grief hasn't stolen, though, is my hearing. Oh, I wish it would take that too.

I want to puncture my ears with scissors. Sound is what's trapping me in reality. Sound is the only thing reminding me that this isn't a bad dream. It's the worst at night.

Kristen and I head to the guest room and close the door. I don't sleep. The mattress is sharp and uncomfortable, a bed of spears. I lay there, and through the walls I can hear my sisters crying. Gentle cries. Feathery cries. Full-body cries. Pillow-hitting cries. Exhausting cries. Their tears and grief and pain sail against the floorboards, through the keyhole, and into my head, rolling back and forth, back and forth in my mind. Who can sleep with that? I want to be mad at them, tell them to keep it down, to get it together, but I can't. That would be too hypocritical, because, yeah, the night crying goes both ways. I haven't sobbed like this in . . . well, ever. And I'm sure my sobs keep them up too. Of course, all of this goes unsaid between us—

I'm so tired. I've never wanted to sleep so badly in my life. It's reached a point of quiet desperation, so I've started taking sleeping pills, little friendly blue ones. At first it was one at a time, then two, and now I'm downing more than I probably should, but I want so badly to sleep, to just sleep, to flee this place, I don't care. At least if I'm sleeping, I know that I can wake up from my nightmares, contain them, keep them on a leash. But right now, in this restless existence, my nightmares are roaming, running wild and claiming pieces of my life for themselves, squatting, sending up their flags, and it's all happening while I'm awake— All these fools, these Kool-Aid guzzlers who wax poetic about how wonderful life is, have no freaking clue! Well, life may have tricked them, but it can't trick me! No.

Life has been exposed. I see its true colors now.

Life is sadistic. Disappointment knows where we hide. Pain is more reliable than Santa Claus, more determined than a starving thief. It will bang the door, jimmy the lock, crawl through a window, come down the chimney, bypass security; it will find a way in.

In this life, there is no such thing as safe. Insulation is an illusion.

The next day, I wake up to the same life. I wake up and my parents die all over again. It's afternoon and the house is silent. I must be alone. Where did everyone go? I stumble into the kitchen wearing whatever it is that I've been wearing for the last few days and grab the cereal box. I stare at it. With his giant smile, the honeybee mascot is trying to convince me that it's great to be alive. Liar.

The grain rings are clinking into the bowl when I hear the shower hissing. I haven't showered in days. Hygiene was one of the first things to go. Lack of hygiene helps me relate to the dead. The first bite of cereal tastes like plastic—grief has stolen taste too—but I keep eating, listening to the sound of the running shower. Then behind the door, through the hissing water, I hear a soft voice.

Am I delirious? I must be. This could be a side effect of the sleeping pills. I'll reduce my dosage, just to be safe. Am I even awake right now?

I stop crunching the cereal and listen again. It's so faint that I can't tell what the voice is saying. I point my ear toward the door, German shepherd–like, trying my best to catch it—

"I just want my mom back."

It's barely audible, more air than voice, but it's so clear, so painfully clear. Before I can lean away, I hear it again.

"I just want my mom back."

Suddenly I'm heavier, filled with hammers, and sinking. I can't hold myself up. My body dumps forward across the kitchen table, my head falling onto my wrists. The cereal bowl goes skidding away, the milk splashing over the sides and forming a chain of little white pools, and from the behind the door, my sister's voice grows.

"I just want my mom back!"

Her voice swells louder.

"I just want my mom back! I just want my mom back! I just want my mom back!!"

Horses are killed when they're in less pain. I wish someone would put us out of our misery. Be humane. Our hearts, it seems, really can break when struck hard enough.

Without eating another bite or wiping up the milk pools, I go back to the guest room and shut the door tight, trying to soundproof the wood. I sit on the edge of the bed, but no, I can still hear her, again and again and again. I need a distraction, badly now. Ah, television, thank you—by distracting me, you'll heal me. Evasion is the best medicine. The remote control—I grab it and flip channels to a toothpaste commercial, a woman smiling bright, happy, her problems cured by the taste of mint. I flip again, and oh, oh, I've seen this movie! Full of memorable characters and a great surprise ending! Bingo! I'll watch this, splurge on it, and in doing so, I will teleport from my current plot into the movie plot, find myself playing a different role, becoming someone else, swept up in the on-screen emotions. Yes! But I can't. I try and I can't. Pain is too attention-obsessed to let me. I'm still here, stuck, fossilized, and my sister's voice is still banging the drums in my ears. So I turn the television once more, this time to ESPN, and I crank the volume up full blast.

Many Faces

This must be how demon possession feels.

Grief has taken over my body, and every day I'm less and less myself. My emotions and thoughts and feelings are jumpy and unpredictable, which makes everything impossible, impossible on me, on Kristen, on everyone. How do you interact with someone when you don't know what version you're going to get? Are you stepping in front of a gentle kiss or a live grenade? I'm a different person every day, every hour, and I have no clue who I'm going to be next, or what will trigger the change.

Grief has more faces than a clock store.

I can't stop it. It has me. I'm sick.

Or am I getting well?

First Funeral

The air is alert, crackling, and the birds are chatty, all of them vivacious in their explosive flights. Beneath the sun, the road is shining white, and we are driving, all of us, without saying a word, to my mom's funeral.

This should be my second parent funeral, but it won't be. It'll be my first. I don't know why my mom and Corbett and Quinn and I never had a funeral for my dad, but we didn't. We gave him no send-off. There was no gathering, no refreshments. And it isn't right, because he was a better man than our lack of memorial would indicate. He was a good man.

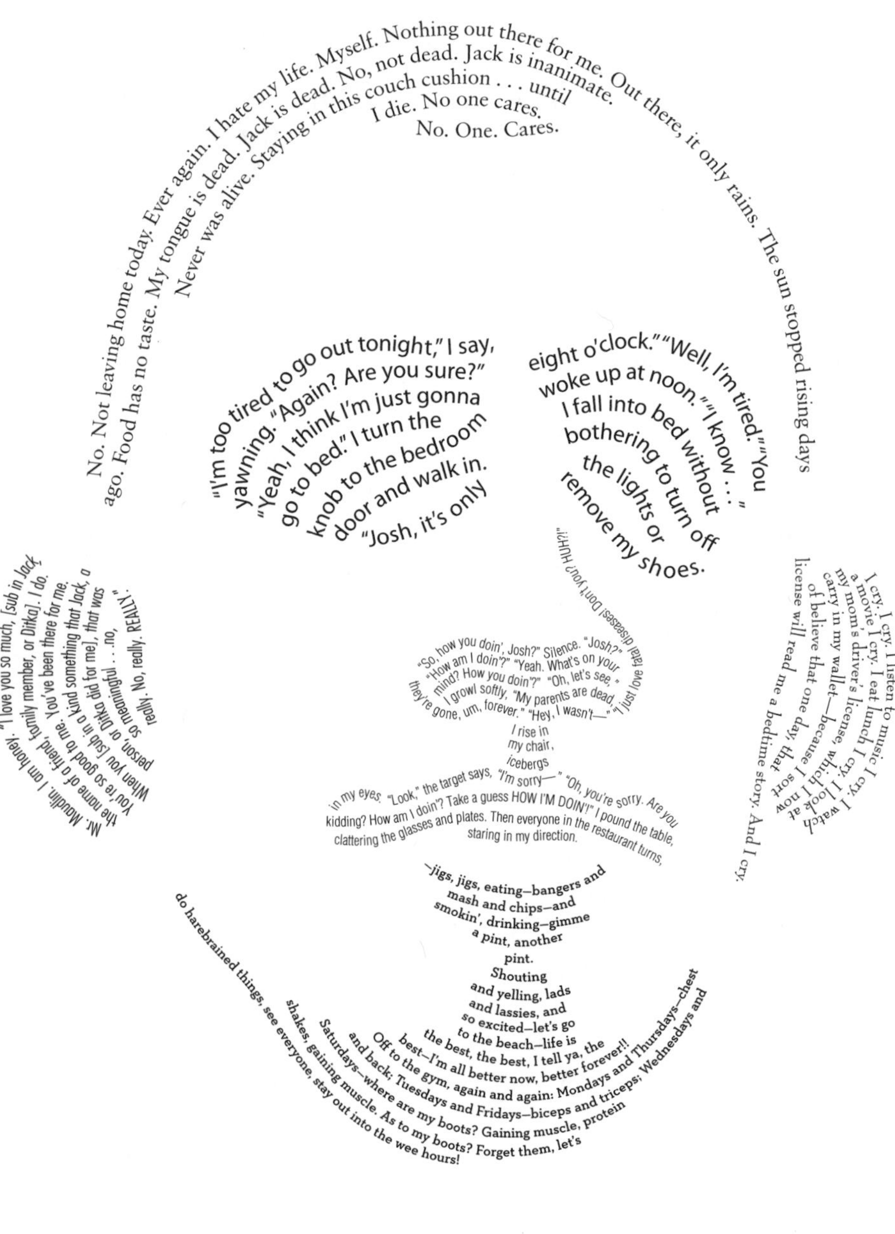

No. Not leaving home today. Ever again. I hate my life. Myself. Nothing out there for me. Out there, it only rains. The sun stopped rising days
ago. Food has no taste. My tongue is dead. Jack is dead. No, not dead. Jack is inanimate.
Never was alive. Staying in this couch cushion . . . until
I die. No one cares.
No. One. Cares.
"I'm too tired to go out tonight," I say,
yawning. "Again? Are you sure?"
"Yeah, I think I'm just gonna
go to bed." I turn the
knob to the bedroom
door and walk in.
"Josh, it's only
eight o'clock." "Well, I'm tired." "You
woke up at noon." "I know . . ."
I fall into bed without
bothering to turn off
the lights or
remove my shoes.
Mr. Maudlin, I am honey: "I love you so much, [sub in Jack,
the name of a friend, family member, or Ditka]. I do.
You're so good to me. You've been there for me.
When you [sub in a kind something that Jack, a
person, or Ditka did for me], that was
so meaningful . . . no,
really. No, really. REALLY."
I cry. I cry. I listen to music I cry. I watch
a movie I cry. I eat lunch I cry. I look at
my mom's driver's license, which I now
carry in my wallet—because I sort
of believe that one day, that
license will read me a bedtime story. And I cry.
"So, how you doin', Josh?" Silence. "Josh?"
"How am I doin'?" "Yeah. What's on your
mind? How you doin'?" "Oh, let's see,"
I growl softly, "My parents are dead,
they're gone, um, forever." "Hey, I wasn't—" "I just love fatal diseases! Don't you? HUH?!"
I rise in
my chair,
icebergs
in my eyes. "Look," the target says, "I'm sorry—" "Oh, you're sorry. Are you
kidding? How am I doin'? Take a guess HOW I'M DOIN'!" I pound the table,
clattering the glasses and plates. Then everyone in the restaurant turns,
staring in my direction.
—jigs, jigs, eating—bangers and
mash and chips—and
smokin', drinking—gimme
a pint, another
pint.
Shouting
and yelling, lads
and lassies, and
so excited—let's go
to the beach—life is
the best, the best, I tell ya, the
best—I'm all better now, better forever!!
Off to the gym, again and again: Mondays and Thursdays—chest
and back; Tuesdays and Fridays—biceps and triceps; Wednesdays and
Saturdays—where are my boots? Gaining muscle, protein
shakes, gaining muscle. As to my boots? Forget them, let's
do harebrained things, see everyone, stay out into the wee hours!

A great man! Right? Yes. Yes? Yes. And now I want everyone to know what a great man he was, is.

But how do you really commemorate a life? Maybe I'll make a banner, hang it out the windows, and in big letters write, "I LOVE MY DAD. A GREAT MAN!" Or I could put it on a shirt, of course! Higher visibility for my message that way! Wait, no, a shirt would seem too spontaneous, like my "Happy Mother's Day" gift years ago, and would only detract, further soiling his name. Maybe I'll include his name, my middle name, James, in all my writings, as a kind of tribute. Oh, he'd love that! Or, I know, maybe it's not too late to have a funeral. I could have my own for him. I could drive up to our old vacation house in Wisconsin, make a weekend out of it. I could make it very private, a small but meaningful tribute, just my dad and me. Yes, that's perfect, fitting; he would find that so— But then again, this may have nothing to do with him and what he would like, what's right. This may be just another way of forcing myself into the spotlight of a moment that doesn't really revolve around me, my way of paying a penance for how I treated him. Sure, maybe he wasn't always a good father. But was I a good son? All the things I failed to say! Those years I wasn't around! All the hugs and phone calls I turned away! Maybe I'm merely trying to atone for another one of my thousand regrets. Oh, if only I were like those freaks who live without regrets, who aren't haunted by past decisions. But I'm not. I have regrets. Lots. This one with my dad is near the top of the list.

"You still want to make a stop at Target, Josh?" Corbett asks.

"Yeah, yeah, for sure. That's cool, right?"

"Yeah. We have time."

My dad did have a funeral, though. Kraig and Kelly are my half siblings, my dad's kids from his first marriage. They had a funeral for him, a nice one, from what I hear. I didn't go.

Thinking I'd be there, Norton and some of my other friends went. They dressed up, wore suits and shiny shoes and everything, walked in quietly, and sat in the last row of the church, looking for me. But once the service got under way and I was nowhere to be found, they feared that they were at the funeral of a total stranger.

Eventually they figured it out. They were at the right funeral, my dad's funeral, I just wasn't there. Later, Norton asked me why I didn't go. He couldn't understand why I wouldn't show up.

I don't think I answered the question. I'm not sure I have an answer yet.

Grief has this tendency to not always explain itself.

Target feels busier than usual, the parking lot stacked. Inside, I wander the aisles, looking for something to wear. When I came to Chicago from Austin to visit my mom in the hospital, I didn't think to pack any formal clothing, didn't consider that I might need something funeral appropriate, so now I'm forced to improvise. The selection is limited, but with Kristen's help, I find cheap black pants—the kind mechanics wear—and a Beatles T-shirt. On our way to the cashier, I consider stealing the whole outfit. If ever I had a right to steal something, now is the time. This wouldn't even be stealing, not really. This would be my way of beginning to collect on the massive debt that life owes me. And life does owe me. No one is looking. Under my shirt, that's where I could stuff it, and then walk out, nonchalant. On the other hand, none of the employees here know how much life owes me, which means there is a risk involved, the chance of being arrested, of missing another funeral, a possibly lengthy prison term, that standard-issue orange— I opt for the legal route. I hand the elderly cashier twenty dollars. That's all it cost. Sure, my clothing choice isn't exactly swanky, dressy, but Mom was in the Beatles fan club as a kid. She loved them, sang their songs to us. That makes this getup completely appropriate. Plus, all of this goes with my Converse shoes.

But I know what message this will send.

The fact that I didn't plan for this tragedy will be obvious to everyone. The moment I step behind the stiff podium, surrounded by a million donated flowers, a drab dot among the fresh and colorful, the moment I start talking, people will know. My clothing will be a symbol of the suddenness, of my trauma. They'll see.

The auditorium is filled. I'm washing my hands, lingering in the bathroom, thinking about what I should say about her, trying so hard to come up with some story, *the* story that will encapsulate her completely. How she used to read to me? The crush she had on Tom Selleck? Her love for teaching? Maybe about the time she ran over my foot with the car? That would be good, would temporarily lighten the mood and garner some chuckles, then allow me to get serious, sentimental even, away from the jocular.

Oh, this is impossible. She can't be summed up. She is more than words. I'm overwhelmed. Why the heck did I agree to speak at my mom's funeral? I'd rather be at my funeral, not hers, not hers. This wasn't supposed to happen. Take me instead, Jack, make it my funeral, then everyone could come casual, enjoy bubbly music, and tell stories, after which they'd watch a lighthearted video montage like a television series finale. Bring her back to me, Jack, bring her back. I don't want to do this—

"Josh."

Father Mack, my mom's priest, exits a stall to the sound of flushing, wearing his black and white priest outfit. He is dressed nice, more prepared than I am.

"Yeah."

"I want to tell you something, Josh."

"Okay."

"And I know you probably don't want to hear this."

His black hair clings tight around his chiseled face, his concave eyes darting back and forth, X-raying me, all of me,

seeing everything. I want to cover up. He moves closer. Before he says anything, I agree with him. Whatever he's about to say, I don't want to hear it.

"Josh, I'm so sorry this happened. All those people out there—we all are."

"Yeah, I know. Me too."

"Your mom was an amazing woman, she really was, so special, so brave. And she will be so missed, so missed."

"Yeah."

"But, Josh, this is a crucible for you. This event is going to prepare you for everything that lies ahead of you."

His words echo off the tile and streaked mirror in exaggerated ways. I am outnumbered.

"Josh, look at me."

No thank you.

"Josh, this had to happen."

I hate that he's telling me this. This had to happen? In order to accomplish what? What could be so important that this had to happen? An impossible anger floods through me, setting off a raging metamorphosis. My skin boils, my eyes go yellow, spikes grow up through my shirt, everything tearing— Father Mack throws his arms around me and squeezes. It feels good. Paternal, momentarily calming me. But his words, I hate them. I'm swinging a rusty bike chain at his words, burning with an appetite for destruction— Now my feet double in size, turning sharp and scaly, bursting through my shoes, leaving them in rags, my muscles swelling— This tragedy had to happen? Explain. Please, holy man, enlighten me. Share what the cosmos is doing. Actually, no, don't. I've hit my limit. Will this topic ever go away? Why do we have to simplify things that aren't simple? Why are we so obsessed with connecting dots? Not all dots form lines! But ridiculous people keep trying to persuade me otherwise, and I'm tired of it, tired of the trite explanations for why this happened and why I'll be better off as a result and why I should feel okay about it.

I know, I know, if I were a better man, stronger, I'd handle it differently, right? Sure, sure. Well, I'm sorry. I'm sorry that I've proven myself to be weak, unable. I'm sorry that I can't deal with it, with my sadness, with the smell of death, with— The pink of my gums splits, and jagged ivory shoots down, up. I'm about to do animal things, alibi-worthy things, things I never thought I'd do. Yes. Drink. This is the solution. Satisfaction for the beast. The balm of destruction— Oh, naive priest, you have no idea what kind of darkness you're hugging. Close your eyes, priest. Don't watch. Your neck is my cup. I will make your bones like matchsticks, cheap rattan. And then I will be stronger. The streaked mirror is the only witness. So go ahead and cry, priest, scream if you wish. No one will answer. In a few hours, they'll find you, a bag of flesh, human soup. Yes, I will make the world gasp. I will turn heads. I will write headlines. I will give everyone something to talk about other than our loss.

Invisible?

The night after my mom's funeral is the loneliest night of my life. I feel a bit like Tom Hanks in that movie *Castaway*, except for the tropical island part. I'm at Corbett's house, on the couch, all the lights turned out, the sound of wind skipping over the roof. My fingers do laps around the rim of an aluminum can. I'm beginning to smell spongy, how my dad used to smell after one of those nights. Gosh, I want my dad here. I want my mom here. I want Jack here. But none of them are. At least my parents have an excuse. What's Jack's excuse?

I thought pain was his thing. I thought that his eyes were forever peeled for the hurting, the sick and tragic. I've heard that. He told me that. Talk about false advertising. He seems to have made for the hills, so what is going on? Huh? Jack, what's your excuse? Huh? You couldn't make it? You forgot? Here I am in the biggest collapse of my life, and you—you deadbeat, you delinquent—don't even notice.

I crumple the empty can, crack a fresh one, and take a swig.

All I can figure is that Jack has grown tired of me, is bored, is too busy, has moved on to better things and rosier places. Maybe that's the real reason I was contemplating priest-icide at the funeral. Maybe I'm desperately trying to figure out a way to get Jack's attention, and I feel like my best chance is to do something shocking. So maybe I'll get a nose piercing. Maybe I'll leave a vodka flask, porn, or a sweaty wad of cash where he can find it. Maybe I'll draw offensive pictures on his new wallpaper. Maybe I'll break his windows and then open my veins with the shards of glass. Maybe I'll stage my own kidnapping, scribble a note, block-lettered, demanding ransom. All are good options. Then I won't be a phantom to him. Then I'll exist. Then he'll notice me. And above all else, that's what I want right now. I want Jack to notice. I want Jack's attention.

The can is cold, sweating. I take another swig.

Beneath these ribs is a divided heart that is both screaming to be invisible and aching to be noticed. Since I've fallen apart, I've been experiencing the latter desire in painful increments. Right now I want to know that Jack still sees me, that he hasn't forgotten me, that he's here, right here, and not just cheering me on from a distance, shouting, "You can do it, champ," but going through it with me every step of the way.

No one is home. I'm drinking beer.

Since I woke up, I've been set on getting completely drunk. This would be a first for me. I've never been drunk, but most of my friends who have been drunk often mention not remembering things afterward. That sounds heavenly right now. Healing by lobotomy, by temporary dementia, by reality drowning. Sometimes memories are punishment. To forget would be the ultimate gift. So that's been the plan all day. But when I opened the refrigerator a little while ago, I found only a few cans of beer. So classic. Not enough to get drunk. Nothing is going my way. Why am I surprised?

I flip the television to one of those depressing public access stations. The camera is fuzzy and shaky, and based on the hollow sound, I suspect they are filming in a bathtub. Two musicians playing acoustic guitars are sitting on stools, singing. They are good, so I pay attention. The music is honest, simple. They keep repeating the same word over and over again. I'm familiar with this word. This word is another name for Jack. How did this get on my television? Why are these two people singing about Jack?

They sing on and on, and every time they say the word, it stokes something inside me. A faint bead of hope within me begins to flicker, regain consciousness. A hope that maybe I'm not alone, a hope that maybe, even though I can't see Jack, Jack sees me, and that he not only sees me, but perhaps he is with me, honestly and truly with me. A hope that if I hold on to Jack, he will see me through to another side that I can't even see yet, that I have his attention. Oh, this is a massive feeling, a massive need. Please let it be true. Please.

I begin crying. I crumble forward onto my elbows, then into a ball. The tears come in buckets now. I'm crying from everywhere. I've become water. I have to put my beer down or risk dumping it all over myself. I lie down, and as I close my eyes, the world fades to black, and I find myself possessing something I thought I'd lost forever when my dad and mom died. I was sure it was never coming back, so sure, but I was wrong, because here it is, still here, hidden inside me, touchable, fighting for air, barely breathing: faith. If I ripped this faith out of my guts and set it on the table, it wouldn't be much to look at. It'd be shabby, weak, a crumb, because this isn't the kind of faith that calls lightning out of the sky or turns rocks into bread; no, the kind of faith I've found tonight is the kind that's only strong enough to keep hanging on. Fingernail faith. But maybe that's all I need. Maybe I don't need to kill a priest or scrub my brain clean of reality, and maybe I don't need to possess armored-car faith. Maybe all I need is simply enough faith to hang on. I suppose that's all faith really is.

Yes, of course. It makes sense. Finally, something makes sense. There is still sense in this world. In this muddy, murky fog of a black bag over my head, something is finally clear. Oftentimes faith means just barely hanging on.

Ashes, Ashes, We All Rise Up

I know what's waiting for us.

The week after Mom's funeral, we go to my parents' house, all of us, to search for and gather up any items worth hanging on to, along with legal papers and that sort of thing. A group of my mom's co-workers and some family friends, along with Jack, have volunteered to help us. For the most part, they'll be the first outsiders to set foot in here in over a decade. After the house fire emptied this place, my parents moved back in and quickly returned to their hoarding/never cleaning/cat urine ways, and it only became more extreme. So extreme that a few days ago, we were contacted about having our house profiled on *Good Morning America*. They are doing a show on hoarders. And while we considered how cool being on television would be, how sad we could look, painting ourselves as real underdogs, a defy-the-odds angle, how winning the pity of the American public might somehow launch my writing career (I considered this last one), we said no. Still, knowing that our situation is morning-show worthy is flattering, strangely comforting. It justifies how overwhelmed I feel. And I am overwhelmed. Yes, it's that bad. Who knows? Maybe the house finally killed them. Will being in there kill me?

These charitable friends of ours have no idea what they're getting into.

Once they're inside, compassion won't save them. Neither will bravery. Oh, I hope they are iron-willed, iron-nosed; have experience with toxic waste or tombs; have an odd affinity for *The Beverly Hillbillies*; aren't too judgmental; haven't brought cameras; left all valuables at home; remembered to bring bug spray, a mask, oxygen tanks, rubber gloves; and aren't expecting me to make eye contact, to— Kristen slides her hand onto my back, rubbing in circles. Above everybody, she's the one I'm really worried about.

We've been married for nearly two years and she's never been inside my parents' house. Obviously this has been intentional on my part. I don't want to be tied to this disaster and filth, to these things, to these habits. I don't want her to think that this house represents me. I want to protect Kristen from this. I want to protect everyone from this, especially myself. I want to keep the whole world at bay. I don't want anyone to go inside, but I'm not stupid, and I know that our task is impossible without their help. Going through everything on our own would take a lifetime, so the walls that I intended to leave erect forever are coming down. Kristen will see this part of me. Everyone will.

I guess desperation makes a great wrecking ball.

A few hours into the digging, no one has mentioned the condition of the house. I find a stack of books. Like everything in here—the junk, the memories—they remind me of death, so I'm sifting through them at a good pace, mindlessly, without care, flipping them aside, like trash out a window— Wait. I freeze. *Love You Forever*. Dust wraps the cover. I brush it off from corner to corner, wiping every inch of it clean, till it's shiny, restored. I sit down and open it, though I'm unsure why. In every word, I hear Mom's voice. With every page, I see her face beside me, full of expression, drawing me in, just like when I was a kid. I'd like to keep reading, but I can't, so instead, I head for the front door, and a second later I'm watering the lawn with my tears.

On day two, Kristen is upstairs in my dad's room, thumbing her way through a folder of documents. Not wanting to sit on the caked, discolored carpeting, she plops down onto the nearest cardboard box.

"Kristen?" Corbett asks. "Have you found anything?"

"Nothing yet."

"How much more—"

"What'd you say?"

Corbett begins to snicker. The snicker morphs into a giggle. She begins vibrating.

"What? What is it? What?"

Corbett keeps laughing, more and more and more.

"What? What is it?"

"Um . . ."

"Tell me!"

"You're . . . you're sitting on my dad!"

Kristen peers at the cardboard box between her legs. Sure enough, staring up at her is the little box holding my dad's ashes, his remains.

"Oh my gosh!" Kristen jumps off the box.

"That's so awesome!"

"Oh my gosh! Oh my gosh!"

"Nice!"

"That's him! Corbett, he's in there!!"

"Yes! Yes! That's awesome!"

"Oh my gosh!"

Now they laugh in duet, Kristen and Corbett, bent over, grabbing their knees, breath elusive, and instantly they know that this is news, that this is a story that must be told. So without delay, they stampede down the wooden stairs together, into the living room, still laughing together. I hardly notice the uproar. I'm busy with my head in a cabinet, digging through old VHS tapes. One by one, I pick them up and read the labels, those thinly penciled-in titles guiding me on a tour of the past.

Josh's 1st Birthday.

Christmas 86.

Dressed to Kill. (This is an original play that I wrote. My entire family filmed it together. It's one of the last things I remember all of us doing together. I was the first one murdered, I think, something about money being stolen and jealous lovers and lying and a La-Z-Boy chair. Dad and Mom were fantastic in it.)

Dad's Birthday.

Mother's Day Concert 1991.

With each label, finality smacks. I want more of these moments, more of these memories. I want the ability to capture new memories, make new tapes, whatever. But that ability is gone. Our story together is over. The end.

"Josh?"

"What?" My head stays buried inside the cabinet.

"I found something kind of interesting."

"Is it the insurance form? Because we really need to find that—"

"No."

"We'll find it, don't worry. I don't know how in all of this crap, but we will. Something from the IRS?"

"Not exactly."

"Well, what is it?"

"Here's Dad!"

The low thud yanks me away from the cabinet. There it is, sitting lifeless on the table, plain and pathetic, a brown cardboard box, the factory's white sticker placed crooked on its front panel: a dead man's name tag. Coming to my feet, I inch toward the travel-sized casket, wiping my hands on my jeans. How is this possible? A whole man in a six-inch box. Creepy.

For a moment I'm taken back to the house fire. The lesson then is the same lesson now. Everything in life can be reduced to ash.

"Those—those are his ashes? He's in there?"

"Yup," Corbett answers, smirking.

"What's so funny? Where was it?"

"Ummm, well . . ."

Kristen and Corbett are mumbling like fish, not taking this as seriously as they should, as seriously as I'm taking it. They are acting weird, and I don't understand why. Yes I do! They have no respect for the dead, for Dad! They should be acting somber! I always loved him more! I should say that. Now is the perfect opportunity, because I can prove it conclusively, acknowledge their childish, ignorant, insensitive behavior. They don't understand—

"Under your wife's butt!"

The words confetti from Corbett's mouth, colored and triumphant and light, and she points at Kristen, who is now red, rivaling a lobster, covering her face, shaking, losing her mind. Corbett is her twin. Then between breaths, they tell me the story, and while they recount the details, I watch the box, which hasn't walked away or said anything because, after all, it's just a box, a stupid box. Before they can finish the story, I'm laughing too, fat ha-has strung together like pearls. Yes, it's sort of morbid, I'm aware, but dang it, it's also funny, and as a human, still alive, I'm meant to laugh at funny things, so I embrace my humanity, and I keep laughing, freely and without guilt; all of us do, holding our stomachs, palms slapped on our foreheads, stooge-like, spontaneous combustion imminent.

And oh, if our neighbors are spying, they must think we're in denial, dissolving under the searing, hot pain. They must be sighing, throwing their pity toward us, the poor, poor Riebock kids. But if that's the case, they couldn't be more wrong, because this isn't denial or naivete. This is genuine. This is real. This is bright.

Sure, my parents might be dead, but we aren't. Mom and Dad are in matching boxes, but our boxes have not yet been ordered. One day, but not yet. For now, we're still here, alive, healing, and joining the others before us who have been saved by laughter. No one who's ever crossed through pits of grief has ever done it without laughing. Laughter is the evidence that we're still here, the proof that our tragedies will not define us forever. Laughter is the language of the survivor.

And right now, look at us, listen to us, because we are fluent!

Intrigued—alarmed?—by the ruckus, our friends come into the living room. We tell them the story. At first they are unsure if they are allowed to laugh. We are, but are they? They exchange skeptical glances, and then decide that it is within the rules for them to laugh, so they join in the moment, clapping their hands, leaning back, hands on hips, big hearty chuckles and high-pitched giggles ringing out from inside their grins.

Minutes later, the laughter dies down, and all of us, including Jack, are standing in our living room with the box, talking, sharing stories, and comforting one another. The conversation rebounds around the room. And I'm here, watching this new scene, this perfect scene, this scene that I never thought I'd witness. Us, entertaining company in our home, welcoming outsiders in, sharing joy, hosting a New Year's party in September.

X

Back to the Difference between Humans and Cows

Oh, it is white! Much whiter than I expected! Glue comes to mind, and eggshells, clam chowder. For reasons that are unclear, I shaved my head, right down to the skin. No, it doesn't suit me and grotesquely accentuates my facial features the way those street caricatures do, gives me the look of smoothed cauliflower, but I don't really care. Yes, my scalp is alarmingly pale, but so what? Dad's been gone four months now. Mom's been gone for almost two—is that all? Or, wait, maybe I mean *has it been that*

long already? When you aren't doing anything, I guess time becomes indiscernible, formless. And I haven't been doing anything. What's the point? I know, I know, I'm wallowing, but I just can't seem to spot the beauty of life anymore, the good—is there good?

Recently I had a stretch where my lack of productivity was nothing short of staggering. A legendary stretch where I never got out of bed before lunchtime—some days didn't leave bed at all—where the blinds were sealed shut, where I lived in the dark, bat-like, a stretch where I listened only to sad music, Sarah McLachlan kind of stuff, where I completely neglected my new job, my dream, where the only friend I talked to was Ditka. I didn't talk to Jack, not even to Kristen. And no, I didn't feel guilty about any of this.

I can credit my clear conscience to a one-trick word: tomorrow. That word I simply repeated over and over.

Decaying on the couch, watching another bad movie, I'd tell myself that I'd get back into the swing of things tomorrow. I just need one more day, I'd tell myself, and tomorrow I'll get back to engaging Kristen and the world, trying, writing, doing something useful. And the more grandiose the promise I made to myself, the more at peace I was with putting it off. Tomorrow I'll seek to rediscover why life matters! Tomorrow I'll capitalize on (exploit?) my family catastrophe by spinning it into an inspiring story that everyone can read! Tomorrow I'll captain the *Titanic* safely into harbor, win an Olympic gold medal in fencing, and build a ladder to heaven and kiss the sun. Tomorrow is *the* day!

With all that practice, I became a master of making promises that I'd never have to keep. It really was magic, and it worked for a while, but then, *poof*, it sort of just stopped working. I'm not sure why. I suppose all tricks—even the ones we pull on ourselves—have an expiration date. Ever since my trick expired, I see the true but equally obnoxious self-help reality.

Everyone can change tomorrow. Everyone solves problems tomorrow. But the only changes that matter are the ones I make today. Tomorrow is the easiest day I'll ever live. Today is the scary one, which is probably why I've spent so much time avoiding it.

But now I'm facing it. I'm trying to live again.

Rather than watching another bad movie, I sit down at my desk (the dining room table) to write. Before I start I want to stop. Everything I've written this week and over the past few months has been junk. My creative strength has left me. But when strength leaves, where does it go? If I knew, I could go find it. Words feel like such strangers. My fingers, it seems, have forgotten how to fly. But today I'm choosing to be hopeful. I'm hopeful that over the next few hours I can write something worthwhile, that flocks of majestic words will migrate toward my page. Okay, so— Suddenly I'm crying. This doesn't surprise me. These days I cry often, and as usual, I don't really know why. I set my head down. After a minute, the tears stop. They start again. They stop. This repeats a few more times. Finally, I crack my knuckles, fanning my fingers across the keyboard . . .

On the jukebox, it's Jay and the Americans and Frankie Valli. The third time tonight that he's heard these songs. Their songs. With a flip of his wrist, he orders another drink. Taking the glass, he chugs till it's empty. He swirls the ice around, sliding a cube into his mouth, biting down, all while humming along to the music. He swivels toward the empty dance floor, smiles. Even now, he can see her out there, her ghost swaying in his arms, the two of them swinging as one, the smell of her just-shampooed hair, the rhythm in their blood.

Those years with her were the best years of his life. They were the kind of years, the kind of love, that don't let you move on but instead leave you forever pointed backward, because the future has nothing for you but pale substitutions. Bliss truly is a dangerous game. Oh, he'd do anything to travel back to when he had it perfect. Anything. Until he finds a way, he'll continue coming here, every night, and asking her ghost for a dance.

A stranger grates a barstool across the floor, sits, and says hello, and she slips away. He turns from the stranger and says nothing. Undeterred, the stranger begins talking about the end of the world, wondering if people are doomed to the same fate as dinosaurs, and then mentions his new experiment in time trav—

Ugh.

I stop mid-sentence, roll my eyes. This is horrible. Literary excrement. This is worse than my story about the mom chasing the daughter chasing the dog chasing the squirrel chasing the acorn rolling down the sidewalk toward a busy intersection. I want to purge my screen, myself, so I slap the delete key silly till it's all gone, leaving only a blank page. The white of it mocks me. This is what I have to show for an entire day's work, for months of dreaming! I quit my job for this— Yes, I'm frustrated! I picture myself flinging the laptop through the window, this overpriced plastic spaceship soaring high before plummeting, smashing into the street, wires and glass and tiny letters strewn about—

I decide to check my email, hoping that someone has responded to one of the billion messages that I've launched into space.

Nothing.

Not.

One.

Response.

Finding writing jobs and speaking engagements is harder than I expected. I expected a challenge, but this? Every magazine and publishing house and speaking venue seems to have rejected me at least once, and the ones that haven't rejected me have ignored me. And I have no idea what to do about it, how to move forward, or if I can move forward. I have no plan. Oh, I should have formed a plan before I set out on this idiotic quest of mine, but I didn't. So now, inside, I feel my fears gain velocity.

Wilting away from my desk, I palm the sandpaper of my scalp. I stare at my laptop screen, at the empty email box, the empty document, the empty dream, the empty day, and my empty reflection, which, oh great, here we go, is now staring right back at me.

"It's not the magic carpet ride your hoofed friend made it out to be, is it?"

Freckled with words and icons, the reflected me is back.

"Not at all."

"It never is, Josh. You know what a dream is?"

"What?"

"A dream is a piano without keys. Sure, you can touch it. You can hear the tune in your head, but you can't actually make any music with it. Dreams are the ultimate teases. They consume space in your life and lead you to believe that you're something you'll never be, that you're meant to create something gorgeous, so you live in this perpetual state of misplaced hope, of falling short, and yet for some reason, you keep hanging on to that dream. It's like you can't get away from it. You're stuck with it, carrying it on your back, sinking. Sound familiar?"

"Yeah. It does. I'm so afraid. I know that's part of why I've been delaying my life so much lately. I'm afraid that quitting my job was a huge mistake, too hasty, afraid that I'm wasting my time, that this whole fledgling attempt at writing and speaking is stupid, that I'm stupid, afraid that I'll never get beyond my parents' deaths enough to do anything else, afraid that I'm on the fast track to failure."

"Fear calls everyone a friend, Josh. But dreamers, well, fear cozies up to them most. When you try to do the things that really matter to you—love, family, all of your dreams—you invite fear to come further in. Dreaming dumps blood in the water. Dreaming attracts fear. Dreams are the mothers of fear."

I pinch the inside of my cheek between my teeth. This helps me think.

"Look, Josh, no one believes in you more than I do, but in light of what's happened to your family—and man, I feel for you—maybe you should just let this writing thing go. Besides, you aren't Daniel Wallace or Dave Eggers. You aren't Chuck Palahniuk or Sara Gruen or Robin Williams or Michelangelo—"

"So what are you saying?"

"I guess what I'm saying is that you should be afraid. You should be scared. I know you better than anyone, and you don't have it in you."

"Thanks."

"I'm just trying to be honest. And it's true."

"I don't know about that."

"I do. Everyone knows but you—everyone sees it! Open your eyes! You can't do this!"

I stand up from the desk/dining room table, look to the ceiling, rubbing my neck, mulling his words. "Maybe I can't do this."

"You're too fragile."

"I just feel so fragile."

"People are laughing at you."

"People are laughing at me."

"What made you think you—"

"—could do this?"

"There's nothing special—"

"—about me."

"You're terrified."

"I'm terrified."

"Yes."

"So then what am I supposed to do? Just be afraid forever?"

"No. I want what's best for you, Josh. You believe that, don't you?"

I nod to the reflected me.

"Josh, there's another way. A better way."

"What?"

"You tell me."

"I don't know!"

"Yes. You. Do."

"I don't!"

"Josh, if dreams are the mothers of fear, then—"

"Give up on my dreams, and my fears will go with it?"

"Kill the mother, and the children die."

"If I want to drive out my fears, then I need to drive out my dreams."

"Smart boy. Stop trying to play this keyless piano, Josh." The reflected me gives me a wink.

"Maybe you're right . . ."

"I am. Freedom is the middling soul."

I close the laptop and walk to the window. On the other side of the glass, people across Austin are preparing for Halloween, considering decorations, rubber masks, that awful candy corn. In here, I'm considering driving out my dreams. I have to admit; it does sound good, so good, better, less cumbersome! Maybe that's the ticket! I'll give myself permission to wallow! I'll do something else with my life—a banker, or a waiter maybe—and I'll spare myself the drawn-out-but-guaranteed humiliation and disappointment! Wow that sounds freeing, so freeing! I'll bury my dreams alive, and in doing so, I'll suffocate my fears, leave them scratching on the lid of a pine box! Yes, the reflected me is spot-on, the discerning devil inside . . . but then again, this could be a lie. Sure, I want to believe everything he's telling me, but something inside won't let me. Something is resisting. I just can't help but feel that there's another way.

Whirling away from the window, I restart my laptop. I open a blank document. Cracking my knuckles again, I ask Jack for help, then begin writing, sending more emails out, hoping that someone, anyone, will answer me and give me a chance.

Circling Flies

The curtain smells musty and feels unnecessary. I tug at it and slink my head around, giraffelike. The room is mostly empty: fifty people, maybe forty, less. That's okay. No problem. Looking for familiarity, I scan. In the front row, legs kicked out and scissor-crossed, is Jack. I knew he'd be here. He gives me a wave. I wave back, then continue scanning, hoping to see Kristen, Gus, my mom and dad—

"You ready for this?"

"Absolutely I am."

I am not ready for this, but since I'm backstage, it's important that I plagiarize the coolness of others and act like a pro.

The members of a band, who are all very musicianish—relaxed, eating organic finger foods, wiry legs, aggressive hair, patchy beards—are mingling, waiting to go on stage. As we chitchat, I adjust the tiny microphone around my ear again and again. It doesn't need adjusting, but I'm nervous to the moon, bending under the heaviness of the moment, this moment that came out of nowhere, this moment that is an actual speaking gig, this moment that comes on the heels of having two articles published at obscure online magazines and therefore generating a bit of momentum, this moment—this actual speaking gig—that was perhaps given to me out of charity but is nevertheless a chance, a colossal break, this moment where I need to do well. No, not just *well*, because *well* isn't good enough! I need to do way more than *well*! Tonight I need every cell in my being to circle the wagons, to link arms and form greatness! And not just for my sake, no! Tonight—and forever—I'm living and dreaming for three. In order to honor my parents, I must summon three times the talent, three times the charisma, three times the wow factor!

Attempting to gather myself, I sit down on a wooden stool and review what I'm going to say. I review my first story. I review my, my— Panic. Suddenly I can't remember my characters, my transitions, my point. I begin racking my brain: which part comes first again?

"See you on the other side, man."

The curtain splits, and the band enters the stage, met by cheering. Will I be cheered? I will, right? I hope. No, because the audience—fellow twentysomethings who, like me, consider themselves to be fashion-savvy intellectuals—will quickly recognize that the band guys have more to offer, that they were the high point of the evening. A coup will be staged. They will demand more music.

The band begins the first song. It's all guitars and kick drum, each beat punching my chest. People are clapping, singing, soaring. When am I supposed to go out there? After four songs? Or is it five— My breathing becomes erratic. I try to control it, to settle my nerves down, settle, settle, settle, but they won't listen to me. They are insolent, a team of screaming two-year-olds, throwing toys, kicking furniture. I begin coughing, hacking, so afraid, oozing sweat now and repeatedly checking my zipper. The reflected me was right! I should have listened to him! Why didn't I listen? Because I was dumb enough to think that this is what I've wanted, that's why. Because no one told me that realized dreams are scarier than failed ones.

From backstage, the band sounds invincible. My opposite. In long loops I'm pacing now, careful not to trip over the floor cables, trying to clear my head, to concentrate, trying to think of serene things like babbling brooks, wind chimes. But oh, every word and story that I'm supposed to remember has become stew. This is just great! This is just like the first time I ever spoke in public.

I was in seventh grade, giving a speech in front of my whole junior high, plus everyone's grandparents, for Grandparents' Day. I decided to talk about my dad. The entire week leading up to it, the fear owned me. I tried to get sick, contract a fever, break a bone, anything to get out of it, but I couldn't, and the day arrived.

The place was packed, a thousand ears cast in my direction, waiting for the car crash. With short little steps and jittery hands, I walked to the podium. Every person in that gymnasium was ten feet tall, a sea of Greek gods with lightning in their eyes, ready to destroy me.

I started. Voice shaking. Young Aaron Neville. After surviving the introduction, I thought I might actually get through it, but then, in front of everyone, my voice locked up. I tried to talk, but I couldn't. I couldn't do anything.

After a dead minute, my eyes sank. The only thing I saw was the fake wood of the podium. Then a tear, one really big tear, fell right onto my notes and bled through the paper. From there, I couldn't stop. In front of the entire assembly, I lost it. The tears just kept spilling out, spilling and spilling, my body's response to emotional hyperdrive, to utter confusion, to being overwhelmed. Yup, everyone got to witness the crash they came to see. I wished right then that an asteroid would strike the school, but no such luck came my way, and I just stood there, my sniffles amplified at a million decibels through the sound system, every snort and whimper playing as a soundtrack for the entire planet. I was sure it was never going to end.

But then one of the grandparents in the third row rose to his feet. Straightening his grandpa sweater and smiling kindly, he met my eyes. Then he cleared his throat, and in front of the whole place, he began talking to me, then to everyone else, telling the whole gym that they needed to support me, applaud me for my courage. He began applauding. And then everyone else followed his lead, applauding along with him. He more or less finished the speech for me. He rescued me. After that, I said a few words, I think, and as I walked away, the place applauded again.

I'd almost forgotten about that.

And yeah, it's certainly sentimental, a great testament to the tender spirit of humanity, to the elderly, and how grandparents keep the world twirling, but I'd prefer not to tell that story again. I don't want this to be another instance when some stranger has to bail me out. I don't want to crash and burn in silence again. But I could. I might. What if I blow it? Mess up? Fail? This could be my only chance to get this dream off the ground, myself off the ground, to piece a little bit of normal life back together, and I'm already so fragile, a leaf on a fall branch, ready to tumble away—

"Yer gonna do just fine."

Startled, I nearly fall off the stool. The metal backstage door closes shut, and my hoofed friend is here. With the band playing, I didn't even hear his clomping.

"I hope so."

"You will."

"I want to believe that, I do, but right now I'm terrified."

"Of what?"

"I don't know. Everything. Being laughed at. Rejected. Bombing. I'm afraid that this whole writing and speaking venture is a stupid idea, that I'll fail, that we'll lose our house because I fail, that I'm going to let everyone down, that if I'm not good at this then I'm not good at anything, and if I'm not good at anything then I'm worthless, that this thin thread I'm hanging on by can't support the weight of any more disappointment."

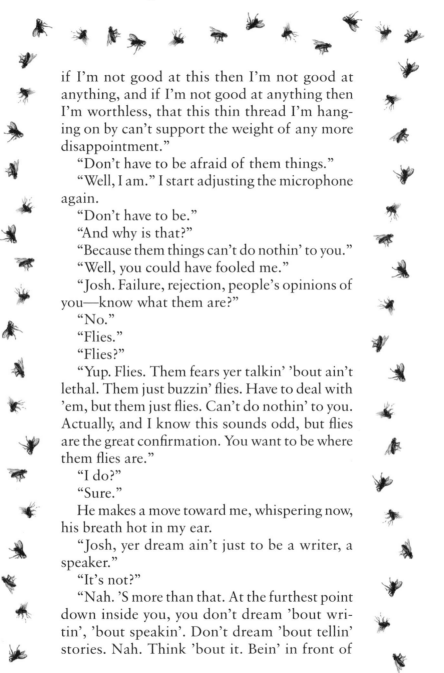

"Don't have to be afraid of them things."

"Well, I am." I start adjusting the microphone again.

"Don't have to be."

"And why is that?"

"Because them things can't do nothin' to you."

"Well, you could have fooled me."

"Josh. Failure, rejection, people's opinions of you—know what them are?"

"No."

"Flies."

"Flies?"

"Yup. Flies. Them fears yer talkin' 'bout ain't lethal. Them just buzzin' flies. Have to deal with 'em, but them just flies. Can't do nothin' to you. Actually, and I know this sounds odd, but flies are the great confirmation. You want to be where them flies are."

"I do?"

"Sure."

He makes a move toward me, whispering now, his breath hot in my ear.

"Josh, yer dream ain't just to be a writer, a speaker."

"It's not?"

"Nah. 'S more than that. At the furthest point down inside you, you don't dream 'bout writin', 'bout speakin'. Don't dream 'bout tellin' stories. Nah. Think 'bout it. Bein' in front of people. Lettin' people into yer mind, yer heart, them things terrify you. So why in the world would you choose this? Because above all else you wanna be free. You dream of a life where the possibility of failure and folks' opinions don't control you, where unknowns don't boss you 'round, a life where fear ain't yer dictator. And if them fears, them flies, weren't 'round now, well, it would only mean you were chasin' the wrong dream. In order to find freedom, to overthrow the flies in yer life, you have to stand among 'em. Can't swat flies from a mile away. And now here you are, swarmed. Right where you should be."

I grin because he's right.

"Now, the reflected you is tellin' you different, right? Tellin' you that freedom is drivin' out yer dreams. But he's wrong. The greatest freedoms is found when you face yer greatest fears. Yer dreams is the map to freedom. So chase yer dream, Josh, and yer fears'll run."

From the stage, someone introduces me over a microphone, and people start clapping, sort of. Hearing my name through speakers makes it sound dumb, the syllables all wrong. I want to leave, sneak out.

"Be free of them flies, Josh. Run toward yer fears. Yer dreams are yer freedom."

He points his big face toward the curtain, and now my hoofed friend clomps slowly toward the metal door.

"Wait! You're leaving?"

"For now. I'll come back and see you."

"I hope so."

"Count on it."

The faint applause is dwindling. It's time. Deep breath and I pull the curtain aside. The yellow lights explode, scorching my retinas. I'm seeing spots. Good. This way I can't see the lightning in the audience's eyes, can't see the flies, their kaleidoscopic heads, each of them zigging and zagging around the room, can't see my fears swarming, waiting. But I can hear them. The whole room is buzzing.

I inch forward across the stage, feeling small. My heart shakes against my ribs like a convulsing chimp trying to break out of its cage. To hide the trembling, I slide my hands into my pockets. Now I swallow big, without thinking, and my mouth begins moving, and success! I think sounds are coming out, words too, perhaps in intelligible sentences. No one has booed yet, so I keep going. I tell a story. Insert a clever comment. Mild laughter—

What's that thumping sound? From somewhere out in the darkness, behind the lights, I hear it, a sound not unlike—

Dang it, Josh! Concentrate!

I keep going, hands out of my pockets now, gesturing, the way my mom did—

Bah! There's the thumping sound again. Does anyone else hear it? What is that? Audio feedback? A raccoon in an air duct?

Kristen walks in. Just outside the lights I see her. She made it. Sure, she's late, but she's here. Her presence brings me my second wind. I leap into another story, telling the heck out of it, no longer thinking, just feeling, my instincts at the helm.

Before I know it, I'm wrapping up, and the audience hasn't walked out. They're still here. I'm still here. The buzzing, though, seems to be fading. Is it? Yes, with each thump, the buzzing grows a bit quieter, and now the thumps are coming faster and closer together, *thump thump*, and faster, piggybacking one another, *thumpthumpthump*, but because I am in a focused tai chi state of mind, I don't veer from the task at hand. And the moment I say the final word, the word that is supposed to clinch the whole thing—the second that it leaves my lips, the thumping abruptly ceases.

Applause. I exhale.

I squint through the lights, looking for Kristen, for Jack, for Mom and Dad. That would be something, the two of them in the back, haloed and proud, my allies. I smirk at the thought.

I scoot off the stage, the hands keep clapping, and obviously this gesture is just a courtesy, nothing more, which sucks, because I secretly want these strangers to clap because they think I'm talented, legitimate, because that sort of affirmation would mean I'm not crazy, that yes, I should be doing this, that this is a worthwhile dream, that I'm not wasting my life, that I'm doing what I'm meant to do. And yet, even though I'm not sure why they are clapping, there is one thing that I am sure of: I'm doing it.

Today I'm doing it.

Jack and Kristen envelop me in their arms and smiles, and I'm glowing, because for one night, today—not tomorrow, today—my fears have grown quiet. For one night I'm free of fear and disappointment and sadness and all the dead things that have defined me of late. And one night of freedom can sometimes make life worthwhile. True, I don't know what will happen tomorrow. In all likelihood, my fears will return, and in greater force, but right now that doesn't matter, not at all, because tonight I'm free. Not because I'm living the dream, but simply because I'm chasing it.

Jack and Kristen and I walk out, but with each step, something is crunching beneath our feet. I lift my shoes to find out what, and oh, disgusting, but yes, of course. The crunching explains the thumping sound, which also explains the dwindling buzzing sound. On the floor and throughout the room—on the chairs, in the rafters, down the steps—sweet piles of flies lay fallen, upturned, their wings broken off into tiny pieces that remind me of toy church stained glass.

XI

Little Sister, Which One of These Is Your Costa Rican Husband?

A mad jungle of tanned faces and gesturing and whistling and straw hats and honking and short-sleeve linen button-down shirts and crackly intercom announcements and vendors selling I'm-not-sure-what greets Kristen and me in the terminal of the San Jose airport. It's a thousand degrees here, wall-to-wall humidity, and most everything is in Spanish. Even the birds flying around the overhead rafters are speaking Spanish. Fortunately, I took seven years of this language in school, so I'm still able to understand a little, about every other word, maybe.

"Car . . . cheap . . . good . . . American."

"Five dollars . . . your bags . . . pretty lady."

"Water . . . Coca-Cola . . . candy bar."

"Visit . . . your trip . . . hotel . . . by the beach."

Corbett, the other Josh, Quinn, and Jack are meeting us here, along with Nelson, my future brother-in-law, whom I've never met. Where are they? I'm trying to follow the signs but not having much luck. Kristen wants me to ask for help. No chance. I'll figure it out myself. Doesn't she know I can figure a way out of any predicament? Doesn't she know the dangers of asking for help? In this world that preys on weakness, asking for help is the fastest way to get swindled or robbed or chopped into pieces with a machete.

In all directions, everything looks the same now, the walls and walkways, even the people—a house of mirrors. I hesitate, realizing that any one of the ten billion men in front of me could be Nelson. I could be staring at him right now, and I wouldn't even— Yep! There's the other Josh, towering above the crowd, waving in our direction as if drifting at sea, waiting to be rescued. Taking Kristen by the hand, I begin barging my way through, our carry-on luggage banging off surrounding shoulders and hips, repeatedly excusing myself.

"Hey, braather!"

A man in a soccer jersey grabs my arm, taps it, and smiles a half moon up at me, rocking back and forth from his heels to his toes.

"Joash? Joash? Nelson! Es me, Nelson!"

Well, here he is, Nelson, the stranger who stole my sister's heart, the stranger who in two days is marrying Quinn and joining the family. This whole thing is surreal, a bit out-of-body. How did this happen? Ah, I feel a quick recap coming on . . .

After college, Quinn, always the adventurer, moved to Costa Rica to work as a schoolteacher. While she was there, living in some remote mountain village, she met and eventually fell in love with Nelson. I've known about their shared affections for a while, but it was only ten weeks ago that I heard about this whole marriage thing.

It was the night before my mom died. Corbett and Quinn and I were sitting on vinyl furniture in the hospital lounge, awaiting the surgery, speaking in late-night whispers. That's when Quinn told us about the wedding plans. Originally they were going to get married next summer, but once Mom died, delaying it seemed—well, we all had to move forward, right? For me, moving forward meant diving into my dream, my writing, my work, and for Quinn, it meant diving into love.

Anyway, she dropped this on us and, of course, wanted us to be excited, sharing in her bridal-cake enthusiasm, and while I tried to pretend I was, I wasn't. How could I be? My sister, my baby sister, tells me that she's getting married, and I didn't know anything about the guy. I'd never met him. I'd never even seen a picture of him.

So I've spent the last few months trying to guess what Nelson is like. Based on what I know about Quinn, I've been expecting a Don Quixote-Enrique Iglesias mashup. Smoldering tempter meets eccentric warrior.

Or maybe, in the off chance that my first guess was wrong, a shoeless poet, someone walking through the woods with a quill in his hand and a telescope in his back pocket. Yes, yes, I was sure that's what he'd be like. The Quinn I knew would choose a man like that.

But now, as I return from the recap, here he is, right in front of me, and he isn't that at all. Both of my hypotheses are wildly wrong.

This guy is short and pensive-looking with a modest haircut, a sort of science-teacher thing, and yet passionate, childlike, completely untangled in the opinions of the world. Wonderful, but not at all what I pictured, and since my guesses were based on what I know about Quinn, then perhaps my notions of Quinn are a bit antiquated, skewed even. Skewed?

The pieces click into place. It all makes sense now. The reason I couldn't share in her excitement that night in the hospital, the reason I haven't been able to get excited about this wedding, isn't because I don't know *him*; it's because I don't know *her*.

Below me, Nelson's smile is still flashing, begging for a response, but nothing is coming to mind. I want to say something, but I can't. My brain is underwater, drowning in questions, questions . . . Do I know my sister at all? Anything about her? Don't be silly, of course I do.

No. I don't. Not even simple things, like what does Quinn dream about? Who's her best friend? Does she have a job? Favorite movie? What does she believe? To me, these are great riddles. I'm confounded, coming up blank. This is worse than I thought. Sure, sure, I knew we'd grown a bit distant, hadn't been close in years—since I was in high school maybe—that I've been a tad wrapped up in my own stuff, my own life. That's obvious, but this! Oh, what kind of brother am I? What kind of family are we?

The answers are clear. I'm a rotten brother, and we are a disjointed family, have been for years, and not even the death of our parents—with three weeks of living under the same roof afterward to grieve and deal with all the logistics, those days and moments that could've (should've?) altered our sibling dynamic, bonded us, turned us practically Siamese—could bring us together.

So now here we are, the three of us, and we aren't so much a family but more like friends of friends, people who signed each other's yearbooks in another era of life. I am with my sisters the way I am with people I've met at Fourth of July parties, sat next to in a movie theater, the DMV. This isn't connection. Please. I'm as connected to my sisters as a moose is to the Empire State Building. I don't know Corbett, and I don't know Quinn, the bride. I'm here this week not as a wedding guest but as a wedding crasher.

"Joash! *Bienvenido a Costa Rica!*"

"Nelson. Hey, man! So great to meet you."

"Yes! Braather! Braather!"

"I know!"

"Braather!"

I move to shake his hand, but in mid-reach I change my mind, and trying to hug, we nearly kiss.

That Quinn's Brother

The ceremony is intimate, thirty people or so, in a low-ceilinged room with a view of the mountains. My dad is not here. My mom is not here. I sit in the front row, scalp freshly shaved, skinny tie and no jacket, alongside Corbett, the other Josh, and Kristen: the gringo row. Oh, except for Jack. He's on the end, along the aisle.

Quinn floats in, hovering, all of her snow white, down the aisle. Disposable cameras click and flash. A baby screams. Nelson's face stretches wide and he shakes his head, admiring his lady, treasuring her. She means so much to him.

She used to mean so much to me. Everything we did together, every memory—it all meant the world to me. The home videos we made, washing Corbett's calculator, camping in the backyard in our crappy, mosquito-filled blue tent, eating the blueberries from Mrs. Hanson's backyard, stealing money from Mom, our shared diet of McNuggets. We were partners. Me and this bride. Quinn. The girl I knew inside and out—

"God . . . holy . . . man . . . woman . . . health . . . poorer."

The pastor is talking in Spanish, so again I'm tracking with every other word.

"America . . . dream . . . love . . . family."

"Quinn . . . travel . . . forever."

Nelson and Quinn hold hands and begin exchanging vows. Nelson's mom is dotting her eyes with a handkerchief, the wet mascara etching black roots across her cheeks. Now Quinn starts crying, and yes, Corbett too, I think. I'm teetering, my eyes beginning to condensate, but in a different way, not in the happy, mystical, wedding kind of way. Out of sadness. This girl here, this bride, I knew her, but I don't know her anymore. Every meaningful moment we've shared is at least a decade old, and now we're left holding only nostalgia. Now I'm a brother to Quinn and Corbett only in photographs and grade-school stories. Now I'm just some guy dressed as a brother, a brother impersonator— How did I not see this coming? I should have!

For all of its surprises, life can be so predictable. And this is the typical script: a family dissolving between birth and death. This is the way it usually works, because everyone is born into a family, but few die in one. And yes, of course, of course, many have no control over that. Dad bails. Sister runs away. Mom isn't interested. Someone dies. I get it. But the rest choose to be orphans. The rest are too busy with career and bitterness and altering the fabric of the universe, the rest are too afraid, too engaged in other fights, the rest lose interest, grow bored, the rest let family slip away.

Nelson slides the ring onto Quinn's finger.

My family, the only family I have left, is slipping away, and I'm letting it happen—

Nelson and Quinn kiss, making their marriage official, and instantly the thirty witnesses get rowdy, clapping and singing, Costa Rican chanting of some kind. Yes, their love is touchable, dazzling, and each of these witnesses sees it, feels it, and is now sharing in the spoils of having played a part, the spoils of being involved in the lives of others. But not me. There are no spoils for me. Oh, sure, I'm clapping, pumping my fist, side-hugging Kristen around the shoulder, preparing my party face, pretending to throw rice and release doves, but far below this flood, underneath my skin, I'm small in the front row, an anonymous passerby, filled with the special kind of hollowness that comes only when we're missing out on the most important things in life.

Redemption has longer arms than you think.

EJ

XII

Marrying God for the Money

We meet at a dark wood place, a German place, the kind of place where Gandalf might sit in the shadows, massively cloaked, smoking his pipe, blowing entire fleets of ashy ships into the air. Everything smells like old cigarettes, and the dartboard is busy, occupied by high-fiving guys in khaki shorts and backward hats. We pick a table in the corner and gather around it. The phrase "88 miles per hour" is carved into the wood. A pitcher of beer arrives, and I am handed a cold glass. Someone gives a toast. We all participate. Taking my first sip, I'm trying to figure out why I came tonight.

Oh. Right. I'm here because of some heavy coaxing.

With seemingly no explanation, the job side of life has hit an unexpected *whoosh*, and now I'm flying around the country on speaking trips. I've signed a book contract. I have a manager. (Technically he's a friend volunteering as my manager. And while this is a wildly unnecessary role, it enables me to coyly drop the expression "I'll have to check with my manager" in the middle of conversations, making it seem as if big things are happening.) Yes, it's all in front of me. The masterpiece I was hoping for when I quit my other job is now being painted, stroke by stroke, producing a by-product of thankfulness and an additional sense of fortune, as if the gardens of success will all continue blossoming until I direct otherwise. Obviously this is life's way of balancing the scales again, tipping them back in my favor in light of how out of whack they've been. Yes. Life is grand.

But not in Austin. Austin has become Mars. I'm feeling more and more disconnected from everything in Austin, so when I'm home, I don't like going out or seeing my friends, and I've become a bit of a shut-in, which is fine with me, because all I need are words. They'll keep me company, centered. I don't need to be around other people. I don't need to be known. I don't need to go out— Okay, fine, so this life of isolation isn't healthy, is probably evidence that I'm ignoring my still-lingering grief and a cluster of deeply recessed fears, only exacerbating them, proof that I'm still, just like when I left for college, on the run.

Everyone is here: Gus, his wife Bell, Webber—whom I met while at my last church job and who currently has the beard of a grizzled prospector, Kristen, and a few others. It is a real reunion, very *St. Elmo's Fire*. Tucked in our corner, our conversation ping-pongs, different ends of the table talking back and forth about different things, relationships, quoting

Seinfeld, hahaha, discussing why we prefer cold pizza to hot pizza, and has anyone ever been to Germany? Our collective mood is relaxed and good, very unattached and breezy and—

"So, Josh."

"Yeah, Gus."

"I got a question for you."

"Okay."

"What do you think the point of a relationship with Jack is?"

This is not why I came out. Doesn't Gus know I'm not here for this? Tonight is supposed to be about sharing a few laughs, a few beers, catching up in purely nonintrusive ways, putting in my time, and then going home. That's it. But now stupid Gus is striking the match on meaningful talk, depth—on things that will potentially tie all of us further together, which is no good. I don't want that. I'll resist. There's something in all of us that resists depth.

Now is the perfect opportunity to offer Gus a lesson about this very thing. Time to snuff this conversation out. Besides, I didn't even know there was a point to a relationship with Jack. Is there one? Wait, now I'm thinking about it, engaging! No! The seed of intrigue has been planted, and it's sprouting in me, I can't help it. I've never even considered Gus's question before, but I have a terrible habit of trying to sound smart and philosophical, very professorlike, so I stammer around for a bit, trying to find my way, giving him useless responses—

"You want me to just tell you?"

"Sure," I say, shrugging. "I'd love to know what the point of having a relationship with Jack is." (Lie.)

"I'm being serious."

"I know that."

"Really, do you want to know the point?"

"You're going to tell me the point of a relationship with Jack?"

"Actually, yeah, if you want to know."

"Yeah. I really do." (Lie.)

"Intimacy."

"What?"

"Yeah," Gus says, wiping his mouth. "Intimacy. The point is being with him, knowing him, letting him know you. It's about keeping nothing from him, sharing yourself, being together, being deeply connected."

The other end of our table is listening to Gus now.

"It's about letting Jack into all of you, being completely naked, so to speak, with Jack, just like things were in the very beginning. That must've been something. Back then there was no pretending, no games, no hiding, no shame. It must have been awesome."

"You think?"

"Absolutely! Are you kidding? Nothing got in the way, you know? They didn't even wear clothes, not even a leaf covering . . . well, anything. Just honest, beautiful, naked vulnerability. Complete connection. Intimacy. That's the point."

I take another sip, finishing my glass, and then I hold it. It isn't cold anymore.

"You don't seem too pumped about that idea, Josh."

"Well, that's because it just sounds kind of . . ."

"What?"

"You know, just kind of . . ."

"Yeah?"

"Nothing. Forget it."

The dark wood is unkind on my back. As I lean against it, vanishing into the shadows and cigarette smell, the others jump in—Webber and Bell and Kristen—talking and discussing and using hand motions to explain what they are thinking and feeling. I already know what I'm feeling. I don't want to be here anymore, don't want this conversation, sort of wish I'd stayed home, so I slide out of the booth and walk into the restroom through the swinging door. It's empty. I'm alone. Safe in the expanse. The lights barely work, which makes everything in here muted and tiny. I have to bend down to see my face in the mirror. One of the dartboard guys stumbles in, whistling. I start drying my hands to demonstrate that I am a normal guy doing normal things, just like him. He walks from the urinal to the mirror, still whistling, flicks his hair back, then leaves without washing his hands, gross.

Once the door shuts, I stare at the mirror again, into my face, into me, into the truth, and it's oh, offensive. Many truths are offensive. I don't want to see it. Why would I let anyone else see it? Why would I let anyone else in? Sure, loneliness is a frightening prospect, but intimacy is the real horror film. Compared to deep connection, loneliness is a snow cone in August, which, yes, is a stupid analogy, but the fact remains. I grip the porcelain sink, my eyes drop down into the white of the bowl, down to the silver drain plug, and I think about how I would feel standing there without distance, without secrets, a lifetime of emotions and feelings and questions and struggles and ideas and mistakes and private dirty thoughts and ambitions typed onto my body, my flesh bound in pages, me as public literature—completely vulnerable, deeply connected, and naked with the world around me, with Jack.

I don't think I'd be able to do it unless I drank way more beer.

One Really Long (And Long Overdue) Conversation

A few days later, Ditka is sitting at the door, sniper focused, panting and panicked, glancing back in my direction every so often. I'm occupied with writing, so I'm not paying much attention until he starts scratching the door, ripping paw-sized strips of paint off. Apparently the matter is urgent. I relent. We go to the park.

Ordinarily this place is active, but today it's barren. The dog walkers aren't here. The son-dad baseball-tossing duos aren't here. The ambitious picnickers aren't here either. Our only company is the endless blanket of bluebells covering the ground. Striding through them ankle deep, I feel a bit like Alice, whimsically making my way through Wonderl— My mind returns to all the intimacy talk. Again. Yeah, ever since that conversation at the German place, I haven't been able to shake it. It's been sort of gnawing on me.

Intimacy with anyone—Kristen, friends, my sisters—is foreign to me. Again, secrets, whispers, and locking myself down—but with Jack, it's an extraterrestrial concept, so far out there I don't even know where to begin. Sure, we spend time together, talk most days, but intimacy the way Gus described it is a realm I've not ventured into. I don't even really know what it would look like to be intimate with Jack, but the way Gus talked about it all, it seems right. And in spite of my fears and trepidations and insecurities and how completely ridiculous it sounds, perhaps borderline inappropriate, impossible even, there is something intriguing about it, as if intimacy is an act of rebellion, ultimate lawlessness, a way of breaking out of the prisons we lock ourselves in. So although I'm probably about to get in way over my head . . .

"Jack? You around?"

. . .

"Jack?"

"Yeah, Josh."

He comes out of nowhere. This doesn't catch me off guard anymore. He's always doing this, materializing out of the wind, from the shadows.

"Hey, Jack."

"So, what's up?"

"Nothing much."

"Nothing much?"

"Well, it's just this conversation I had with Gus the other night—"

"At the German place?"

"Yeah. Well, I've been thinking about it ever since."

The three of us keep walking, Ditka more trotting, the way he does when he's excited.

"Oh? And why is that?"

"It's just that, listening to Gus talk about intimacy and you, the way he talked about it—I don't think that's what you and I have. So if Gus is right, if intimacy is the point, then I think I'm kind of missing the point."

"Well, let's just be honest about it. What Gus talked about is not what you and I have."

"Yeah."

"Does that bother you?"

"A little, maybe, but I'm just not sure I want to be *that* close to you, or anyone. I mean, being really open, letting you in—all the different things Gus said—all that vulnerability and connection? I don't live that way with anyone, never have."

"Why not?"

"Are you kidding me? It's dangerous."

"Dangerous how?"

"Well, the way I see it, every day I'm building a case for why I'm worthy of love, why I'm good enough. And pretty much everything I do is an attempt to strengthen my case, to prove it to myself and to this world. The clothes I wear. The things I say. My writing. Is my skin clear? The number of dollar signs in our bank account. How's my credit score? The number of people in my cell phone. Am I funny? Do 'important' people think I'm important? Do I give good advice? I could go on and on. Anyway, that case is much easier to prove if I hold people at a distance. I can be attractive from far away, drag that honeymoon first impression out for a while, make myself seem special or witty or successful in the short term. But if I stick around too long, the jig is up. Once I start letting people get close, and once I start getting really close to others, well, I risk being exposed. Getting too close to others is the greatest threat to my case. Intimacy would destroy my life's work. Also, it's just horribly inconvenient."

"Okay. You're right. Intimacy could destroy your life's work. But couldn't it also complete it? I mean, don't you miss out on a lot of life this way? Don't you think you limit our relationship this way?"

"Probably. Does that bother you?"

"Do you really want to know, Josh?"

"Probably not."

. . .

"Okay fine, yes, I want to know."

"Well, if you really want to know, yeah, it does bother me. It bothers me a lot—"

"But it's not like we aren't close. I feel like we've got a good thing going here—better than most, right? You have to admit—come on, admit it, we do stuff together, we talk all the time!"

"And what do we talk about, Josh?"

"I don't know. Who keeps track of this stuff?" I stuff my hands into my jacket pockets. "Earlier this week I thanked you for taking me out to lunch, and for the sunny day—you know how much I love it when it's sunny. Lately I've been asking you to help me get my book written. And then, oh, this morning I asked if you could help us pay the bill for our car, because the dang coolant system in the Jeep isn't working again. Um, I always ask if you can check on my sisters and my friends and if you can make sure Kristen gets home from work safely—that kind of stuff. And we do that all the time."

Ditka stops to pee on a patch of weeds. The urine runs toward me, forming a liquid yellow Florida at my feet. From my pocket, I tug on the leash, and Ditka gets the message. The three of us move on through the park, walking as we talk.

"Have you ever put orange juice on cereal, Josh?"

"What does that have to do with any—"

"Just humor me. Have you?"

"Actually, yeah. That's so weird. I haven't thought about this in forever, but one day when I was a little kid, I really wanted some cereal. I poured a bowl and then went to the fridge to get the milk, but we didn't have any, which was common for us. Going to the grocery store and having food in the fridge were rarities. Both my parents were in education and worked a lot, all the time, so we neglected things like that and ate out mostly. McDonald's. Pizza. Sometimes my dad would bring home those nasty sandwiches from the gas station—"

"The milk, Josh?"

"Right, sorry. So when I opened the refrigerator, there was no milk. Man, I was crushed. But I still wanted to eat the cereal, so I used orange juice instead. I figured it would work fine since I like orange juice."

"How was it?"

"Are you kidding? It was horrible. But why? That's a totally random question."

"Volume isn't a very good substitute for depth."

"Oh, I get it, like with the orange juice and the milk, and how you and I may spend a lot of time together but it's all superficial—very clever. Look, Jack, what are you getting at? What do you want from me?"

"What do you want from me?"

"I . . . I don't know."

"You don't?"

"No."

"Well, let me tell you, and you stop me when any of this sounds familiar, okay?"

"Sure."

"You want me to give you things like food and health, to fill you with a holistic peace that you can't quite describe."

I nod.

"You want my protection and you want me to help you with your career."

I nod.

"You want me to take you to the new world someday. You want me to clear up confusing things. You want me to acquit your conscience when you blow it, for me to assure you that you're a good person, that we're on good terms—"

"And is something wrong with all that?"

"No, not at all. Josh, I want to do that for you, all of it—"

"Then what's the problem?" I take my hands out of my pockets and stop walking. "What's the big deal?"

"You don't want *me*, Josh! You want all this stuff *from* me, but you don't want *me*. You don't want to be connected to *me*. You know what you are? You're like one of those people who loiter around expensive hotels and movie premieres hoping to land an eight-figure spouse, someone who marries for money. You're a gold digger."

Lava pumps through my veins. I'm burning, tempted to go all Tonya Harding on him, all Cobra Kai. Where does he get off talking to me this way? Whatever. I turn and show him my back, and we don't say anything for a while. I don't ever want to say anything again. I wish he'd go away, allow me to go away, to morph into a canine like Ditka here. Then I too could sprawl out in the grass, belly to the sun, responsible only for performing simple tricks, occasionally fetching sticks and small balls—slippers if I opt for the honors track—barking when I sense intruders, and allowing my ears to be stroked, but never facing this kind of prying, these inquisitions. Dogs really do have it better. Blessed mutts.

"Josh, do you remember Sara?"

. . .

"Josh?"

"Yes. I. Remember. Sara."

"Do you remember your relationship with her?"

"Sure."

"Tell me about it."

"Why? That was forever ago."

"I don't know. We've never talked about it before."

Reluctantly, I pivot toward him. Ditka comes to his paws. We start moving again.

"Well, it was toxic mostly, and we stayed together way longer than we should've. You know, the only thing worse than a bad relationship is a long-term bad relationship. But I guess it just goes to show you that people chase the familiar, even if it's detrimental. Anyway, by the end I couldn't stand her. Don't get me wrong, at first I was crazy about her. We met while I was at the second of the three colleges I attended.

I was still reeling from a breakup with a girl named Emily, so I wasn't looking for a relationship. But my buddies and I were at a restaurant in Chicago, and there she was, waitressing. She had these silky eyes, so brown, and black velvet hair, ivory skin. She was smart and fun and wholesome too. She was the closest thing I knew to a freaking Disney princess! It really was great for a while.

"But then everything changed. I didn't like her anymore, and to make things worse—or better, I'm not sure which—after a while, she didn't like me much either. I guess we fell out of what we called love. She didn't like my friends, my clothes, my music, my demeanor, or most of what I enjoyed doing, and she tried really hard to change all of it, to whittle me into that white-collar, well-behaved guy who would someday resemble one of the Ivy Leaguers her older sisters had married, be a congressman—you know, smile, wink, kiss the baby, pose for the cameras. That whole deal. She was using me to get what she wanted. But I wasn't exactly a victim; I was using her to get what I wanted too."

"And what was that?"

"The usual stuff. I wanted to be wanted, some hot physical times. I wanted a place in society's aristocracy, someone to be with on lonely nights. I guess we were using each other."

"Yeah, people are always using each other and trying to pass it off as love."

"It seems that way."

"And now you're doing that with me."

"Yeah. I guess I am—Ditka, no! Wait! Wait!" Yanking the leash, I drag Ditka away from a thorny bush.

"But then things ended, right? Between you and Sara?"

"Do we really have to talk about this?"

"Yes."

"I really don't want to. And this is rapidly becoming the longest conversation ever."

"The longest conversation ever?"

"The longest conversation ever."

"Well, so what if it's a long conversation? I want to have it."

"*Why?* Why do we have to visit stuff that happened years ago, stuff that I don't want to talk about?"

"Because that's what intimacy is, Josh! Because this is where connection happens: in the places you try the hardest to hide. Naked, remember? So why did it end between you and Sara?"

"It ended because . . . because Sara sat me down one day and told me that she was . . . pregnant."

My last word is void of syllables, no enunciation, because I want it to be fiction, to evaporate. But here it is, true, existing, floating in the cool air in front of me, in front of Jack.

"That must've been a jolt."

"It was."

"Then what happened?"

"Do you ever stop with this?"

"With what?"

"The questions. The wanting in."

"No. I don't."

I catch his smile out of the corner of my eye.

"Well . . . I was coaching a little kids' basketball camp the week that I found out, so all day I was surrounded by boys and girls, hundreds. It was awful. I blew my whistle, helped the kids dribble through cones, talked about teamwork and shooting, and said coachy things like, 'That's okay, good shot!' 'Great job!' 'Okay, now you can't just run around with the ball. Remember dribbling?' And every time I looked at one of them—into those round, sweaty faces, those pink cheeks, the pigtails clipped with barrettes, whatever—I saw the kid that I was about to have, my son, my daughter, my little Josh. Every one was a walking, talking sonogram. Every time I heard one of them yell 'Daddy,' I turned and looked. That week, I was coaching my own unborn offspring."

"You've never told me about any of this."

"It's not just you."

"Why, though?"

"I couldn't tell anyone."

"Why not?"

"ISN'T IT OBVIOUS?"

As quickly as my voice spikes, I bind it to a hush because a man in sunglasses is looking my direction with a suspicious tilt, as if he knows my secret, as if he's been listening in and is now going to share this information with the universe. Oh gosh, he will. I try to act nonchalant—nothing to see here—but it's too late. He knows. He's appalled. Oh, wait. No. He's just talking on a cell phone.

"Go on, Josh."

"I was too ashamed, too freaked out. Every night I sat there in bed, my mind climbing the walls, constantly wondering how I was going to support this baby, this baby's mom who I didn't even want to be with, and myself. I had visions of working as a taxidermist, those fake marble eyes staring down at me all day, or at a bowling alley, spraying that mystery stuff into the shoes and lugging balls from rack to rack for the next fifty years. I wouldn't graduate from college. I thought about what the heck I was going to tell my friends and my parents, about what people would think of me, the things they'd say about me, the inevitable nicknames, me as the source of their fodder, about whether or not I should dump my girlfriend and if doing that would make me a total jerk. And then at one point I thought about suggesting to Sara that she get an abortion, and then I thought about whether or not I'd be able to live with myself if she actually did. So why didn't I tell you? Are you kidding me? You don't want to hear this!"

"Yes I do."

"No! You don't! Not really."

"I do."

"Stop! You don't! You don't want to be a part of it, a part of me! Not really. You don't want to hear what I *really* think and feel. You don't want to hear that I'm afraid that everyone sees me the way I see myself, or that I partially despise this sheltered life I've lived, that I sometimes bask in the tragedy of my parents, because at least I'm relevant now. And you don't want to know how badly I really miss them either, that every day I want to ask you to send them back to me for one day, one lunch, one hug, one touch! You don't want to hear that I hardly know my sisters and that I can be a disastrous husband and that I don't have a clue what I'm doing and that sometimes I feel more lost now than ever, feel sometimes like you're not here or real or alive, like maybe I've just invented you so I have some sense of comfort in this world—"

Completely unfazed by my ranting, Jack steps toward me, but I step away.

"Oh yeah, you said you'd make me fully alive, but you left out the part about how long that would take—I mean, sometimes it feels like we're all trapped in a hurricane, being tossed around on tin rafts, helpless, just riding the roll of the dice, and there's nothing more to life than that. That's what you want? No. You don't want to know that I think I may have become a writer only because I want to be famous and I believe this is my best shot at getting there, because I'm enough of a narcissist to think I'm very, very important, important enough to be famous and to write about my life, to tell my stories, my fabulous stories! You don't want to know that I sometimes doubt the kind of eternal life you promised and instead believe that true eternal life, true salvation, is just doing something great enough, renowned enough, that you're remembered forever, bronzed in the minds of people for years to come!"

Again Jack steps toward me, still toward me, but again I step away.

"You want into this? I'm a bog, a freaking labyrinth, and you don't want to get stuck in this, lost in me, so stop pretending that you do, that this is our *Good Will Hunting* moment, where it's all going to come together, that some bumper sticker quote you give me can make it better, liberate me, soothe some wound! You don't want this! I don't even want this! I'd love to be anyone else! Anything else! I want to forget so much of what's inside me. So why on earth would I let someone into the things that I'm trying so hard to forget? Huh? If I do, then it all just lives on in another person! That's what relationships do! They multiply us! And if that's the case, then I'm just multiplying the things I wish I could erase! And every time I let another person in, I'll only give all the things I'm trying to forget about myself new life, more territory, and I don't want that! No one does! You don't! You don't! You don't want this—"

My eyes tear up, wet and runny and bare, and I fold, staring at nothing but flowers and grass and dirt. Cupping his gloved hand around the base of my neck, Jack pulls me in, and through his shirt, I feel his heart beating against my cheek.

Arnold, the Giant's Umbrella

The back of the park is dried up, all brush, but there he is—Arnold, my favorite tree in the world, fully alive. With a trunk the size of five people, his branches grow up and out, so high, so many, so impressive, so complex and dense, climbing, climbing, a bridge to outer space. If any of the giants roaming this world are ever in desperate need of an umbrella, that he-giant or she-giant is going to uproot Arnold, and he will shelter them from the rain.

Jack and Ditka and I approach Arnold—

Wait. There are boards nailed into his trunk. I've seen Arnold so many times, but I've never noticed this before. Have they always been here? Impossible. I would've noticed this, right? Maybe not, though. After all, it's weird how you can look at something so many times and still never really see it. Seven billion people in the world, all of us visually impaired.

The three of us creep in for a closer look. From beneath his branches, I can see the boards scaling up, leading to platforms scattered throughout Arnold, as if constructed by a master carpenter or those cookie-making elves. My eyes scan Arnold top to bottom, and for the first time, I think about climbing Arnold. Oh, the fun I'd have, the perspective I'd gain! But when did I last climb a tree? Like twenty years ago? That's a long time, too long. I may not be able to climb a tree anymore, may have forgotten how, lost the skills of youth—yes! Youth is a skill—but even if I can recall how, aren't I too old to be climbing trees? Shouldn't I be more mature? No, no, no, no, that's a heart-shrinking thought! I never want to be a person who thinks he's too old to climb a tree!

"Josh, you going to climb it or not?"

"You up for coming with me?"

"I'm in."

I tie Ditka to a stump so he won't run away and wrap my hands around the lowest board, and Jack and I begin scaling Arnold's trunk. I am careful, so careful, so as not to fall and break my leg or neck, or worse, my ego. The spot we choose is perfect, a wide palm with thick branch fingers spreading out around us, and here, upon our timber thrones, Jack and I sit against Arnold's rough bark, reveling in our collaborative accomplishment.

A minute passes without either of us saying a word. At first, the silence feels good, but it quickly becomes uncomfortable. Another minute passes. Now the silence is an itch that I want to scratch. I must say something, anything, because this silence isn't golden—is it ever? Why does the quiet make me so jittery? Probably because in the quiet, even sound is stripped away, leaving me more vulnerable, without the garments of noise, naked, more connected to everything in this world. Another minute passes and suddenly the park looks different. More detailed. Filled in. I'm beginning to see the world, Jack, life, just a bit differently, viewing each of them from a position that only silence can provide.

"So then what happened?"

"What?"

"What happened? With Sara."

"Oh, right. Well, a week later she stopped by my parents' house—where I was living at the time—and let me know that she got her period. She wasn't pregnant. And then she broke

up with me—it all happened in the same conversation, all on the front porch, all with her friend waiting in the car, watching us, the engine idling. It's kind of funny, but I still remember standing there as the two of them drove away. After that, I went to my bedroom, sat down on the floor by the closet, right up against the door, holding the knob, and just cried. Man, that was so hard, but at the same time, it's exactly what I wanted. I knew I didn't love her. That was obvious. You know, the whole time I thought she was pregnant, I never even considered how having a baby would affect *her*. It never crossed my mind. I didn't even think about the life of the kid! It was all about me. I didn't know what I was doing or who I was becoming. I wasn't sure which way was up anymore. And then for some reason, once I knew I wasn't going to be a dad, there was the whole question of why it would have been such a bad thing if I were. I mean—why did I think this way?

"Well, I ended up attributing my mind-set to two things. First, every young, unmarried dad I'd seen on television was a dropout, hillbilly, or thug, someone in a tank top with greasy hair. So apparently, culture wanted me to think that being a young, unmarried father is a calamity of some kind, and if I became one, I'd be like them too. Culture was defining *ideal* and *mistake* for me. Culture was warning me. Second, I'd already drafted the perfect hypothetical future for myself in my head—college grad, good-paying job, my awesome wife and me traveling the world, without kids, me publicly embodying the good guy—and this terrible event of fatherhood would have destroyed that future. Right? That's what I thought.

"Only then it kind of occurred to me that maybe, sometimes, when something 'terrible' happens, I only think it's terrible because I'm comparing it to another image I've set my sights on. So really, the 'problem' isn't the problem. The problem is the delusion I've created and become attached to. The problem is the delusion that what I'm picturing is a far better option. I know that isn't true all the time, but in some cases, it is. And all that stuff really messed with me. Everything in my life felt uncertain, like it was changing so fast, but—and I felt so guilty about this—I also had this massive sense of relief. She wasn't pregnant. We were done. I got to move on. I had the next fifty years back, you know?

"Like I told you, I haven't shared any of this with anyone until now. But who would, you know? The way of life Gus was talking about—normal people don't do that. The way you and I interact is the way most people do."

"Well, you're right about that. But that doesn't mean it's what I want."

"Yeah, you never really answered that part. What do you want?"

"You know, I don't get asked that very often, but I want you to let me love you. I want you to give me every part of you, the good and the bad, the exciting parts and the shameful parts, the things that you can't wait to wake up to and the things that keep you up at night. I want all of you."

"All of me."

"Of course."

"Kind of demanding, don't you think? All of me?"

"And you think I deserve less than that?"

The sun is tired now, and an evening wind sifts through the park, swaying Arnold's branches, turning the leaves giddy as if they've just heard a real gem of a joke.

"You know, Josh, it's interesting. In all these movies you watch, *The Notebook*, *Phantom of the Opera*, *Big Fish*, whatever, whenever some guy says, 'I love you, I want you, all of you, forever, every single part, the depths of you, blah, blah, blah,' it's romantic, everyone swoons, and he's just Mr. Incredible. Right?"

"Yeah."

"And I'll bet when you see that, you know, you just know, that you're seeing an incredible love on display, because there's no part of the girl that the guy doesn't want—the good, the bad, all of it—right?"

"Yeah."

"Okay, but then when I say that, you recoil, because in your mind, it's not loving. It's just demanding. It's unfair. But intimacy has nothing to do with what's fair, Josh. Intimacy isn't fair. If you want what's fair, become a lawyer. Intimacy is about what's real. Sometimes the difference between intimacy and unfairness is simply a matter of perspective."

"I guess so."

"Josh, I know that relationships are hard for you—with Kristen, with everyone. It's going to take time. I get that. And I'm okay with it. I do patience. But if you interacted with Kristen the way you do with me, what would happen?"

"We'd probably have been divorced already, or we'd be like my parents."

"That's where we've been heading. I mean, when's the last time we had a memorable talk or a memorable moment? Months? Years? Josh, you don't talk to me about your parents dying or about the struggle and excitement of writing or about your anger, how weak you feel, your marriage, the things you daydream about. You don't talk about feeling lonely, but I know you are. When's the last time we had a moment that really meant something to you?"

"I don't know. But today certainly counts. I'll remember this one."

"Me too. I want more of this for you and me."

"Well, like you said, it's going to take me some time to get used to it, but I think I'd like that. I'd like to start getting the point."

"You already are, Josh."

Far below, Ditka barks. He's mad, throwing a tantrum, sick of being tied up, of waiting for us to climb down, of wondering what Jack and I are doing in this tree, this giant's umbrella.

XIII

About Feeling Fine

"So, Josh, how are you feeling?"

My therapist's office has cream-colored walls and a picture of a farmhouse. On the floor beneath it are two plastic plants, strategically placed to assure me that like a plant, I'm growing, alive, helping the world breathe.

"Actually, Lydia, I feel fine."

I am confident in my statement, and I show this by leaning back into the couch cushions, arms wide. Kristen is beside me. I look to her to confirm. Without hesitation, her eyes, shining and brave, say, *Yes, you do feel fine. I can tell that you've felt fine lately.* I beam at her, at Lydia, at all corners of this room that I've come to know so well. Yes, doing this every week for a year has given me plenty of opportunity to familiarize myself with these surroundings, though I almost didn't make that first appointment.

When Kristen first suggested therapy, I was resistant, because, obvious to me, I didn't need it. I was fine. So I wasn't about to needlessly subject myself to psychological dissection, the probing of every word, inflection, and movement. I'd heard stories. Beyond that, I really wasn't about to pay a moderate fee for a captive audience, which I briefly argued would be the equivalent of visiting a mental prostitute, whereby making me a john. A john! Yes, I was being a bit absurd. Kristen had to practically drag me here those first few weeks.

Now, though, being in this place is no punishment. Actually, I really enjoy my time here every Wednesday, because unlike everywhere else, here I'm supposed to be frazzled, emotionally vaudevillian. Being a mess keeps me in this club, and thus far I've been a fine member. And though I'm not quite sure how it's happened, this hour has healed me. Lydia, my current therapist, and Gene, my first therapist, have helped put me back together.

"Really? You feel fine?"

"Yeah, really, I do. I'm fine."

"Well, that's great, isn't it?"

"I think so. Why wouldn't it be?"

"No reason. So, how are you feeling about feeling fine?"

The nearby trees have cast skinny, shadowy branches across Lydia's face, transforming her into a work of modern art. Her cropped gray hair doesn't move. The whites of her eyes glow out at me. *How am I feeling about feeling fine?*

My mind goes to a hundred faces and a thousand conversations. Friends, acquaintances, everyone—they've wanted me to feel fine for a while. Move on, they tell me. Plunge into work, they tell me. Look to the future, they tell me. Whatever. They say it all kinds of ways, but the message never changes and, when stripped of all its lacy rhetoric, is simple: get over it.

No, I'm not judging. In fact, I've tried to give the benefit of the doubt and believe that the bulk of this is coming from a tender place, is the right thing to say, but even so, pieces of it, I think, are something else. I've been in their shoes; I've wanted to comfort someone, to say the right thing. I've made similar statements, and on the whole, whenever I've said those things to grieving people, it's not because I want *them* to move on or get over it. Usually it's because *I* want to move on. I want to get over it, because if they stay in their sad place, then as their friend I have to either abandon them or abandon my desire for happy places and maintain residence in the sad place with them, and I hate sad places. My desire for them to move on is fueled by my desire to move on. It's my longing to get back to normal life, to how life was before they fell apart, thinking that if I move quickly enough, then maybe everything will return to the way it was, the way a snapping rubber band does—

"Josh? Are you with me?" In therapist fashion, Lydia presses a finger into her temple, evaluation forthcoming.

"Oh, uh, yeah, sorry. How am I feeling about feeling fine? Hmm. How am I feeling about feeling fine? Well . . ."

I want to let the word *fine* flop off my lips again. Although if done wrong, that could, I suppose, come across as snarky, adolescent, as if I'm hiding some dark secret, and that's no good. So instead, I'll say that I feel *fine*, only emphatically, with methodic nodding. Yes. That's what I'll do. But then just as I'm about to say it, I feel something, something suggesting that I don't feel *fine* about feeling fine—a vacancy, as if a piece of me is missing. In need of a closer look, I peek deep within myself, and there it is, I see it. Something is leaving.

In his black suit and fedora, he's there, a little man, at the bottom of the staircase, bag packed, bus ticket in hand. Grief. He's moving out of me. He's leaving. And yet I feel terrible. This doesn't make sense. If Grief is leaving, I shouldn't feel empty. I should feel happy, right? Unless—and I know this may not make sense—unless I don't want him to leave. But why wouldn't I want him to— Has Grief become my friend? Can that happen?

Yes. That's it. Sure, he was a bully at first, but Grief, it seems, has become an ally. I've come to rely on him. He's become the surest way of holding my parents close. Grief has been the link, my only way of relating to them. My tears and my dreariness and my anger provide me with daily assurance that my parents are still near. Now that he's leaving, how am I going to—

Peering within myself again, I watch the scene continue to unfold.

From the top of the stairs, I'm trying to reason with Grief. *Please, don't go. Don't leave me. I need you if I'm going to remember them.*

But he stays quiet, neutral, then checks his pocket watch, straightens his tie, grabs his bag—

Sure, my parents have been dead for a while. But now they feel gone, light-years away, rubbed out. How did I miss this? All the signs were here! I'm no longer wearing my dad's ring or carrying my mom's driver's license in my wallet, and I don't think about them when I watch the Home Shopping Network or smell a cloud of Aqua Net hairspray, and I've deleted both of their numbers from my phone, and I've stopped shaving my head, and I haven't cried over them in weeks, and what did Mom's laugh sound like? Oh gosh, what's happening?

Back inside me, I'm pleading, *Please, Grief. Stay. I need you, I need—*

My words don't even make a dent. As he steps outside, the daylight sprays in through the open door. To no one in particular, Grief tips his hat, and then the door shuts.

Now I understand. I know exactly why I don't feel *fine* about feeling fine. I know why I feel this sudden void, and I don't want it to be true, but it is true. Grief isn't the only one moving on, closing the door behind him, saying goodbye. So am I. I'm moving on. I'm saying goodbye.

Scrambling for Kristen with one hand, I squeeze the couch pillow with my other. "I guess I didn't know it, but feeling fine doesn't feel that great."

"And why is that, Josh?"

My chin bows into my chest. "I'm afraid that if I feel fine, then that means I didn't love them, that I'm forgetting them, that this is the end, that they can't be a part of my life anymore."

"Oh, Josh . . . do you really think that?"

"I don't know."

Lydia scoots to the edge of her chair. She might reach for me, hug me—is this allowed? Is she beginning to cry? Is this in violation of some code? Maybe. But those rules no longer apply. Right now she's more friend than therapist.

"Josh, maybe feeling fine doesn't mean that you didn't love them or that you're forgetting them or that this is the end. Maybe feeling fine means that you don't have to connect with them only through the pain anymore. Josh, maybe you're okay now. Maybe you're living your life again, your new life, a different life, and because of that, maybe you're free to enjoy your parents again, enjoy everything again."

Kristen drags her fingers against my neck. She plays with my hair. And for the first time in a while, I can feel it, the electricity of human contact. I can feel her. The shroud of pain is lifting, finally lifting, and in the lifting, I now understand this thing called grief a bit more. Wow, I drastically underestimated it, downplayed it. It isn't just our way of coping with the death of something, someone. No. It's our way of fighting mortality, of prolonging connection for as long as possible, our way of hitchhiking to the other side with that person or thing that we've lost, our way of accompanying the dead. In grief, we taste the grave. And then when grief leaves, we're deported, sent out of the grave and back to life.

Lydia is right. Life outside of loss exists again. I exist again outside of loss.

In the window, the sun is yellow, highlighter yellow, canary-yolk, lemon yellow—has the sun always been this yellow? And that grass, so green, surely home to a trillion species—ants and crickets and spiders and slugs, gophers too! Amazing! Endless life packed into a few inches of earth! Life right there, life right here, life within reach— Oh, I want it! Life! Every drop! I want to try new food, Ethiopian maybe, to suck on Jolly Ranchers, then take them out of my mouth and hold them up to the light, and I want to go to Italy with Kristen, to discover new music, great bands, and shout their songs at concerts in unison with others, all of us rocking out in our skinny jeans, and I want to ride a majestic horse, my butt growing swollen in the saddle, and I want to go to a musical, sit close enough to see the performers' sweat and spit, then have Jack over for dinner, cook for him, bratwurst maybe, anything on that George Foreman grill, and I'll watch the grease dribble into the plastic tray, swirling brown and purple, and I want to learn—relearn—how to play piano, and go for a drive with Ditka, his head joyfully out the window in the wind, and I want to call my sisters—oh, my sisters—yes, that should be near the top of the list, this list that symbolizes my resurrection, this list of exploding life things that I'm ready to drink, hold, sing, promenade, ingest—

Lydia reaches into her bag and removes an official-looking sheet of paper. With a click of her pen, she scribbles on it, grinning proudly as if something massive has happened. I suppose it has. Though it seemed impossible for a while, I've been put back together—not necessarily the way I was before, because once life falls apart, we're never put back together the same way. We're different. Life is different. Changed. It's only once we've been near death that we can really experience life. And that, I suppose, is why pain and grief affect us so much, and why, in some odd way, our lives aren't complete without it—

Coming to her feet, Lydia picks a piece of lint from her skirt. Five o'clock already. Time is up. I thank her. She thanks me. I'm not sure why. We shake hands—

Gosh, no—I'm not over losing my parents! I haven't forgotten them! Grief may have moved out, but he'll visit. He'll pop in unannounced. I'll never be completely past this pain, because some wounds don't ever completely heal. Some aren't meant to. With some wounds, the complete healing would be the greatest wound of all. I'll carry this forever, and forever it'll remind me of how much I lost and how much what I lost meant to me.

Kristen and I walk out the door and down the hallway, holding hands, discussing what we're going to eat. I tell her that Chinese food sounds good.

What's Left of Corbett . . .

Supplemental income was needed. Yes, the writing and speaking side of things is still progressing, I think, but we've yet to reap any of the impending and surely enormous financial windfall. And since Kristen already has a full-time job working at a photography studio and is great at it, and because her boss embodies everything someone could possibly love about Texas and humanity in general, and because I apparently have loads of free time to watch talk shows, I needed to come up with something.

I decided to try my most brilliant idea first, so I signed up for a job taking online surveys. Their-oh-so golden promises sounded beautiful, so I gave them my secret numbers and paid thirty dollars, expecting quick dividends, but received only spam email in return, no money. I then considered that maybe as a way to offset some of our expenses, and rather than getting a second job, I could gather throwaway sandwiches, the way Wallace and I did in college. It worked then! Surely it could work for Kristen and me now! Right? I dismissed that idea quickly. It's strange, though, how ten years can pass and we can find ourselves in the exact same place. Maybe I haven't changed as much as I think I have. Maybe nothing does—

But I did find a job.

I've taken a position teaching sex education in Austin public high schools. No, seriously. Gus set me up with the whole thing. He's my boss. As he first described the role, I couldn't stop giggling. The idea of talking about love and condoms (hee-hee) and STDs and penises (hee-hee) all day, aided by full-color pictures—my gosh, you wouldn't believe the pictures!— seemed absurd. Especially since my knowledge of those subjects isn't exactly, well— But it pays! And it's flexible enough that it won't interfere with my dream, will allow me to write and to take off when I get a speaking gig somewhere, and they offered to train me really well, so I took the job.

This is my second week. I'm in a classroom. Showtime.

I print my name on the board. It's sloppy, as if I'm missing three fingers. I erase it and try again. Then I underline it, because the bold emphasis will demonstrate my authority, make it evident as to who is the expert here, and then a tornado of respect will touch down.

"Hey, guys, my name is Josh. I'm from Chicago. I'm married to an amazing girl named Kristen, and when I'm not working here, I'm a writer. And I think we're going to have a good time together."

Chairs shift. A girl cracks her gum. There's way too much red lipstick in this room, too much angst, too many whizzing hormones. Eyes roll. Are they rolling at me? No, that can't be! I'm so— More eyes roll. Oh, these young people are smug, all of them, with their sideways glances and smirks. Little do they know that while I am an authority, I am also a cool teacher, the teacher they have been waiting for since their formal education began, a teacher who, like them, also participates in the latest crazes. Obviously this last part cannot be emphasized enough.

So I down sit on the nearest desk, casual, my hair tactically messed, one jeaned leg up on the chair, every inch of me trying to demonstrate that I'm one of them, and that they could do worse hoping to someday be one of me.

"For the next couple days, we're going to talk about sex and relationships and love and all kinds of other interesting things. You guys ready? Well then, let's get started."

I turn out the lights. The room squeals at the first image.

Eight hours later, and because we have only one car, I'm picking Kristen up from work. Traffic is light, so I'm paying little attention to the lane lines and enjoying the open space, king of the road. As has been the case for months now, the car speakers are broken, making everything squeaky, lacking bass, like all the vocalists have been sucking helium, but I'm listening to the radio anyway, singing along, louder than one should. It's the end of what's been an ordinary day, a day that I'll never think about again, which is how many days are. It's as if they never even happened. Most of us only really live about a year, I guess.

"It's time! It's time!"

The little human inside Corbett is ready to roll.

"Huh? What?! Are you serious?"

"Yeah!"

"You sure?"

"What kind of question is that? Yes! Come on!"

"Alright. Alright. Stay calm."

"I am calm. Is everything going to be okay? I mean, it's early! Weeks early!"

"Yes. Everything is going to be fine. Just fine. Let's go. I'll get our stuff."

"But how do you know?"

"Honey, I just do. Everything is going to be okay." Corbett's husband, the other Josh, grabs the ready bag.

"I'm scared. I wish my mom was here. I really wish she was here."

"I know, Corbett. I know."

Rushing out into the cold Chicago air, the other Josh helps Corbett waddle to the car, then hurries to the driver's side and slams the door. He buckles the seat belt. As the engine comes to life, Corbett begins to sniffle.

"I want to call my brother."

Back in Austin, I'm in the photography studio where Kristen works. Ditka is here too, having spent the day with his mom. I'm facing a portrait of an old Irishman, getting lost in it, thinking about how he very well could be the greatest sales pitch ever for a trip to see those rolling green hills of his homeland. I'm ready to get on a plane right now. Ireland must be the greatest freaking country in the world!

"Josh, you want to take Ditka potty while I close up the studio?"

"Yeah, babe. I'll meet you outside. Ditka, you wanna go for a walk?"

He runs to the door.

"Wanna go outside?"

As I'm leashing him, my phone rings—a ridiculous ringtone called Calypso. Oh, it's disgraceful, a source of massive embarrassment. Each time it goes off in public, I feel compelled to stand up on a chair and apologize, to tell everyone it's not my fault, explain that if I'd had better options, a wider selection, I'd have chosen differently; to promise everyone that I'll do better, try harder, assure everyone that I'm not as obnoxious as my ringtone, that my ringtone doesn't define me.

After a few seconds of fumbling, I answer it.

"Hey, Corbett."

"Josh?"

Her voice is deeper than usual. She's upset.

"Corbett, are you okay?"

"Um . . ."

I can see her on the other end of the phone, flung limp and boneless across the floor, a virtual rag doll, her makeup cried off, and I brace myself for word of our next tragedy. Is her husband dead? Did she fall down the steps? What now?

Ever since Mom and Dad died, it's been this way. My head is now wired with a doomsday clock, constantly ticking down toward another terrible thing, more sadness, a bubble waiting to burst. I'm always expecting it. Every time someone hugs me, I assume it's goodbye. Every piece of mail is an eviction notice. Every knock at the door is a repo man or a police officer, and I'm going to jail, Kristen is leaving me, my friends have been eaten by deranged zoo animals, Corbett has been kidnapped, our condo blew up, Ditka contracted rabies, Quinn has scurvy, and what's that spot on my chest?

"Josh, I'm having the baby right now."

"What?"

"Yeah. Right now. We're on our way to the hospital."

The leash falls from my hand to the floor.

Kristen looks at me, concerned, mouthing something. I miss what she said, so I mouth, *What?* Kristen mouths again, slower, with big hand movements, *Is ev-er-y-thing o-kay?* I nod back, mouthing, *She's having the baby!*

"Okay, okay, I'll catch the first plane up there," I say to Corbett. "I'm not sure if that'll be tonight, but early tomorrow at the latest. I love you guys. Keep me in the loop."

"Okay. Thank you so much, Josh."

"Corbett, you're gonna do great. I love you."

"Love you too. Thank you."

I slip the phone back into my pocket, and all thoughts of Ireland evaporate. Yes, Chicago will be gray and cruel, but I will be there! I will not miss this. I've missed too much of my sisters' lives already—additionally, I'm not going to launch my uncle-hood on the wrong foot. No, I'll be there, and whenever this story is shared, I'll be included, seen in photographs, and my nephew/niece will know how much I cared about him/her even then—and a few months ago, I decided that I wasn't going to be absent and detached anymore. But even after that therapy session proclamation, it took one more moment to bring it all together.

It was Christmas, our second without Dad and Mom. Kristen and I were in Chicago with Corbett and the other Josh. Quinn and Nelson were there too, in town from Costa Rica. Though things between us all were still awkward and distant, no different from the way they were at Quinn's wedding, we were determined to make it an enjoyable holiday, full of holly and good tidings, fa la la la la! The greatest holiday in history!

And we actually pulled it off. Like we have since we were kids, we exchanged pajamas on Christmas Eve, donned them immediately, and then did an informal sort of fashion show, remarking about how "snazzy" we all looked. Then we danced around the tree, singing the *Charlie Brown Christmas* theme, heads tilted up like in the cartoons, followed by pictures, assorted poses, one of us in a human pyramid, one of the boys flexing, a wacky-face one, and then we drank eggnog (I drank eggnog), and eventually we fell asleep watching *It's a Wonderful Life*. And never at any point did we succumb to the "I wish Mom and Dad were here" moments that we all felt pressing down on us. We couldn't. We had to prove to ourselves that though our lives had changed so much, holidays could still be familiar.

I mean, sure, it went unspoken between us, but we knew this Christmas was about sustaining normalcy in any way we could, maintaining our long-standing traditions. We knew that traditions were the only way to preserve our sanity, the only way of feeling, even just for a moment, that life was in our hands, cooperating. So while we were keeping our traditions alive this Christmas, our traditions were, in a way, keeping us alive.

Later that week, Kristen and I were preparing to fly back to Austin, but before we left, Corbett and Quinn and I decided to go to breakfast. I'm not sure why we did this. It's never been our habit to eat meals together, but apparently our out-of-character choices can end up being our best.

Everything inside the restaurant fit a country store motif: ceramic roosters and weather vanes and barns and washboards. We sat in a booth, perusing the menus, but didn't talk. Don't get me wrong. Our mouths moved and sounds came out, but it was hardly talking. It was more of our typical mindless noise, mechanical, the way we've been communicating for years. It was almost like we were giving PowerPoint presentations.

I went first—cue first slide.

Job.
Next slide.

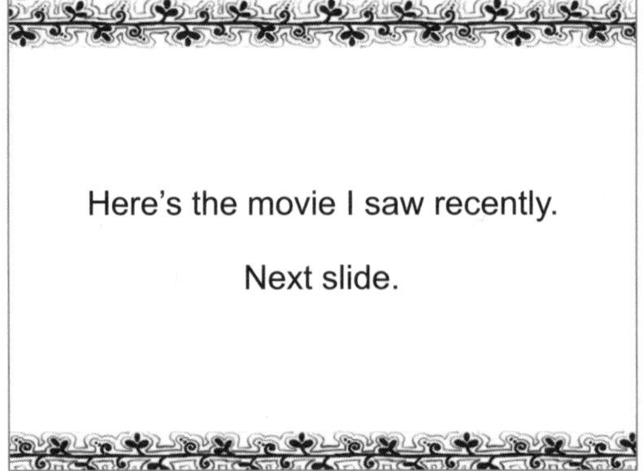
Here’s the movie I saw recently.
Next slide.

Kristen.
Next slide.

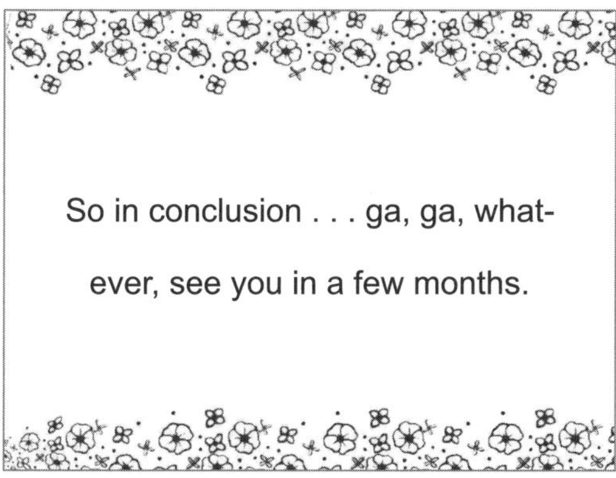

So in conclusion . . . ga, ga, whatever, see you in a few months.

The waitress came to the table. We ordered. Then Corbett did her presentation.

Review of
So You Think You Can Dance.
Next slide.

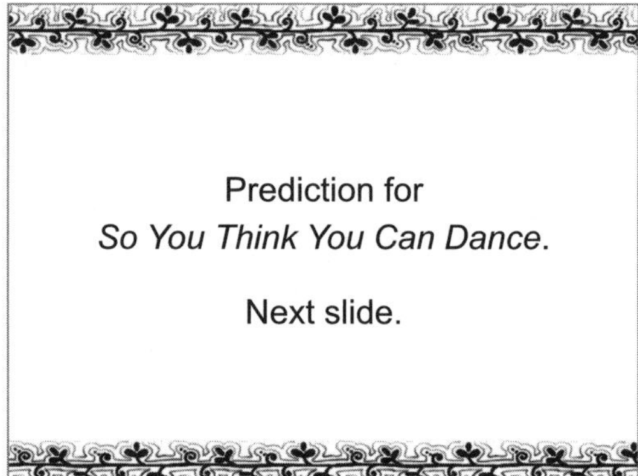
Prediction for
So You Think You Can Dance.
Next slide.

Blah, blah.
In conclusion, blah.

The food came. My eggs were runny, but I ate them anyway, and as I wiped the plate clean with an English muffin, Quinn was finishing up her presentation.

"So I think Nelson and I are going to move back to the US."

"Really? That's great," Corbett said. "You guys thinking of coming back to the Chicago area?"

"Yeah, I think so."

"Well, as your sister, I have to say that would be so cool!"

"How long have you been thinking about this?" I asked.

"Oh, a while, I guess."

"A long time?"

"I don't know. I guess."

"How long?"

"I really don't know, Josh."

"Like a month, since before you guys got married?"

"Yeah, something like that, at least a few months. I don't know."

"And didn't you think that I'd want to know about that?"

"Well, to be honest, Josh, no—"

The waitress returned. I gave her the "come back later" look. She left.

"I didn't think you wanted to know any of that." Quinn said it plainly, which riled me up, so I crowded the table, trying to intimidate.

"Why not?"

"Really, Josh?"

"Yeah!" When I smacked the table, a man slid his glasses down his nose and looked at me. I stared bloody daggers right back—

"Because I didn't think you cared! What about the way you are with me would indicate that you wanted to be a part of my life at all?"

I sipped my coffee, hot, hoping to drown the lump in my throat.

"You never call. You never write. You never email. You never ask me anything about myself. You never tell me anything about you. Why would I think you wanted to know? And why would I think to tell you?"

Suddenly everything hurt, like I'd been beaten with sticks. Piñata boy. The pain was everywhere, and it needed to be dulled, so I reached into my medicine-cabinet brain, clawing around the shelves for something that would do the trick, an icepack maybe, or no, even better—a painkiller, a mind-bendingly gorgeous, pure, dirty painkiller; hello, old reliable. Yes. That would do the trick; it always had. As had been my routine for years, when faced with unpleasant life moments, I wanted to inject nature's Novocain: the lie. Lies, lies, those little miracle drugs—they're so dependable, so slippery, and they can do so much. Lies numb us to the pain, to the truth. Watch . . .

"It's not my fault."

"They started it."

"It's no big deal."

"Things aren't as bad as they seem."

"I didn't mean it."

We the punctured-arm people, our colander skin—we shoot ourselves full of lies, and pretty soon our hearts become barefoot, hippie flower children, dancing in a world without feeling. Lies are our most organic painkiller.

There at the table, I wanted to take another hit, to release myself of conviction and responsibility, to mask the pain, so I grabbed a vile out of my brain and plunged the needle in. *It's Quinn's fault! She's the one who moved to Costa Rica! This is just like her and Corbett to blow everything out of proportion! All families are like this, so who cares? Not me. I don't care. So we've grown apart, moved on; that's what being an adult is about: leaving family behind—*

But then I felt it: Jack's hand in my chest, squeezing, telling me that regardless of how much I didn't want this to be true, it was true, that Quinn was right, that she'd just verbalized what I'd felt at her wedding, and after Mom died, what we'd all been feeling for years—the elephant in the room. I felt Jack's hand telling me that this had to be reversed, that this new level of depth and connection and life that I was just now beginning to explore with the world around me had to include Corbett and Quinn, my family, and Jack's hand showed me that deep down, though I'd been too scared to admit it, I longed to know my sisters, so badly, to connect with them, to love them, and most of all, to be known, loved, and chosen by them—yes, chosen.

That's when the long, winding strand of holiday lights lining my insides switched on. Of course!

This is perhaps the greatest human desire: to be asked to prom, to be declared the winner of *American Idol*, to be given the promotion, to have that rock star in a stadium full of fans point right at us—us, us! To be chosen! The universal ambition! The human heart cannot rest until it is chosen! We want to be chosen, especially by our families, by the people who could so easily settle for simply being stuck with us.

Jack's hand kept squeezing, and I knew I had to do something, because in some ways I'd recognized all this for a while, but recognizing it hadn't changed it. Now it was time to do something about it. Sometimes you just have to go out and do something! True? True. Otherwise we're just living the same dreary rerun over and over.

I stopped crowding the table.

"Quinn. I—I'm so sorry. You're right. And I do care, but I just haven't showed you. You either, Corbett. And I've only had a harder time with it now that Dad and Mom are gone. I relied on Mom to fill me in on both of you, to connect me to you. Everything I know about you guys these days, I knew through her. We haven't been close in so long, but now that Mom's gone, it's like we aren't even related. I do love you guys and care about you, but I just haven't done anything about it. And I don't feel like you guys have either. I'm so afraid that you guys don't really care about me."

Quinn and Corbett were crying now. I kept going.

"You guys never ask me how I'm doing or how my marriage is or how writing is going or what's really going on. But you know what? Things are hard. They're really, really hard. And I'm jealous of both of you because you have this whole sister thing. I hate it! I hate the ways things are with us. You guys, I'm so sorry. I want to be your brother, and I want so badly for you guys to be my sisters."

"Josh, I'm sorry too. I had no idea you felt that way. I don't want things this way either."

"Me neither," Corbett said, wiping her eyes.

The waitress came back to the table, dropped the check, and told us to stay as long as we liked.

The Splatter on the Walls

The sun isn't up yet when Kristen and I board a flight from Austin to Chicago to be with Corbett, the other Josh, and the tiny little human who arrived in the middle of the night, a boy named Syrus. A few hours later, we land at O'Hare International Airport, grab our bags off the carousel, catch a ride, and pull into the hospital. We haven't eaten. I'm exhausted, dolphin-colored bags under my eyes. My face hurts. I can't rest, though, because Corbett needs me now. She needs me to be her brother—no, more than her brother, her brother and her dad, our dad, and our mom too, our entire family tree. And while the weight of her massive needs would overwhelm a normal human, I will meet them all. I will be her root system, her means of water and nutrients, her very survival!

I convince myself of all this as Kristen and I run through the parking lot, our fists and legs beating the winter air. We reach the glass entryway. I bend over, grabbing my knees, trying to catch my breath. Why the heck is it so hot in here? It shouldn't be this hot. I'm boiling, my head in flames, and suddenly my stomach is coming up into my mouth and things are spinning. I'm nauseous from the lack of sleep, from the running. Mostly the running, I think. How long has it been since I exercised?

"Can I help you?"

The woman behind the information desk is giving me a look, the kind of look you give to people you *know* are going to rob you.

"Yeah. I'm looking for Corbett Burick. She came in last night."

As my stomach slithers back down to where it belongs, she frowns and checks a clipboard, still looking suspicious of me, scrolling through a list of terrible things that I might possibly do to her. The silent alarm must be tripped. She knows it.

"Yes. Let me call the room and see if they can take a visitor. Your name?"

"Josh Riebock. I'm her brother."

While the desk woman makes the call, I pace around the lobby, hands on my hips, my breath and temperature returning to normal. This room is soothing. The walls have pictures of sailboats and kids flying kites, and one of a mountain with an inspirational phrase underneath, something about peaks. The automatic security doors fling open, and Jack and the other Josh appear. The other Josh is coated in that new father glow, overjoyed, ready to keel over.

"Hey, guys."

"Hey."

"Hey."

We all hug. Jack asks about the flight. I say that it was good, then say something about how cold it is. It is so wickedly cold!

"How's my sister doing, Josh?"

"Good, man, really good. She's doing really good."

"And you? The new papa?"

"Tired, dude. It's definitely been a long night. But I'm good. Everybody's really good."

We begin walking.

"That's awesome, man. Kristen and I have definitely been thinking of you guys."

"Well, thanks so much for coming."

"Of course."

Through the automatic security doors is a gallery of balloons and potted plants and stuffed animals, a story behind each one. The doors go on and on. The four of us move quickly, and finally the other Josh pushes one open.

"Hello?"

"Hey! It's Uncle Josh and Aunt Kristen!"

What's left of Corbett is propped up in the bed, draped in ten feet of baggy hospital gown, that plastic bracelet around her wrist, wires and tubes poking out of her arms, each one linked to some machine, all of them blipping and beeping. She is a cyborg, a land octopus, nothing like the new-mom pictures used in promotional materials, but a mom nonetheless. My sister. I laugh to myself because when we were little, she'd sometimes pretend that she had a kid, carrying a doll around, giving it a bottle, excessively burping it, putting it to bed, wiping its tears. She's doing that again, only now she isn't playing. The dress rehearsal is over. That lump in her arms now isn't plastic. It's flesh, bone. It's hers. It's amazing. She's amazing, and probably has been for years. I've just been too selfish to see it. But then again, if you never get outside yourself, you never see anyone else.

"Hey, Corbett . . ."

I begin creeping toward her for a hug, but then I freeze when a tiny noise squeaks out from the package blanketed in her arms.

"Corbett, he is absolutely adorable."

I'm holding the little plum-faced bundle and talking in my baby voice, and I realize that this is the same voice I use when I'm talking to Ditka. Naturally, this raises an important question: does it mean that I see my dog as a person? Or do I see this person as a dog? And what kind of uncle am I if I see my nephew as an animal? I take a moment to ponder this, along with the far-reaching ramifications of all scenarios, before eventually deciding that this is not an issue of how I view either, but rather evidence pointing to my limitations in the field of voice creation—

"He doesn't really cry much."

"Really? Does he eat much?"

"No."

"What color eyes does he have?"

"I'm pretty sure they're blue, but they're closed most of the time."

"Does he open them ever?"

"Every now and again, but then he shuts them. It's the cutest thing."

"Love it—"

A nurse walks in. She says she has to take Syrus back to the little baby incubator room with all the other incubating babies, so I hand him over. She leaves. And now, for the first time since I got here, Corbett and I are alone. I sit down in one of the plastic hospital chairs.

"So, how are you feeling about all of this? I mean, you're a mom! And that's incredible, but how are you feeling about it?"

"It's kind of hard to take in right now, you know?"

"Actually, I don't know."

"Right."

"Yeah."

"Well, I already love him so much. He's perfect. I can't even describe it. But it's been hard too. Like last night was really hard. Just without Dad or Mom. It's like this is one of those moments that they should've been here for. And I just really want them here. Really badly. I don't know . . ."

I hand her a box of tissues. She pulls one out and plays with it, spreading it wide, then folding it over, then rolling it up.

"Sorry." Corbett dabs her eyes, then makes more shapes with the tissue.

"I'm really glad that you called me, Corbett. Seriously, it's so cool to be here with you guys. And you guys are going to be amazing parents. I just know it."

"Thanks."

The door opens again, and this time a short Asian doctor in blue scrubs and a white lab jacket shuffles in. Seeing him, and that he is Asian, I feel confidence rush over me. Surely he is not just a doctor but a doctor of doctors, smarter than his Harvard or MIT classmates, than Stephen Hawking, than Patch Adams. I'll bet he had a perfect score on his MCATs. Yuck, me and my stereotypes.

"And how is Mom feeling?"

"Good. I feel really good. By the way, this is my brother, Josh. He flew up here from Austin."

"Nice to meet you, Josh."

I stand stiff and severe and act professional, as if I too have a prestigious degree hanging in my office. We shake hands, but he isn't interested in me.

"Corbett, is your husband around?"

"Yeah, he just went out to get some coffee. There he is now."

The other Josh and Jack walk back into the room carrying small steaming cups. The other Josh squeezes onto the bed with Corbett. He makes a joke about how small the bed is, and we laugh.

"Well, we've received some of Syrus's test results, and we've found an abnormality."

Dr. Perfect MCAT kills the mood with one sentence.

"We aren't going to know for sure for about forty-eight hours or so, but it looks like Syrus has either Edwards syndrome or Down syndrome."

"What?" Corbett's face shrivels, the other Josh's too. "What does that mean?"

"Well, in very basic terms, if Syrus has Down syndrome, it means that he'll be a bit slower developmentally, but otherwise healthy. We won't know the extent of his developmental limitations until months, even years down the road. It's one of those things where you just kind of find out when you find out. But if he has Edwards syndrome, then he probably won't live longer than twelve months."

"He may not live to be one?!"

"You know, Corbett, it's best not to jump to that just yet."

Dr. Perfect MCAT is speaking in an even tone, calm, but how can he be calm? Huh? What the heck is wrong with this guy? This monster, this heartless charlatan—

"Like I said, we won't know anything for a little while yet. But as soon as we have something more concrete, I'll fill you in on where we go from there."

Hugging his clipboard, he shuffles out of the room the same way he shuffled in, and as the door latches behind him, a bomb detonates, splattering limbs and children's books and hospital gowns and hopes and dreams and joy against the walls and windows and—

"YOU'VE GOT TO BE KIDDING ME!" As soon as she says it, Corbett collapses into the other Josh, his arms shaking around her body, wishing he could grip her tight enough to make this go away. "Why would this happen? And he might only live for a few months? I just can't do this! I can't—"

It goes on like this for I don't know how long, every emotion and thought reminding us of how helpless we are, so needy, newborns eternal. Then we go quiet. No one says anything. The overhead fluorescent lights buzz. No one is hungry. No one knows what time it is. We hold each other. Sometimes that's all we can do.

The News

We haven't heard any news from Dr. Perfect MCAT yet. Over the last thirty-six hours, our outlook has bounded from good to bad, from optimistic to bleak. All is fine. All is lost. Everyone, it seems, except for Jack, is beginning to crack, complaining about the hospital food, the weird smells, the limited number of television channels. As for me, I'm doing my best to hide my anxiety, attempting to be the joy generator into which all can plug in, attempting to rescue us all. I have to. This is my shot. I couldn't rescue us from the fire, or when Mom and Dad died, and I couldn't rescue us from my parents' marriage or our suffocating, nasty house, but yes, this is my chance; maybe I can rescue us from this, swoop in— Minutes are hours, hours are weeks. The room has shrunk. The symphony of tears plays on. This whole experience is too familiar. We've been here. We are platinum grievers.

Along with the crying, we've been talking a lot, not in a PowerPoint-presentation way, but in a real way, about our dream kids, about my new sex ed job and my accompanying newfound knowledge of safe sex, about not wanting to be disappointed with the hand that life deals us. When Jack goes to stretch his legs or get more coffee, we talk about him, wondering why he does the things he does and how we know he loves us, but at the same time, we don't understand him one bit, can't even begin to, and how if this whole abnormality thing with Syrus is Jack's way of teaching Corbett and the other Josh a lesson, punishing them or something—if that's how Jack works, then how can we possibly— And what about Syrus? If he has Edwards syndrome and is going to die within a year, aren't we doomed to spend the entire year crossing days off until he expires? Wouldn't we prefer to never have him at all? But then again, isn't that what life is anyway, regardless of how long someone lives? Isn't each of us an hourglass? These conversations end prematurely, though, because we fear where they lead, and can't bear to follow them to a conclusion. We don't want to. No, right now we only want to hear that Syrus will be okay. We're begging for that.

Our hearts are begging to hear that Syrus will have birthday parties—first, sixteenth, twenty-first—and crushes on girls, and detention. We're begging to see pictures of him at a Cubs game and at the beach, sunburned beside his sandcastle, and we're begging to see pictures of him in front of the Grand Canyon and at prom in a white tuxedo. He'll wear a white tuxedo because he'll be confident, and he'll be confident because, duh, we will have loved him well, and beyond that, he'll have every reason to be confident, because he'll be a great kid, a prodigy, and he'll wear a white tuxedo because he'll like being different, will embrace the nonconformist life, but mostly because he'll have waited to go to the tuxedo store until the last minute and all they'll have left are the white ones. Naturally, I'll give him a hard time about this, as any uncle should, strengthening our bond through gentle teasing, but he'll no doubt be like his mother and the grandmother he never met, witty and sarcastic, deadly in word duels, a Billy the Kid of comebacks . . .

"Uncle Josh, didn't you wear a white tuxedo once too?"

"Uh, no."

"Ha-ha, you did."

"That sounds made up."

"You totally did! You wore it when you were in that musical, *The Big Picture*! The tails and the bow tie and everything!"

"Who told you that?"

"Mom did."

"Corbett!"

Yes, waiting in this hospital room, we're begging to know that Syrus will live, because if he lives, we'll live, and if he dies, a part of us will die too. A piece of us that has come to life through him, only him, will disappear forever if he doesn't make it. So for our sakes, we need him to make it. We don't want to lose that part of ourselves. We don't want to lose Syrus. We don't want him to die! We don't want to die! I don't want Corbett and the other Josh to die! In begging for Syrus's life, we're begging for our lives. Oh, we're symbiotic—

The door cracks open, and Dr. Perfect MCAT walks in, squeezing his clipboard against his chest. Corbett sits up on the bed, legs straight, mannequin-like. The other Josh moves to the mattress, presses in against Corbett, without the jokes this time. Jack moves a plastic chair next to the bed. He sits. I stay in my chair beside Kristen, my hands clenched, my heart guitar-string tight, one twist away from snapping.

"Well, you guys . . ."

Life-and-death moment. Life-and-death moment.

"I've got some news for you."

Corbett and the other Josh lean together. Jack puts a hand on each of them. And though I'm trying to make it seem like I'm not watching them, I am, and I know that, no matter what, they are in this together. Even if the sky falls, they are in this together. We all are. I'm not running anymore. Now I choose family. I choose this. And if the sky does fall, well, then I'll let it land on me.

"Your son . . ."

I stare right at Jack. *Jack, please let him live. Please let my nephew live. Please let my sister's heart live. Please, Jack. Please, Jack.*

". . . doesn't have Edwards syndrome. He's going to be okay."

Lessons! Pictures! Dances! Crushes! Birthday parties!

"Now, he does have Down syndrome, so we're going to connect you to some therapists who will work with him on his physical and mental development, speech development, that kind of stuff. But as long as you're aggressive in your approach, he'll do just fine."

"Wow. Thank you so much, Doctor."

"Do you guys have any questions at this point? Mom? Dad? Uncle?"

"So," Corbett says cautiously, "as far as him living, you expect him to be fine?"

Please, Jack. Please, Jack. Please, Jack.

"Absolutely."

"Thank you, Doctor."

Thank you, Jack.

XV

A Minnesotan, a Southerner, and an Addict

He said he'd show up again, and now here he is, packed tight into the kitchen, chewing and stinking, muddy tracks everywhere, his horns scraping the cabinets.

"Oops. Sorry 'bout that."

Great. He's torn one of the doors clean off.

"That's okay." I pick it up off the floor, set it on the counter. "So, you ready?"

"For what?"

"Yer a bit restless, ain't you?"

"Actually, yeah. I am, but how did you—"

"Almost like yer insides are a honeycomb, crawling with hornets, stingin'."

"That's not the way I would've described it, but that is how I feel. I feel it all the time. When I wake up. In the shower. When I'm driving. But I'm not even sure what it is. I just know that I've been feeling it for a while now. It's like it's time for something new." I hop up on the counter and sit, legs hanging, staring this agricultural mime in the face.

"U' course it is."

"What do you mean?"

"You've limited yer dreams."

"Limited? I haven't limited—"

"You have."

"No way. Have you been paying attention at all? I'm halfway done with my book. I'm traveling around the country speaking, not a lot or anything, but some of the gigs are kind of a big deal. At least to me they are. And I'm working this sex ed deal to help us while I'm chasing the dream. And we're about to launch an internet marketing campaign, some really creative videos, one in a cartoon format, another in the sci-fi genre, futuristic, a commentary on technology and the human soul, and we're hoping that one of them will go viral, spread like crazy. And I'm already thinking about another book, one with illustrations, maybe. I'm not limiting anything! I'm reaching for the stars. Aiming high. I'm lassoing the moon here!"

"Yer full of clichés."

"So I'm not working hard enough?"

"Never said that."

"Whatever."

I'm annoyed, so naturally I think about lulling him to sleep, then tipping him over. He is big, though. I'd have to push really hard while keeping my balance and . . . what's the word? Ah, leverage. It would be all about leverage.

"So what else can I do? Try to reach a bigger audience? Expose myself to better authors? Network with more people, more important people?"

"No."

"Upgrade the website? Host a radio program?"

"No."

"Launch a short story publication? Follow up with that guy I know who's in television?"

"No."

"Then what? How could I possibly dream bigger?"

He blinks, then curls his tongue over his lips, vacuuming up the stalactites of drool. "I ain't talkin' 'bout dreamin' bigger. In some ways, bigger is yer problem. Bigger is exactly what's limitin' yer dreams. You humans got such a supersized mind-set. If it ain't big, it ain't worth it. If someone ain't doin' something global, with a flashy slogan attached to it and millions of folks interested, then they must be wastin' their life. People confuse dreams with grandeur all the time, but they ain't the same thing."

"What then? If this isn't about dreaming bigger, then what are you talking about?"

"I'm talkin' 'bout dreamin' different. Right now yer dreamin' so much 'bout what yer gonna do, and barely dreamin' at all 'bout who yer gonna be. Now don't get me wrong, yer relationship with yer sisters is a great start, and the sex ed work and therapy stuff you done, all good. But what yer feelin' inside is the need to go further. There's so much more . . . Josh, yer obsessed with this career of yers. Yer givin' every ounce of yer imagination to yer career, and still so little of it to yer character. Yer imagination ain't hardly touchin' yer character. You ain't dreamin' 'bout one of the most important parts of yer life. The only part that's guar'nteed to be with you every day till you die."

I think he's just put words to my feelings, labeled the internal hornets, but oh, I don't like this idea at all. Character dreaming sounds risky—a kind of soul hammering, surgery with blunt objects—so only part of me wants to do it. My heart wants to, but my head is resisting. Or is it my head wants to, and my heart is resisting? I don't know. But how the different parts of me sometimes disagree, it's a wonder this body doesn't shatter—

"You know, Josh, bold people dream 'bout careers. But character dreams is reserved for the bravest. 'S too bad, though. If people was less obsessed with changin' the world and more concerned 'bout changin' themselves and playin' a role in the few lives around 'em, then the world wouldn't need so much changin' to begin with."

"For some reason, that's a lot harder to do."

"No question 'bout it. This can't be done alone."

I clamp my teeth around my already bitten fingernails and begin pulling skin off. "So if I was going to do this, where would I start? This kind of dreaming you're talking about seems so . . ."

"Ambiguous. Yup, it is. But the ones who're willin' to dream this way, 'bout who they are, always figure it out."

"Gee, thanks for the cryptic advice. That's all you're going to give me?"

"'S all you need now."

"Alright. Well, speaking of figuring it out, can you help me fix this cabinet door? Kristen is going to be home from work soon. You don't happen to have a screwdriver, do you?"

A couple days pass, and I'm at a coffee shop with Kristen, still thinking about my hoofed friend, when we bump into Chuck. Chuck is an acquaintance. We've met a few times, done the small talk thing, but we don't really know each other. His face is scruffy, his skin tanned to oak, a lumberjack surfer. We exchange pleasantries. I introduce him to Kristen. And then, perhaps pressured by the fact that we have some mutual friends, we decide to have breakfast. Later that week, Chuck and I meet at Kerbey Lane and begin swapping stories.

Chuck goes first, and within two minutes, it becomes evident that Chuck is hugely flawed, which is good. Flawed people I don't mind; it's the perfect ones who scare me.

No. I take it back. Suddenly his flaws are no longer comforting, because the story of his life, though marked with egregious mistakes (because of the egregious mistakes?), is growing far more interesting than mine, scintillating, peppered with provocative words and phrases like "cocaine" and "alcoholic" and "illegal casino" and "bags of cash," the kind of things that make someone larger than life.

The more Chuck shares, the more inadequate my made-for-floundering-network-television life feels compared to his Hollywood-A-list-movie-ready life. Just a few minutes ago I was confident that my life was a juggernaut worthy of ooh's and aah's, but now, faced with Chuck's riveting saga, I'm not so sure. What makes me memorable? Unique? Not my race. No. I'm not black or Hispanic or some cool exotic blend of a few races. I don't even have an accent, something really ear-grabbing. I'm just plain boring white, and I'm crippled with an equally vanilla name. So few have ever made it with the name Josh. Josh Groban. That guy from *The Mighty Ducks*. It's so unfair! My sisters were blessed with such distinctive names! Born for superstardom—

Chuck's story changes tones, transitions, and hits bottom. His health failed. He watched his friends die at the hands of the same lifestyle he was living. Shortly after, he found rehab. Rehab found him. Chuck describes it both ways. Following a few rounds of treatment, and with the support of his family and friends and Jack, the addictions lost their grip on his life.

"I've been sober for seven years now. And these days," Chuck concludes, pouring orange juice in through the gap in his beard, "I run a food service company."

"That's crazy, man. Seven years sober."

"Yeah. Isn't it?"

"That casino part sounds pretty awesome though."

"Yeah, well, it didn't work out too well."

"Right. So when you aren't working, what do you do?"

"Well, usual stuff, I suppose. But one of the things that takes a lot of my time is being a twelve-step sponsor."

My heart jerks at the phrase. I've heard this phrase plenty over the last few months. First, a friend told me he was starting the twelve steps for alcohol, and then another friend for sex. In both cases, I left the interaction patting myself on the back, certain that I—as any friend workshop would instruct—had exuded empathy, that I'd encouraged them to recover, to address their glaring flaws, and also silently wondering if maybe I too should— Ha, no. I don't need to do the twelve steps, and no, I'm not acting defensive. Sure, I have my issues, but the fact that I accept this and am willing to verbalize it means that I'm not in denial, that my issues can therefore only be the garden-variety issue, on par with any good person/angelic being. I'm no addict, no burnout, no Chuck. My face doesn't belong in some black-and-white infomercial outlining the perils of bad choices and befriending the wrong crowd. My issues are different, less hazardous to me and the world, not at all like my dad's issues, the type that warrant such severity and introspection and help, lots of it, and extended time in a controlled environment like AA, in the company of others who've lost control, fellow bottom dwellers.

"What about you, Josh? Tell me about you."

"Where do you want me to start?"

"Wherever."

Because I want my story to sound as interesting as Chuck's, I share for fifteen minutes, using lots of adjectives and metaphors, and I include a few random stories about when I met or almost met celebrities. Andy Roddick. Sandra Bullock. Ted Nugent. Quentin Tarantino. A celebrity interaction makes every story better.

Maybe I do have a disease.

"So your dad was an alcoholic?"

"Yeah."

"And you went through the twelve steps with him?"

"Yeah. I was about seven, so I only remember pieces. But every week, our whole family went to the meetings together. Everyone sat in a circle. I remember a guy in a leather jacket and ponytail. Everyone smoked. The smell in the room was always so different after the breaks. I remember a bit of the recovery language. And I remember being in the circle with my dad when he was on step nine, the making amends part. He and I sat there. My legs were too short to reach the ground, so I kept swinging them. I guess I was nervous. Then he asked if there were ways that he'd hurt me. The answer was yes, but I couldn't bear to tell him anything. I didn't want to hurt him. Or maybe I just didn't want to let him into my hurt. All I could get out was how I wished that he'd throw the football with me more. I just wanted him to play with me. I just wanted his attention. He cried when I said that."

"So have you done the twelve steps before?"

"No."

"I see."

"You see?"

"Yeah, I see."

"You see what?"

"Well, do you think you should?"

I try forcing a laugh. "Why would I?"

"Well, I think everyone could benefit from the program. It's fantastic."

"I'm sure it is, but I don't have an addiction. I'm not an alcoholic or a gambler. I've never done a drug, unless you count steroids—"

"Josh, the program isn't just for those kinds of things. It's for anything that you haven't been able to overcome on your own, anything that's been dragging you down, haunting you, year after year. Think of it this way. What's the easiest way to get at you? If you were the force of evil in the world, how would you attack Josh Riebock?"

"You have some really interesting questions, don't you?"

"I guess."

"Well, if I were the force of evil, I'd do everything I could to convince Josh that he's worthless, a waste of time, and ugly, and that unless he achieves amazing things and is wildly successful, no one will want him or love him, everyone will abandon him, and eventually he'll die alone . . ." I start spinning my knife on the table, fidgeting. "Chuck, I hear that in my head every day. I tell myself that all the time. I've been telling myself that for as long as I can remember."

"There's a term for that, you know."

"Oh?"

"Yeah. It's called self-hate."

"No, no. Hold on a second. I think you misunderstood me. I'm insecure, sure. I don't love myself as well as I could, or whatever, but self-hate? That's overstating it."

"Really?"

"Yeah."

Chuck extends his finger, pointing to the middle of the crowded restaurant.

"Okay, Josh. Let's do an experiment. Walk over to our waitress right there and tell her that she's worthless, and tell her that unless she achieves great things, no one will love her and she'll die alone. And when you're done telling her that, ask the people listening at nearby tables if they think what you said is hateful. What do you think they'll say?"

His words cut through me, severing arteries and veins, spilling hurt and cholesterol and blood everywhere.

"Josh, you said it yourself: you hear that every day. So, doesn't that mean you hate yourself?"

Whoever said the truth hurts was putting it mildly. The truth gashes. And for some reason, Chuck, my new friend, is willing to gash me. I don't like it, but better to be gashed by a friend than a stranger, I guess.

"Josh, I can tell that this is hard for you; going deep inside ourselves always is. That's why most never do it. But the twelve steps could be really powerful for you. Imagine loving

yourself. Imagine being able to enjoy who you are. Imagine not having to compare yourself to other people . . ."

The visionary words of my hoofed friend are coming out through Chuck.

". . . And imagine being able to celebrate others! Imagine writing, doing your job, not to prove your identity or worth but as an expression of it! Imagine knowing you have value!"

"That does sound pretty awesome."

"Well, what do you think?"

"I have to think about it. I want to do the bold thing and just say that I'll do it. Everybody wants to be bold, you know? But I don't want to tell you I will if I'm not really going to do it."

"I get it."

"I'll let you know. Okay?"

"Okay."

We pay the check. I walk home, but before I get there I already know my answer. The parts of me aren't in full agreement, but majority rules.

Emotional Sobriety

Other than Kristen and Jack, I don't mention this twelve-step stuff to anyone, not even to Gus or Webber, or Wallace via phone. That would play out all too horribly.

The moment the words come out of my mouth, the casual listener, half-listening, would become hyper-focused, their eyes trained on mine, cell phone now switched to silent. At that point, I'd be doomed, because no matter what I say, they'd assume I've been leading a double life, that everything I've been portraying is an elaborate hoax, a sham, and they would then begin to create memories, fictional vignettes where they sensed I was acting "a bit funny," where though they didn't say anything, they saw the warning signs and could tell *something wasn't right*. Yes, they'd do that. They'd have to in order to assure themselves that their intuitions are infallible, that their ironclad psyche is a reliable life compass, to assure themselves that they are equipped for danger, aren't grossly oblivious. Then they'd feel safer, as if they are prepared for whatever life might throw at them, as if there's no chance—no chance!—a wolf of a man could ever get that close without them already knowing full well the horrible fangs that he bares, the atrocities he might commit, the inherent risk involved in mingling with every single member of humanity. Yeah, there's no way I'm sharing any of—

But soon after, Chuck tells me I need to share this process with my friends and family, so reluctantly I tell them. A few furrow their eyebrows, confused at what I'm actually doing, but everyone is supportive.

From there, we execute Chuck's plan. One chapter at a time, I go through a twelve-steps workbook, reflecting, burrowing into the origins of my dysfunction, writing my answers in a spiral notebook I bought at CVS. Then Chuck and I meet at a restaurant or a park and discuss it. This element is more thrilling than expected and happens in an intense prison kind of way. He asks me something (attack). I give an answer (defense). We circle. We grapple. It's Thunderdome! If he thinks there's more to it, he presses, digs, asks stormy questions like, "Why do you think that is, Josh?" "Do you love your work more than Kristen?" "What is this wound costing you?" "Are you being fully honest with me?" "Where are you in the wrong here, Josh?" "It sounds as if your life has been mostly about image management, true?" "That sounds prideful, Josh, don't you think?" Ahhh!

By the end of each session, and after Chuck has successfully pushed my buttons, I find myself liking him less and less. But still, he is my friend—my twelve-step sponsor and my friend. And as improbable as it seems, I'm finding a unique beauty in being friends with someone I don't like. Unlike my friends who don't push my buttons, Chuck reminds me that I'm not indestructible, not immune to anger or frustration, that I have buttons to be pushed. Who knows? Maybe the friend I don't like will do more for me than the friends I do like ever will.

But oh man, I'd love to land just one uppercut on his bearded jaw or shoot him with a tranquilizer. Or maybe I'll just key his car.

I haven't left our bathroom in two hours. The door is locked. I'm spread out across the concrete floor, along with my book, my spiral notebook, and a pen. Tonight's twelve-step exercise is listing all the ways I've been hurt throughout my life, all the moments that have contributed to my self-hate. It sounds awful. It is awful. I want to cry before I even begin, but I do begin.

Some of the events I scribble about are massive, and others seem inconsequential, but Chuck told me to include both. I do.

> The car accident in the cornfield.
>
> Crapping my pants at my elementary school, being made fun of by everyone. The laughing. The jokes. I skipped school for two days after that.
>
> In high school, having a group of girls, hot girls, give me the nickname "Beak Boy," then drawing a picture of me with a beak, gathering around the desk in Mr. Harper's history class, giggling.
>
> ~~Two~~ Three girlfriends cheating on me.

I fill a page. Tears fall. I fill another page.

I fill five, more tears.

I fill and cry through nine pages, until my shoulders hurt, until my hand is sharp and immobile—a talon—until I can't write anymore, until I'm too scared to dig any deeper, scared of the prehistoric creatures and wounds that might lie even further down, until I'm certain that the scariest place I'll ever go is deep inside myself.

I shove the notepad aside. I curl up into the fetal position along the bathtub and shut my eyes. Yes, I want to be humble and courageous and honest and selfless, to be a modern-day saint, and I want to love others, love myself. I don't want to hate myself anymore, but here, floating in the black, healing feels so far away. Change feels so far away. This is what the dark does. The dark makes good things seem far away and makes terrible things seem close, that feeling of being chased through the woods. Right now, becoming who I want to be seems like another one of life's rigged carnival games: alluring but impossible.

I've never felt so insufficient.

My whole life I've been in the self-sufficiency business, pretended to be. It seemed like the only option. Self-sufficiency is the mark of an adult. Of the achiever. And I must achieve! I must be enough, be a source of strength, a sort of human Stonehenge, unshakable! I don't hurt! I don't ask for help, no! I give it! Because if I'm not sufficient, then what am I? I'm needy. Deadweight. Insufficient. And I can't bear to be branded with the Scarlet I! The insufficient get nothing! Blessed are the self-sufficient.

Unless . . .

Is it possible that I've misunderstood self-sufficiency? Maybe self-sufficiency is part of my prob—

I open my eyes. Teary-eyed oil slicks pulse around the bathroom lights. As I sit up against the tub, I can hear my hoofed friend's voice pouring through me. Self-sufficiency is the mark of the limited dream. It's only when we possess great dreams for who we can be that we possess great desperation for the help to make it happen. Yes.

Suddenly I'm on all fours, crawling across the bathroom floor, more insect than man. When I reach the door, I kneel and tell Jack that I'm hurt. I'm not completely sure if he's listening, but I tell him I can't do this alone. And then I begin asking Jack, wherever he is, to heal me of my self-hatred, of all these memories, to help me reach this dream. Then I ask again. And again. My body withers. I collapse on my face—the concrete ironing the wrinkles from my forehead—pleading with him, pleading, a beggar, a cockroach, a nothing man, self-will dried up, an ego famine, hitting both a literal and figurative bottom— Oh, I know it may not have the pomp and glamour of Chuck's cocaine bottom, with illicit paraphernalia and law enforcement badges, but that doesn't matter, because it's my bottom, mine! And no one is going to take it away from me or belittle it, because here at the bottom, my bottom, in this lovely surrender, I feel a grand release, my burdens turning to feathers. Wonderful. I don't know why I waited so long to get here.

Eventually I stand up. My knees and elbows are pink from the floor, the surrounding hair kinked. Chuck will want to hear about this. A breakthrough, he'll call it. He'll be excited, will understand, and will recall his own breakthroughs. We'll have a moment. I should call him right now. I check the time, but it's late. I'll call tomorrow. Still, it's nice to know that if I did call now, he'd answer, on the first ring probably.

I suppose he's a polite friend that way. After all, if you're going to gash someone, you should have the courtesy to walk alongside as they bleed.

I hate myself. I love myself? I hate myself. I love myself? Hate self. Love self? Self-hate. Self-love? Hate. Love? Hate. Love? Hate-me love. Love-me hate. Love-me love?

The mirror is swaddled in the steam of a satisfying shower. I towel-dry my hair, then step to the fogged glass, cutting out a clear circle with my hand. I study myself in the mirror.

My pug eyes aren't quite symmetrical. The right appears to be a bit bigger than the left, which is more almond-shaped, kind of feline. And wow, my eyebrows are unruly, two gardens overrun with weeds. I exaggerate my grin to see my teeth. I'm still missing a molar that fell out a few years ago following an incident with hard candy. I never got it fixed. The surrounding gums are now gray and colorless, still embedded with a few jagged shards of dead brown tooth that smell of decay. I step toward the mirror. From here, the wrinkles, blemishes, and scars stand out like Braille, like journal pages, chronicling the places I've gone, the person I've been. To hide acne, I used to slice a razor over my skin. Slipping it sideways across my forehead or chin, mean and deep, I'd bleed out everywhere, red falling onto the sink and then crawling in drunken patterns down the drain, leaving a crusty bacon scab for days. Better to be injured than flawed, I thought.

But now, studying this haggard face, which hasn't been shaved in two weeks, and my body, which is skinnier and paler than it's been in warmer, more gym-frequented days, I don't feel shame or malevolence—

"Liar."

"No. Really. I'm starting to like what I see."

"Sure you are."

"I mean it. I'm seeing less and less of a freak, less of that guy who's dying to save the world. I'm starting to see me. And, well, I kind of enjoy it, and that really is a dream come true. Yeah, I never thought it could happen, but here I am, looking at my face without wanting to crawl out of my skin, without wanting to trade lives with whoever is on the cover of *GQ* this month."

"You're an embarrassment," the shirtless reflected me says from inside the mirror, mimicking my every move.

"You're a liar."

"No. I love you. And you love me."

"I hate you."

"You hate yourself."

"No. Not anymore. That's changing. So go away. Leave."

"Impossible. You're nothing without me. You need me. I'm a part of you. I'm as integral to you as your skeleton."

"Then I'll break you, one bone at a time, for as long as it takes."

As the reflected me fades from the mirror, I grab my toothbrush, scrubbing my teeth good, being careful to avoid the empty slot where that molar used to be, where the nerves now sit peeking out.

XVI

Train over Ocean

The macaroni is mushy again, dissolving into a paste. I can never seem to cook it quite right, which I'm sure is the fault of the utensils and food, not the chef. I fill one bowl halfway. Then I fill the second bowl halfway and open the fridge, looking for orange juice or milk. We have neither. I see eggs, corn tortillas with nothing for them to wrap around, a container of hummus, butter substitute, a bottle of club soda, and a door filled with assorted condiments. The inside of a refrigerator can be the most depressing sight in the world. I pour two glasses of water, sit on the couch, and place the bowls on the ottoman, which has proven itself to be an especially valuable home item, acting as a footrest, a nap zone for Ditka, a makeshift go-cart on which I sometimes ride around the house (it has wheels), and in this case, our table.

I turn on the television. Kristen and I look at our dinner and at each other. We're tired, still sort of eking by. She's working hard at the studio and still carrying us financially. I'm working hard too, still teaching young people who shouldn't even be saying the word sex about sex, but now the initial charm has worn off. It's not humorous or novel anymore. It's embarrassing. Whenever someone asks me what I do during the week, I want to lie or change the subject, and sometimes I do—gosh, I want to quit. And of course, I'm doing this while still trying to manufacture more speaking gigs, doing a bit of traveling, and trying to finish my book (masterpiece?) that will probably never get finished, my book (catastrophe?) that is slated, in all likelihood, to forever linger in literary purgatory. All of this is adding up to obscene work hours. I have little time or energy for Kristen. Oh, and then I'm still involved in the twelve steps too, though as far as that's concerned, I'm pretty sure I've relapsed into self-hate and tumbled headlong off the wagon, which is only taking a further toll on us, on our marriage, our marriage that was supposed to be unlike any before it—the only other couples worthy of a place alongside us atop the Mount Rushmore of romance being Romeo and Juliet, perhaps Harry and Sally.

"Josh, you want to thank Jack for dinner?"

I look into my bowl. The macaroni has morphed from many noodles into one big super noodle. I know I should be thankful for what I have. I'm finding that difficult.

"No, you go ahead."

"You don't want to?"

"You got it."

"Okay, I'll do it," Kristen says.

"Fine."

"Fine?"

"I'll do it. Jack, wherever you're at, thanks for giving us food."

It isn't my best effort. It isn't effort at all. Even talking with Jack has become a chore.

I begin chewing, hoping the macaroni will magically taste better than it usually does. I picture crab legs, strawberries, or real pasta and real cheese, like something a restaurant might sell. No luck. It tastes the same as always. Bland. We both know it. This is about all that Kristen and I seem to agree on these days—

Yes, we've been fighting a lot. Not the Fight Club–category bouts seen on reality television, packed with cursing and door slamming, name-calling, lamps being tossed out windows. No, it's not that extreme. Our fights revolve mostly around tones of voice and envelopes and how loudly one of us eats pretzels, over things that, in past seasons, only enhanced our love. But right now these subjects ruffle us. Right now these subjects threaten our very existence. These meaningless points mean everything.

It's as if I've traveled back in time to an era I know all too well. Oh yes, these fights are familiar. They war inside me. I could, in detail, describe these fights to a police sketch artist, pick them out of a lineup. These fights remind me of home. And now they're happening in my home. My parents' marriage recycled. A hand-me-down romance. These are the kind of fights that happen when you're slowly, slowly growing apart.

And Kristen and I are growing apart. How could we not? We've been so busy. I've been so preoccupied with other things, my heart on furlough, stuck in a marital coma. Chuck has mentioned this to me, other friends have too, but gosh, I didn't even notice it, not really, so I didn't take their warnings seriously. I figured they were overreacting. I assumed they were deluded. They weren't.

Once our bowls are empty, I carry them to the sink and drop them in. My shoulders are sinking under resentment and frustration and embarrassment. I feel three inches shorter than I used to be, struggling with my inability to provide, my failure as a writer that isn't "making it," and our marriage that feels more like my parents' marriage by the day. I'll probably be sleeping in the living room soon, on the couch. Yes, the dominoes are about to fall. This is the end. Personal Armageddon.

Our house will be taken, and with our tails between our legs, we'll move back to Chicago, in with Kristen's parents or into a place overrun with mice, and not the pleasant sort of singing mice found in children's programming with their tiny caps and vests, but angry mice, real biters. I'll be a pastor again, pretending to want to be there, having lied through the interviews in order to get the job, and the mounting stress will break us. Newly divorced, working a job I hate and seeing Ditka only on weekends and holidays, I'll lose my hair, combing over the scraps, and my belly will sag down over my belt. And whenever Kristen and I inadvertently cross paths at the grocery store, I'll see how beautiful she still is, endlessly brilliant, and then I'll be reminded of how I blew it. Our love is ending. The dream is ending. My faith is ending. I'm giving up. I almost want to.

In need of affirmation, I head to Blockbuster, searching for movies about people who triumphantly gave up, something that will inspire me to fade away. But on the racks, I see *Hoosiers* and *The Edge* and *Schindler's List* and *Aladdin* and *Gladiator*, movies that would only entice me into pressing on. I walk up and down the aisles but can't find the "lost hope" section. The really tall film geek behind the counter in the blue-collared shirt and yellow name tag asks me if I need help with anything. Where would I possibly begin?

Defeated, I drive home with nothing, and for the first time ever, I want my phone to ring. I want to hear Norton or Quinn say that they are abandoning their passions in order to do something that will require less endurance, or that they've decided to become more pessimistic. I want Corbett to say that she's converting to a less taxing belief system. I want Gus or Wallace to quote me divorce rates, high ones, absurdly high ones, and to assure me that I shouldn't feel bad about it if that's where I end up. Hearing any of that would be heaven, sheer heaven! That conversation is something I could be thankful for! That would be a moment of complete relief. I guess sometimes what we want most is permission to quit.

I just need someone else to go first, to be my green light, to show me the way. I need a faint breeze to knock me down, and I'll never get up again.

Back at our condo, I open the balcony door, hoping, but the air is permanently still, unwilling to do me any favors.

Free? Cougar

Because I'm not in the mood, I skip church. I don't feel bad about this. Since we still have just the one car, Kristen drops me off at a bar to watch lots and lots of sports on lots and lots of televisions. Earlier this morning, Jack stopped by the house and asked if he could join me. I declined. I told him I wanted to be alone. Alone and in the company of sports, I won't have to think about anything substantive—other than the sports—and that is ideal.

One of the teams I'm rooting for scores early and takes the lead. I made the right choice. This is exactly what I needed. Another team I'm rooting for scores, and as I'm turning warmer and warmer inside, two women claim the table next to me. Hips swinging like a pendulum, the blonde struts over to the bar and is immediately engulfed by a pack of men. The dark-haired one stays at the table, veiled by a newspaper. She is out of place. If a friend were with me, I would mention how out of place she looks. But since I'm alone, I turn my attention back to the televisions. All of my teams are performing as I hoped they would, and I'm officially bouncing in a magical bubble on my own planet, a planet where I'm not thinking about the sex ed job that I want to quit or the book that I'm out of ideas for or the bill that we aren't sure how to pay or the hope that I don't have. On this planet, those sorts of thoughts are quarantined from the general population, excommunicated!

A drink shows up at the veiled woman's table; this is the third drink that has been sent to her. After each drink lands, she pulls the newspaper down and glances around the bar, clearly annoyed, and then a grown man in a jersey winks idiotically. Each time, the veiled woman ignores the drink and goes back to reading, so now three untouched drinks stand in a line across her table.

After the fourth drink comes her way, she drops the newspaper. "All I wanted to do here was read. That's it. Is that too much to ask?"

Seeing her whole face, I know now why men are buying her drinks.

"Nah. That's pretty reasonable."

"Yeah. Are you watching a specific team?"

"A few, actually."

"How they doing?"

"They're doing okay."

"Well, that's great."

"Yeah, it is. What about you? You got a team?"

"Not really. I don't watch a whole lot of sports."

"Oh?"

"I like it, I do, but with my work I don't get to watch a whole lot."

"And what's your work?"

"I'm a writer, a travel writer, actually," she says. "I just got back from Europe writing a piece."

"That's pretty cool."

"Oh, it was, one of the best trips of my life. I didn't get paid much for it. I never do. Maybe someday. I'd love to become an author."

"Well, I certainly wish you the best of luck."

"Wait."

"What?"

"What about you?"

"Me?"

"Well, what do you do?"

"Oh, sorry. Yeah. Well, I guess I'm a writer too."

Her fingers are smudged black from ink. She slides the newspaper aside. Her eyes sparkle, telling me I'm important, better than these other bar drips.

"Really. I had no idea that writers could be so cute."

"Oh . . . yeah."

I know this shouldn't feel this good. I know, I know, I know. Everything in me knows. Bad Josh. Bad Josh. But when life is hard, all the wrong things feel right—

Flirting is happening. I'm flirting. With disaster. But oh my, this disaster, Miss Disaster, has soap-opera lips and the curves of an east coast highway. And since she's quite a bit older than me, that makes her a cougar. I note this. With every not-so-clever comment I make, she purrs and tosses her fountain of chocolate hair. I am in a shampoo commercial. As we discuss writing, she looks on, admiring me, her Han Solo. The good feeling is escalating, and it's all coming so easily. Easily! Like taking candy from a—

Yes, loud within me, I hear the armchair therapist wisdom. I know that the easiest people to be admired by are those we don't know. I understand that in the presence of strangers, everyone is fiction. I get it that this is a mirage, all smoke and mirrors. Cougar hasn't seen my temper; she doesn't know that I bite my nails and have bad credit and watch too much television and am not handy around the house. She doesn't know that I spend a good chunk of my weeks talking about gonorrhea, or that I may still be depressed, or that I'm in the twelve steps, or that I hate myself, or that I'm overly dramatic in all my ways, or that I'm hard to live with, or that—

Yes, fine, this is all a mirage, but sometimes the mirage is better than reality! Sometimes the mirage feels like the only cure for reality! Sometimes I want the mirage. Like now! I want it, because I just want to feel good, and I don't want anything—not Jack, not my conscience or my hoofed friend or anyone else—to convict me, tell me differently, or rob me of this glee!

My eyes zip across the wall of televisions. All my teams are winning. They are flawless today, and in Cougar's eyes, so am I. When's the last time I felt flawless? Oh, flawless is soothing, aloe for the wounded ego—

I take my flirting up a notch. I'm laughing loudly at moderately funny things, periodically biting my lip, pushing my left bicep out with my opposite hand to make it look bigger, staring at her longer than necessary, and then, in response to my adept flirting, she flirts more, so I flirt more. The cycle spins.

"So," she hums, pressing her body forward on the table, enhancing certain attributes, "what are you doing the rest of the day?"

"The rest of the day?"

"Yeah. Because, you know, I live right near here. We could talk about writing, or . . . whatever else you want to do. What are you doing?"

The words rattle around in my head. What am I doing? I'm here, alone, all day. Kristen isn't picking me up for hours. What am I doing? I'll tell you what I'm doing: whatever I want with whomever I want! Today I am the invisible man! I'm doing what feels good, and no one is going to know anything about it!

Cougar starts touching her neck, and I begin to imagine my afternoon.

Cougar and I will ride, top down, in the 1948 Buick convertible that she probably has, feeling so alive, and drive fast to her house with the wooden back porch, with the view overlooking a river. The weather will feel like fall, the leaves changing from green to magenta, and we'll discuss the leaves while listening to Michael Bublé and sampling wines beneath the bigger-than-normal moon. Then the moon will reach his hands down. We'll step onto his cratered palms and he'll lift us up, ushering us into a gravityless ballroom where we'll dance, dance, dance, and moved by this cosmic moment, joyful and priceless tears will float off our faces to form a chandelier, hovering above us.

Then, returning to earth, we'll spin and laugh, and I'll be better looking, a Spanish soccer player kind of handsome, and two inches taller, and rich—not just a writer but a famous writer, and she'll ask me to sign the multiple copies of my many books that she owns and has read many times and loved. I'll tell her about my horse farm and what prompted my walkabout through the Australian outback, and we won't fight or mention chores or insurance bills or feel the pressure to be responsible. We won't speak of money troubles or of dying dreams or about me knowing all there is to know about STDs, and she won't keep me accountable. Nope! Instead, life will be a permanent vacation, and then, after all of that buildup, I'll stare into her admiring wide eyes, it'll be time, and Cougar and I will—

"So," Cougar says in a midnight-radio-host voice, "the rest of the day, you free?"

Free? Me?

Yes. Liberation is here. I'm about to be loosed from this grinding season. I am free. I am free.

The Exhausted Billionaire

My mom is the one who called.

"Hey, Mom!"

"Josh?"

"Yeah. Hold on. Let me turn the TV down. What's going on?"

"Josh, I have something to tell you."

"Okay."

"Oh, this is hard."

"What is it?"

"Your dad is going into hospice."

"He is?"

"You know what that means?"

"Yes, I think I do."

"It means that they aren't going to treat him anymore. They'll take him off all the medication—oh brother—the medication that he's been on for so many—" The phone went quiet as she tried to gather herself. "Sorry."

"That's okay, Mom."

"He probably won't last very long, they said."

"Any idea how long?"

"They don't know for sure, but his body has relied on all those pills for so long, they think it'll be quick. Anyway, you should probably come and see him."

For the first time in years, his beard was gone, and for the first few days, he couldn't get enough of the hospital ice cream. Every time he finished one cup, he was ready for the next. He'd take it in his shaking, blue and purple hands, treasuring it, treasuring every sound, every taste, every sight, every person.

Sometime that week, I don't remember when, Norton came to see him. "How you doing?"

"Norton, if after I die, I wake up surrounded by cats, I'll know I didn't make it."

We all tried to laugh.

On the third or fourth day, his mouth failed, so his eyes had to do the talking. I did whatever he asked for. I had to. I couldn't leave his side. I didn't want him to leave mine. I wanted to stay. I wanted him to stay. I felt like I loved him more if I stayed. I was comforting him. I was comforting myself. Every second became precious, a final harvest of memories. I wanted to burn his face into my chest, to trap the sound of his breathing in my ears.

Few things are as sacred as our memories, and these would be our last, his last. Soon after, he sank into tears; he was afraid of what was next, how the next part would feel, wondering if he'd done this part well. Then he glanced toward my mom. She popped up out of her chair, took urgent steps, and stood pressed up against the side of the hospital bed, finger-combing his unwashed, straw hair, smoothing it back over his head.

"You look real handsome, Jimmy. Jimmy, you look marvelous." She said it in that Fernando Lamas/Billy Crystal voice and kept smoothing his hair. He closed his eyes, chuckled a bit, but then choked on his own emotions. She did too. Taking his hand softly, she bent down and kissed him on the forehead, letting her lips linger for a moment without pulling away. Then she sat down next to him, her eyes glassy, and kept on with the finger-combing.

Gosh, I hadn't seen that kind of affection between them since before I could drive. At first it made me mad. This is what I'd wanted to see all those years, and they waited until now? Are you kidding me? Why is it that we wait until the end to make changes?

Probably because we know that, above all other moments, we are forever defined by how we finish. Fair or not, this is how we often see people. Someone could botch his whole life, run it aground, and then redefine everything in the final, quintessential scene. Monsters become heroes. Of course, the inverse is true as well. Poor Judas. It sounds as if he was a great guy up until the end, but the only way I think of him is—

Anyway, my anger passed, and then watching them was like watching Shakespeare. This was their moment. The decades of mistakes no longer mattered. This was all that mattered. It was their world, the two of them taking the floor for one final waltz. The room felt bright, full of love and resolve, packed with enough energy to power a train over the ocean.

I thought it might fill him enough to give us one more conversation. Chicago's own Lazarus, he'd sit up straight, his beard grown back in, purple spots mopped off his hands, waving to me for another ice cream cup.

"Dad?"

"Yeah, son."

"You feeling okay?"

"I am. How could I not? I made it to the end."

"Yeah."

"You didn't think I would? Well, I'm shocked you'd think that. Your father? I mean, really—"

"Da-ad."

And we'd laugh and laugh. I'd be his audience again.

"You know, son, I didn't do it perfectly. I stumbled a lot. I flat out blew it a bunch, and I've got regrets. I do. It was so hard. There were days twenty years ago when I wanted it all to be over. I wanted to give up."

"But you kept going, Dad. And man, you did a lot. You have people who love you. You made people laugh. You made people feel like they were important. You had that one-night stint as an amateur fashion model. You rode snowmobiles. You taught me how to carve a pumpkin. You got your PhD. You had dinner with Michael Jordan—"

"And don't forget that I'm an author too."

"That's right. *Ant City*."

"It's called *Let's Go to Ant City, USA*. Josh, I wrote that when I was twenty-five years old. Illustrated and everything. And yeah, I suppose it was never officially published, but it wasn't about that. I just wanted to write a story that would make a few people happy."

"You did that, Dad. In a lot of ways, you did that."

"Yeah, I think I did. I gave everything I had here. Now it's my time to go. And I feel okay about that. This isn't quitting, son. I'm not giving up. I've given everything I've got."

"I think a sane person would have given up years ago."

"Ha-ha, you still think I'm crazy after all these years, huh?"

"You bet I do."

"Good. I'm finally ready for what's next. It's time. And yeah, I may have gotten lost in the middle, Josh, but I finished what I started. That's all you can really hope for. You don't get to choose a lot of what happens to you, but you can choose to see life through to the end. I did that. That feeling is a kind of wealth money can't give you. Sure, it would've been nice to have both, but I'm happy with the one I got. This is the end, and for the first time in my life, Josh, I'm rich. I'm a billionaire."

"You're right about all that, Dad. I know it. Still, you have to admit, it's a little cheesy."

"Yeah, I guess it is. But hey, it's your fantasy. Now get me another ice cream."

Lip Tango

". . . You free?"

As the words come out of Cougar's mouth, I'm still replaying the last lesson my dad taught me. And now I have my answer.

I AM FREE . . . but I won't be with Cougar. That would be cheap, and Kristen and I haven't come this far to settle for the cheap route now. We can't just fold up and die now! True, enjoying an afternoon with Cougar would be easy, would demand nothing of me, but how much would it really give me?

Suddenly my mind is thrust back into the blurring pace of early romance again, and I'm thinking about our wedding and about how gorgeous Kristen was, how gorgeous she is—every molecule within her adding to the galaxy's most stunning constellation—and how gorgeous our love is, this difficult/shimmering/brute love that's changed my life, taught me how to trust, taught me that there is a force stronger than anything life can throw at us, and yeah, sure, I annoy her, and we fight, and we're so different, have been parallel to each other lately, but she's my "it" girl, the greatest human I've ever been fortunate enough to stumble across, and right now I just want to hold my "it" girl and never let her go! Wow, love really is a house of limitless lessons! True higher education. And now, aha, my heart and brain have absorbed the most recent slice of learning: love is grueling and life is grueling, so without endurance we get neither! And I want both! Life! Love! Both! Yes, there is a time to be greedy! This kind of greed is good—thank you, Mr. Gecko! I want it all, and no, I will not give any of it in exchange for admiration! Being admired has never made someone who they want to be. EVER! Is our love flawless? No! But way inside me, I don't want to be flawless. Not really! What I really want is the girl who invites me to be free, to be my flawed, quirky, neurotic self! The girl who knows just how deep my imperfections run! I want my wife! Kristen! More than ever, I want Kristen—

"You know," I say, plucking my phone from my pocket and texting Kristen to pick me up right away, to hurry, "actually, I'm not."

"Ohhh."

Kristen texts me back, asking why.

"Yeah. I have to meet someone."

I text Kristen again, telling her to just come.

"Are you sure?" Cougar asks in her best pouty voice, strategically enhancing things again, upping the offer.

"Yeah, I'm sure."

Kristen texts back, asking if I'm okay. I tell her yes, and again say to hurry.

"Well, can I at least have your number?"

"No. I'm sorry, but no."

"Why not?" Cougar leans away now, covering things and reaching for the newspaper.

"Because I love my wife very, very much."

My chair rips loud across the floor. I get up. And without looking at Cougar (and skipping out on the bill?), I leave the sports bar. I stand outside. Waiting. Eager. There she is. The car is still rolling a bit when I jump—very Bo and Luke Duke—into the passenger seat, and taking Kristen's face in my hands, I comb my fingers through her hair. It's soft and blonde and everything. And her eyes, these bright lighthouses, are signaling me to shore, drawing me safely back home. Now I lean over the center console, and we kiss and we kiss, our lips fumbling around, joined in a tango, now the Charleston, the jitterbug—

"I love you, Kristen."

"Thanks, babe. I love you too."

—the cha-cha, the foxtrot. We keep on, like two people who now know that the best kisses are meant be cherished and drawn out, two people who know that life's richest moments don't come cheap, that they are the ones that we almost didn't get, the ones that we had to struggle for. Because without the struggle to endure, we'd never be truly set free. We keep on like two people who know that sometimes you have to fight for the life that you want, two people performing an act of survival, not exactly that lost-in-the-wilderness kind of survival—facing wild beasts and the elements—or the wrongfully imprisoned kind of survival, or the terminal sickness kind of survival, but *our* act of survival, our way of spitting in the face of the apathy that has come to destroy us.

So yes, in our own way we keep on, surviving, refusing to let our love grow stale, refusing to believe that our dreams—any of them—are destined to die, refusing to believe that we were born without the perseverance gene. So yes, we keep on, on, on, for months, months of me not cutting my hair and instead letting it expand, long and curly, its growth representing this softer yet exploding new existence, and all the while I'm writing, doing speaking gigs here and there, still doing that sex ed deal, meeting with Chuck for the twelve steps, climbing back on the wagon, practicing my emotional sobriety, and Kristen working at the photography studio, Ditka being so Ditka, and Jack being forever Jack, the four of us bonded together, resilient to the last drop, the freaking von Trapps!

We keep on, until the nights grow shorter, the days grow longer, and suddenly it's June.

Victory Lap

Today is the last day of school. It's my last day as a sex ed teacher. As I'm concluding the sex presentation, the bell rings. Students, screaming and giddy, barrel down the hallways, cinematic visions of vacation hatching in their minds. A few stop and say goodbye. A few say thank you. I pack up my stuff. Outside it's an oven, and as the sun hits my face, I want to raise my arms, celebrate, do a victory lap, like Tour de France champions do—do they carry a bottle of champagne on that lap? They certainly should. I should do that now, the champagne part, the spraying of it. I will. But I'll wait until I get home to celebrate. I want to celebrate with Kristen and Ditka. There is so much to celebrate. Yes, I did it. I stuck it out.

Sure, maybe it was all in vain. Maybe all those students are blitzing through the steps of physical intimacy right now, passing all sorts of horrible burning sensations among themselves. I don't know. But I know this: I didn't quit. I finished. For many, this wouldn't be a big deal, but for me, the tenured cynic, the kid who's been giving up his whole life, it is. I finished! And not just this, no, I've finished a lot of things over the last few months. I finished the twelve steps. I finished my book, and the speaking side of work is picking up too. I'm not sure why. I'm not sure why anything happens.

Flocks of students are pouring through the glass doors, throwing papers into the air, charging into months of swimming pools and flings and sleeping in and awkward jobs and better, unscripted, lucky, lucky, lucky days. In my own way, so am I.

Funny, I've been growing older my whole life, but now I'm finally growing up.

Jack meets me at the car.

"Hey, Jack."

"I'll bet you're glad to be done with that."

"Oh man, you have no idea."

"You did good."

"Thanks."

Jack and I climb into the Jeep and roll down the windows, and as I'm pulling out of the parking lot, out of this piece of life, I realize something. Life isn't just about me finishing what I started. No, no, it's about Jack finishing in me what he started. It isn't about what I'm doing here. It's about what he's doing here. Though I often lose sight of it, he's still continuing on, doing something in me. Oh, sure, I give up on him, but he doesn't give up on me. He doesn't quit. He won't quit, because this innovative lover is also the master of endurance. Jack is going to finish!

While the car speeds along, our hair jets out behind us in the wind. We're listening to Creedence Clearwater Revival's "Lookin' Out My Back Door," and I'm singing loud, without consciousness, like Robert Plant lives inside me, like I'm headlining a summer festival—

"You seem happy, Josh."

I stop singing, turn down the volume. "I am happy."

"Yeah, but you know, one day that word will be completely redefined for you. One day you'll burst into the new world, and you'll know what *happy* originally meant. Love and life, what they originally meant. What all this was about."

"Sounds amazing."

"It is . . . You want to see it?"

As he's saying this, his words begin to sound distant and muffled, as if we're conversing cross-legged at the bottom of a swimming pool or a lake or a rich person's bathtub.

What's going on? Something else (a vision?) is taking over.

"Uh-huh." It's possible that I say this back to him, but that may or may not be accurate. It's hard to tell because my voice seems to have become endless, echoing on and on into forever, and all sense of my surroundings is disintegrating into a million pieces, like a dandelion in the wind. Now my windshield begins filling with loosely formed images, the lines and details slowly coming into focus, joining together to create a scene—

Okay. I see a room. It has windows. The walls and ceiling are covered in drawings and photographs and phrases, the floor lit by the spark of the flooding sun. And there's a desk too, a handsome and sturdy antique piece, the kind of thing that belongs in a European bookstore. Someone is sitting at it. There's a familiar tapping sound. No, not annoying. It's a sweet sound, as if every tap is softly blowing my ears another sugary kiss . . .

All good things must come
to a beginning. EJ

XVII

So Many Mansions

Ding goes the typewriter   I lean away from the desk, the wooden chair creaking as I rock back and forth   I see the words "The End" printed on the page   I pull the sheet of paper from the spool and set it on top of the others, capping the thick stack, then I smooth it down with my hands and drop it into an envelope   I reach across the desk for my mug   Ahh, still warm   I sip the last of the coffee, so good, and wander over to the window   Just beyond the glass, a bird is sitting in a tree, stuffed among the leaves, his head jutting back and forth, chirping constantly, a feathered auctioneer I chuckle

This place is nothing like I thought it would be

Oh, sure, I had my ideas, bad ones mostly I was picturing something more sterile, neutered, some kind of machine-buffed floating science lab in the sky, something terminal, tedious, like weekend detention, like that movie *The Breakfast Club*, only not as funny and with less cursing Though I never would've admitted it, I figured the new world was worse than the old one, nothing more than a state of mind, a land absent of the physical, a place where I didn't have a body, where there wasn't anything to touch or do or eat or feel

The bird moves to the edge of the branch, beak aimed skyward, and flies, flies, flies, his blue and green reflecting sharply against the sun, his yellow belly matching the yard flowers below What can I say? I was way off about this place True, I've never liked being wrong, but I guess being wrong is sometimes a magical thing

I'm outside on the front porch now, and the world is so very avant-garde, unopened, as if every single molecule is brand new, created only seconds ago Like always, the city is humming, charged by spectacular but ordinary people who aren't wearing robes or playing the harp like they do in cartoons Trotting down the steps, I inhale the smell of burning leaves, my favorite scent No, no, it doesn't smell that way to everyone Some describe it as roses, others as cinnamon, and then there are those eccentric types who mention something about skunk or asparagus or wet grass For me, though, it's burning leaves

I move up the street, passing mansion after mansion—there are so many mansions!—and normally I'd pause to look, to admire the architecture, to wave or greet or hug my neighbors But not right now Now I'm moving quickly with rabbits' feet, envelope in hand, excited, because today I'm meeting someone, someone who's been on my mind for quite a while

No, I'm not worried about coming across as rude, being labeled   Everyone is happy for me   They understand   I know this   I see it bottled in their eyes

Doormat

Out of habit, I keep checking my watch, but the numbers are scattered and the hands are missing   Time doesn't exist here   It wasn't invited   No other rulers are invited   So without time, I won't be early or late   I'll just be there, at the hill   Then I'll pass this envelope into those beautiful hands   Oh, I can't wait!   And to think that I used to question if this moment would come, if this place existed, if maybe certain forces were strong enough to veto this entire thing

I suppose I wasn't alone in that . . .

It was June 25, 2009, in the old world   The sun was shining over Austin, a great smoking tangerine, blazing hot, bobbing in clumps of white cotton   I was at home, writing, listening to Michael Jackson

He always was a hero of mine   I still remember seeing the *Thriller* music video for the first time   It only took once, and after that, I wanted to be Michael Jackson   Wow, the creativity, the innovation, his feet like wheels rolling through time   To me, it was obvious—Michael Jackson was supernatural!   The closest any human could come to being a god!   He blurred the lines between mortal and immortal

But on June 25, 2009, I stopped mid-type as the story leaked out

Michael Jackson Dead at Fifty Years Old

After that, the universe froze, every other headline and talking head became wooly mammoths, and a new ice age began   All the networks were covering it—the conservative one, the liberal one, all of them   The world had come to a screeching halt

On the news, droves of people were gathering outside the Los Angeles hospital where Michael Jackson had been admitted From a nearby balcony, his music was playing loud, all the classics, and the people who weren't crying were dancing, emulating him, which seemed to make some feel better Imitation was their tonic Gawkers abounded too, and the gossip hounds In the middle of it all, a reporter roamed in search of a good interview, someone who would respond to her weird questions

After striking out a few times, she hit the jackpot

Immediately this interviewee caught my attention Why was her hair so frazzled? Combs had been invented She apparently did not own one While the reporter probed, she stared blankly into the camera, sobbing on and off, undergoing an emotional metamorphosis, a snake shedding its skin The reporter asked if she knew Michael Jackson No She didn't Slowly massaging her neck and trying to knead the tension away, the woman erupted, "I just can't believe this! I can't believe it, it can't be! It can't be! Not him! Not him!"

"Ma'am?"

"This isn't right! This isn't right!"

"What isn't right, ma'am?"

"This is the worst day of my life!"

Because it was so raw and unsettling—not to mention bad for television ratings—the camera swept away, leaving me so confused Sure, sure, I was sad that Michael was dead and knew that we'd all lost something in his departure, but come on, this was far from the worst day of my life This day didn't even crack the bottom hundred, probably not even the bottom thousand! But for this woman, this was number one, the worst day of her life! Really? Why was she so upset? There had to be more to it, but what?

There was, of course, the possibility that she was unstable, a nut of some kind, and that this violent outburst was normal for her, a daily expression And then it was also possible that she was already having a terrible week, a tragic year, and this event was the shattering point Or maybe this event, this day, was a stark reminder for her about mortality, a reminder that none of us—even the most supernatural—can escape death

Aha! Yes! I knew that was it! I'd cracked the case wide open! Around the world, Michael Jackson's departure was plunging us headfirst into that murky, bitter swamp of wondering what happens after this, wondering if all the hopeful stories we've heard are true or merely something we share in order to aid our sleep, to help us cope at funerals and crime scenes And we were plunging deeper with swift fear and urgency because the probability of death finding us had just gone from likely to inevitable This moment was the guarantee, because if anyone could escape death, surely it was Michael Jackson, this supreme something or other, this moonwalker And if he could do it, then maybe others had a chance too His life was hope for us over death! But he couldn't Death got him too Life ended for Michael, which meant it would end for all of us For the television woman And . . . for me

Hey, I believed in the new world! I did! Jack told me about it! He promised me! But in that moment, my belief escaped me (as it often did), and I felt it too, that pit in my stomach, something like the floor dropping out beneath me, certain that death was coming, that I was next on the list It had my address, my number It could be dialing right now, en route, and since death was stronger than Michael Jackson, it would certainly be stronger than me There was nothing I could do!

So there I was, just like the television woman, sinking into a chilling swamp, stepping into the ring with a seemingly unbeatable opponent, begging the universe to intervene, to provide any evidence that the new world was real, that life really was stronger than death, and then my body, in that moment, pressed into the couch and turned to ice

But here, in eternity, death has been exposed as the greatest hoax in history In the old world, people fear (as I did) that death is an end, a wall Death tends to agree But with every person who enters the new world, death takes another backhand to the cheek, is proven wrong Each time someone passes into this new world, he gets undressed, knocked out, treaded on

Death is a doormat, so please don't forget to wipe your feet

Early Jones

Crossing the midtown bridge, I'm switching the envelope into my opposite hand when I bump into a friend of mine, Early Jones We shake hands He tells me that he doesn't want to slow me down, so instead of talking, he presses a small, wadded paper into my hand Unfolding it, I find the scribbled words weathered and crimped I read them to myself

Early Jones asks me to read it out loud

"Why?"

"Something this true shouldn't remain silent," Early says

"Wow Setting the bar pretty high, aren't you?"

Early laughs and tells me to go on, to just read it

Love Love Love That's the story, the paper says, I say

I pass the slip of paper back to him, but Early waves his hand, telling me to keep it "It's a gift," he says I fold it I'll add this to my collection of Early's work

We part ways, and I keep on, focused, across the bridge, quickly toward the hill, to meet up with— But that Early Jones, he's really something

In the old world, he was a writer, a fortune cookie writer Don't judge; his fortunes always seemed to outdo the typical cookie drivel His words did something to people A taste of his genius:

Try to fly, you just might

Love is the battery that makes life run

Art make happy

In everything he did, Early was always writing In our own way, I guess we all are You could say that Early's whole life was poetry It makes sense; all lovers are poets And in the old world, Early was a lover—of ideas, all creatures great and small, people, cacti, donkeys, even mosquitoes But above all, Early loved Jack

When he woke up, Jack was the first thing on his mind, and as he fell asleep, it was Jack then too Early was always looking for creative, intentional ways to love him In fact, one of his favorite pastimes was to love Jack in ways—as he put it—that surprised him And of course, Early knew that someday he and Jack would be together in a new way, a deeper way, the fullest way, here in the new world Early dreamed about that moment He knew it would be the greatest moment of his life

By the end of his old world days, Early frequently compared his relationship with Jack to love-struck pen pals writing postcards to one another from across the world In fact, every night (and so spot on with his analogy), Early would climb the fire escape, taking a pen and a stack of thin paper with him And then, from his usual rooftop spot, he'd jot a message to Jack, leaking his heart onto the paper Then he'd take the message, move to the edge of the roof, and stretch his hand high over his head, waiting for the wind to scoop the slip of paper from him Once that gust hit, Early would stand, wet-eyed, and watch his words flap through the sky, over the steel jungle, and into unknown places, until it was gone, and—he hoped—delivered

So on any given night, Early's messages—

Soon, soon, soon . . .

Or

If you lived at the bottom of the sea, I'd happily become a fish

Or

Our time apart has been sweet, but our reunion will be sweeter still

—were traveling from him to Jack, from one lover to another

Another thing about Early has always struck me too Early says that entering the new world means more to some than it does to others, and that it all depends on how we lived our old world lives He says that the more we longed for Jack in the old world, the more we cherish that first embrace with him here The more we loved Jack while we were apart, the more it means to be fully united

I didn't really buy that at first, but man, that was never more obvious than when Early arrived

A bunch of us were waiting on the hill Early entered to the usual celebration, but without hesitation, he sprinted right past us and made a beeline for Jack Without missing a beat, Jack, a fellow poet, started running across the hill to Early It was really something The gap between them was shrinking, shrinking, but then, when they were within maybe fifty feet of each other, Jack just stopped running and raised his palm toward Early, crossing-guard style It was crazy! I'd never seen anything like it None of us had I don't think anyone breathed for a good couple seconds

Jack made the first move He dug deep into his pockets and removed a wad of paper in each fist *Could it be?* I thought Has he been saving them all these years? Yes

The next thing I know, Jack lifted his hands skyward, the countless thin strips of white paper squirming through his fingers, and suddenly a warm wind rolled over us Jack smiled He opened his hands, and then, right then, thousands of worn love notes—Early's rooftop postcards to Jack—took off from his palms, flying through the air toward Early, back to the one who penned them Return to sender

Through the paper blizzard, Jack ran to Early, who broke into a run again, faster and faster, the wind churning the slips of paper along, the two of them sprinting through every correspondence in their long-distance courtship, and then on top of the hill, in the eye of this heartfelt storm, they embraced, embraced, embraced Early squeezed Jack And Jack squeezed Early He squeezed him so tight that Early's feet came right off the ground, dangling as Jack swung him in circles, while the cherished slips of paper floated down onto their shoulders, a snow globe for the ages

Finally, the wait was over

The Professor Was/Is Right

There's an unzipping here, and stepping into that new self takes some getting used to, like extreme jet lag

The first time I cut myself here while slicing up some meat for Ditka and my blood came out as clear liquid, someone had to assure me that it was normal   And without pain and fatigue and mind block, you can run and jump and laugh for as long as you please   Like right now, even though I've been walking awhile, moving fast, I'm not tired   My muscles don't hurt   And that is very nice, I think

Turning the corner, I pass a café where an Echo is taking place   That's where people from all eras, all times, all races, all lands, gather together and share how they got here   Some of the roads traveled!   I've listened to a medieval knight share his life, a 1700s schoolgirl, world leaders, bus drivers, former death row inmates, Civil War slaves—it really is amazing how our old world lives shimmer when we look at them from here

Whenever I'm sharing in an Echo, I always include a specific moment

I was sitting in a classroom at a metal desk   The door opened, sucking the dust right off the chalkboard, and a man walked in, a man that I recognized and yet didn't recognize at all

I knew him

But I didn't

He was a familiar stranger

This man was my dad, but not my version, the version I'd seen most of my life   Gone was the brittle, made-of-glass man   Gone was the sick and hurting, helpless man, the man falling down in the driveway, lying on his side, shouting, "Help me!   Help me!   Is anyone there?   Here!   Here!"   This man wasn't frothing in anger, shame, or beer   No   This man wasn't wounded, betrayed, and abandoned, worn out and pummeled

No

This man, this all-too-familiar stranger, was new This version of my dad was the one I'd always imagined: whole body, whole spirit, wholly alive, and strong He seemed free He was—

The door slammed behind him, rattling my desk His red and black flannel shirt twirled through the air, coming toward me, and his smile was punctuating his black face stubble Every step, each knock of his construction boots against the tile floor, was a guitar chord all the way to my desk I sat up, drawn to the music of my father

I didn't know how any of this was happening, but I didn't care Sometimes how things happen is irrelevant It was happening! My dad was alive, and he looked this way

If I'd reached out, I could've touched him, but I hardly moved I was too afraid that if I did, he'd disappear, that I might smudge the details—

He was looking at me, the way I'd always wanted him to, and he didn't stop, none of him stopped He was a willow tree, and his limbs grew across my desk, tender and sweeping, and somehow I knew that he was proud of me

"Josh . . ."

English Leather floated from his neck to my nose, and he looked at me as if relishing this moment, wanting to multiply it, as if he wanted to stay with me but knew that he couldn't—

Off the blocks my brain went, running laps, once around, faster, twice around, faster still, wanting him to finish his sentence

I waited

I stared into his face, at his hands, back to his face

Please talk Please talk

Please

Talk

My mouth was dry More English Leather into my nose My eyes on his face

I waited more And more

Then rolling his sleeves up tight to the elbow, he reached for me, put both hands around the back of my head, and brought his new face toward mine

"Jack is the only thing that matters"

One month after my dad died, I had that dream I never forgot it I carried it for the rest of my old world life, always wondering if what he said was true Some days it was true to me, other days not so much But once I got here, I found out just how right right right my dad was He's never been more right

I suppose the easiest thing to do in the old world is waste your life, and the easiest way to waste your life is to forget what my dad told me The point is, in that twisted, beautiful old world, and in this new world too, Jack is the only thing that matters

Shotgun

Atop the hill now, the sweat of my palms begins soaking into the envelope as I pinch it tighter between my fingers This is my gift to him He's going to love it! For my part, it felt so good to finish it, the new book I've been working on It's a story about us And it felt so good to write those last words, "The End"

Of course, here in the new world, those are *only* words, nothing more than a matter of speech As for life, that doesn't end Ever

Here in the new world, we live in the eternal beginning, where it's creation every day, all over, for all of us Spinning, I take it in from every direction I take in the beauty of this world without horizons It transcends imagination, even when the mind and heart are extended as far as they possibly can be But that's just about all I can share with you right now Someday soon, I'll meet you at one of the mansions There are so many mansions—did I mention the mansions?—and we'll talk about everything

Even then, though, mysteries will still remain I naively assumed everything would be answered here, but that's not true In the new world, there's even more to be fascinated by, and here, we are the truly fascinated All of us, we're still asking questions, seeking, exploring the deepest spaces of love, and my gosh, I adore it We all do Here, we can enjoy the craziness without going crazy Come on, it wouldn't be much of a new world if all the mystery were gone, now would it? Mystery is what keeps us alive Without mystery, we'd fade away Like dying stars, we'd burn out, disappear, choke on the boredom

In retrospect, I can say that I had a good run in the old world And now I know that in the grand scheme of it, I was a speck A speck that mattered, yes, but just a tiny, replaceable speck No matter how old, smart, strong, or holy I became, I was still always just a little child in a cornfield, running my fingers over my body, checking to make sure I was okay, with more questions than answers And whether I liked it or not, admitted it or not, I was dependent upon the only one who could keep me from drifting off into oblivion, upon the only one who knew the way through the old world, through my old heart And now, here in the new world, I see and I know that when you're trying to find your way through a great big field, there's no greater guide/friend/lover/Lord than Jack

I hear the soft rumble of tires and an engine approaching, slowing at the base of the hill He's here, and in one way or another, we all meet here, right here at the hill The hill that made all of this possible

Okay, so should I just hand him the envelope without any explanation? Or do I preface it? Oh, even better! I'll construct an elaborate story, an urban legend, say that I found this manuscript buried somewhere, that it's ancient, capable of powerful things, which is why the peasants took such care to hide it for so long and keep it to themselves until I discovered it Yes! He'll love that! I could even hide in the tall grass, lead him to think I'm not here, and then, ha-ha, I'll rise and jump out in full character, some kind of hillside creature

I laugh to myself, at myself The presentation doesn't really matter, I suppose I just want to enjoy him And I know I will And I know he'll enjoy me too

Today I'm going to make him smile big Today he's my audience

So until we talk again, or see each other face-to-face, enjoy your old world life as best you can Embrace it, play in it, wake up and live, because you are in the middle of it all—the sweet, wonderful, cruel, drive-you-mad middle!—and hopefully this inspires you along the way, lifts you up, does something, stirs your affections for your heroic and monstrous life, your interesting life, and for the one who made it all so interesting

Life is a field You aren't alone

With a meow of the brakes, the maroon wagon stops, and now, like I said, I have to run My dad told me that he'd keep the car running, and that I could ride shotgun

The End

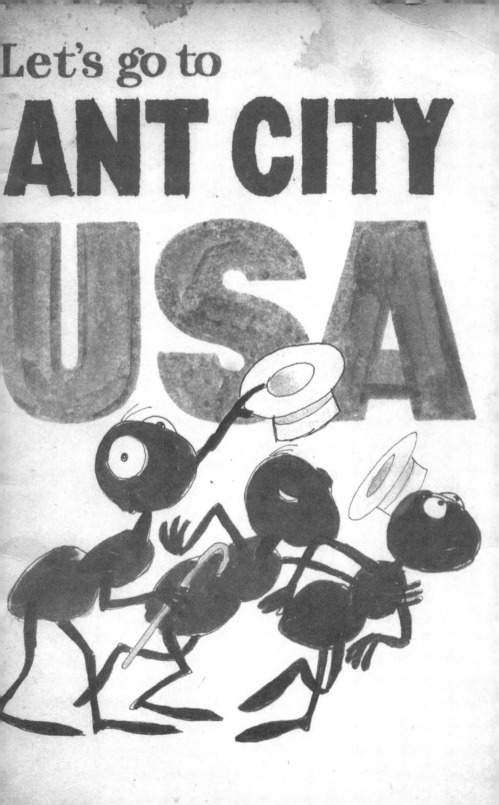

Let's go to ANT CITY USA

Let's Go To Ant City U.S.A.

James Riebock

Illustrator.......John Ortman

July 9, 1965

"Hello!" said the ant.
"I am Mr. Ant.
I am happy you came today.
I would like you to see my house and meet my friends.
Follow me!
I will show you the way.
Ooopps!
Hold on!
This hole is deep and sometimes it is wet."

"Here comes Billy Ant.

He looks for food for all of us.

Billy, come here!" called Mr. Ant.

"I want you to meet a visitor.

Billy! Billy!" he called again.

"Oh, well! I guess he is too busy."

"Look out!" cried Mr. Ant.

"Stand over here!

I wonder where everyone is going.

Say, here comes Freddy Ant.

Let's ask him where everyone is going.

Freddy! Freddy! Come here!" called Mr. Ant.

"Hello!" said Freddy as he ran over to us.

"Where is everyone going, Freddy?" asked Mr. Ant.

"We are going to get the food that Billy found.

Come on with us!" Freddy called as he ran off.

"We don't have time now," called Mr. Ant.

"Let's go on now," he said.

"These ants are worker ants.

They carry the seeds of corn into our house and keep them warm and dry.

If we get many seeds, we will have enough food to last all winter.

Shall we move on now?"

"I want you to meet another friend," said Mr. Ant.

"Down this path, please! This is Huey Ant."

"Hello!" said Huey.

"My job is to put all of these corn seeds in these rooms so they will stay dry.

If a seed begins to grow, I must have one of the other workers take the seed outside."

"Thank you for telling us what you and your workers do," said Mr. Ant.

"We must go now and see the Queen before it gets too late.

Good-bye, Huey!"

"Turn here please!

Here is her room and there is the Queen," said Mr. Ant.

"Good afternoon," said the Queen with a smile.

"We are glad you came today.

I hope you had a good time visiting our home.

Will you have some tea with us?" she asked.

Then a little worker ant came into the room.

"Here comes our tea now," said the Queen.

The little ant put three little cups on the table in front of the Queen.

"Please, sit down and have some tea," she said.

"Thank you!" said Mr. Ant.

Then the Queen said, "I do hope you had fun today.

When you visit us, we like it, too.

We like to have visitors see how we live and work.

I hope you come back again soon.

Next time, bring a friend with you."

Then Mr. Ant stood up and said, "We must go now.

It is late and I must help with the work."

"Good-bye and come again soon!" said the Queen.

Vocabulary List

1. ant
1. follow
2. Billy
2. visitor
3. everyone
3. Freddy
4. worker
5. Huey
5. job
5. Queen
6. tea
7. hope
8. ....

Josh James Riebock is a sought-after speaker at conferences, colleges, and churches across the country. The author of *mY Generation*, he lives with his wife, Kristen, in Texas.

Also by Josh James Riebock

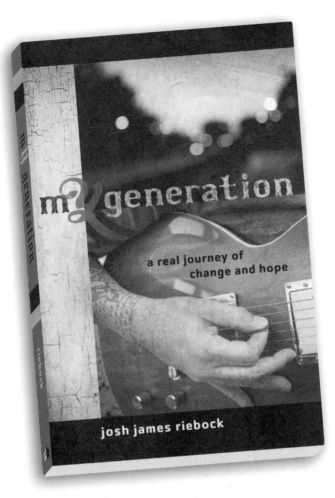

"A must-read for anyone seeking to understand Gen Y. . . . Not only will Josh's imaginative, insightful, and gritty inside look prepare you to engage a new generation, but God might just change you in the process."

—**John Burke**, author of *No Perfect People Allowed* and *Soul Revolution*

Relevant. Intelligent. Engaging.

Available wherever books are sold.

Like us on • Follow us on ReadBakerBooks • Read our blog: relligent.wordpress.com

Visit **joshriebock.com,** where you'll find Josh's

- speaking schedule
- booking information
- blog
- bio

Also follow him on Twitter

 www.twitter.com/#!/joshriebock

And find him on Facebook

 www.facebook.com/pages/Josh-Riebock/221730051185951